Machine Learning and AI in Finance

The significant amount of information available in any field requires a systematic and analytical approach to select the most critical information and anticipate major events. During the last decade, the world has witnessed a rapid expansion of applications of artificial intelligence (AI) and machine learning (ML) algorithms to an increasingly broad range of financial markets and problems. Machine learning and AI algorithms facilitate this process understanding, modelling and forecasting the behaviour of the most relevant financial variables.

The main contribution of this book is the presentation of new theoretical and applied AI perspectives to find solutions to unsolved finance questions. This volume proposes an optimal model for the volatility smile, for modelling high-frequency liquidity demand and supply and for the simulation of market microstructure features. Other new AI developments explored in this book include building a universal model for a large number of stocks, developing predictive models based on the average price of the crowd, forecasting the stock price using the attention mechanism in a neural network, clustering multivariate time series into different market states, proposing a multivariate distance nonlinear causality test and filtering out false investment strategies with an unsupervised learning algorithm.

Machine Learning and AI in Finance explores the most recent advances in the application of innovative machine learning and artificial intelligence models to predict financial time series, to simulate the structure of the financial markets, to explore nonlinear causality models, to test investment strategies and to price financial options.

The chapters in this book were originally published as a special issue of the *Quantitative Finance* journal.

Germán G. Creamer is Associate Professor at Stevens Institute of Technology. He is also a visiting scholar at Stern School of Business, NYU; Adjunct Associate Professor, Columbia University and former Senior Manager, American Express.

Gary Kazantsev is the Head of Quant Technology Strategy, Office of the CTO at Bloomberg L. P., New York, USA.

Tomaso Aste is Professor of Complexity Science, Department of Computer Science, University College London, UK.

Machine Learning and AI in Finance

Edited by
Germán G. Creamer, Gary Kazantsev and Tomaso Aste

Foreword by Marcos López de Prado

Routledge
Taylor & Francis Group

LONDON AND NEW YORK

First published 2021
by Routledge
2 Park Square, Milton Park, Abingdon, Oxon OX14 4RN

and by Routledge
52 Vanderbilt Avenue, New York, NY 10017

Routledge is an imprint of the Taylor & Francis Group, an informa business

© 2021 Taylor & Francis

British Library Cataloguing in Publication Data
A catalogue record for this book is available from the British Library

ISBN: 978-0-367-70332-5 (hbk)
ISBN: 978-0-367-70333-2 (pbk)
ISBN: 978-1-003-14571-4 (ebk)

Typeset in Times
by Newgen Publishing UK

Publisher's Note
The publisher accepts responsibility for any inconsistencies that may have arisen during the conversion of this book from journal articles to book chapters, namely the inclusion of journal terminology.

Disclaimer
Every effort has been made to contact copyright holders for their permission to reprint material in this book. The publishers would be grateful to hear from any copyright holder who is not here acknowledged and will undertake to rectify any errors or omissions in future editions of this book.

Contents

Citation Information

The chapters in this book were originally published in *Quantitative Finance*, volume 19, issue 9 (September 2019). When citing this material, please use the original page numbering for each article, as follows:

Chapter 9

The QLBS Q-Learner goes NuQLear: fitted Q iteration, inverse RL, and option portfolios
Igor Halperin
Quantitative Finance, volume 19, issue 9 (September 2019), pp. 1543–1553

Chapter 10

Detection of false investment strategies using unsupervised learning methods
Marcos López de Prado and Michael J. Lewis
Quantitative Finance, volume 19, issue 9 (September 2019), pp. 1555–1565

For any permission-related enquiries please visit:
www.tandfonline.com/page/help/permissions

Notes on Contributors

Tomaso Aste, Department of Computer Science, University College London, UK.

Giulio Bottazzi, Institute of Economics and EMbeDS Department, Scuola Superiore Sant'Anna, Pisa, Italy.

Shun Chen, School of Economics, Huazhong University of Science and Technology, Wuhan, Hubei, People's Republic of China.

Ying Chen, Department of Mathematics, Faculty of Science, National University of Singapore, Singapore.

Wee Song Chua, Department of Statistics & Applied Probability, Faculty of Science, National University of Singapore, Singapore.

Rama Cont, Mathematical Institute, University of Oxford, UK.

Germán G. Creamer, School of Business, Stevens Institute of Technology, Hoboken, NJ, USA; Visiting Scholar, Stern School of Business, New York University, NY, USA.

Lei Ge, School of Finance, Southwestern University of Finance and Economics, Chengdu, Sichuan, People's Republic of China.

Daniele Giachini, Institute of Economics and EMbeDS Department, Scuola Superiore Sant'Anna, Pisa, Italy.

Igor Halperin, Department of Financial Engineering, NYU Tandon School of Engineering, New York, NY, USA.

Wolfgang Karl Härdle, Ladislaus von Bortkiewicz Chair of Statistics, C.A.S.E. – Center for Applied Statistics & Economics, Humboldt-Universität zu Berlin, Germany; Sim Kee Boon Institute for Financial Economics, Singapore Management University, Singapore.

Kiyoshi Izumi, Graduate School of Engineering, The University of Tokyo, Japan.

Geonhwan Ju, Department of Industrial and Systems Engineering, Korea Advanced Institute of Science and Technology (KAIST), South Korea.

Gary Kazantsev, Bloomberg, New York, NY, USA.

Kyoung-Kuk Kim, Department of Industrial and Systems Engineering, Korea Advanced Institute of Science and Technology (KAIST), South Korea.

Dong-Young Lim, School of Mathematics, The University of Edinburgh, UK.

Chihoon Lee, School of Business, Stevens Institute of Technology, Hoboken, NJ, USA.

Michael J. Lewis, Guggenheim Partners, New York, NY, USA.

Marcos López de Prado, Global Head of Quantitative Research and Development, Abu Dhabi Investment Authority; Professor of Practice, Cornell University, Ithaca, NY, USA.

Hiroyasu Matsushima, Graduate School of Engineering, The University of Tokyo, Japan.

Pier Francesco Procacci, Department of Computer Science, University College London, UK.

Hiroki Sakaji, Graduate School of Engineering, The University of Tokyo, Japan.

Justin Sirignano, Mathematical Institute, University of Oxford, UK.

Daigo Tashiro, Graduate School of Engineering, The University of Tokyo, Japan.

Foreword

Markets are extremely complex and dynamic systems developed by humans to exchange goods and services. They have existed since at least 5,000 years ago, when Mesopotamian cities first designated specific areas where trade was allowed, regulated, and protected. Those original *bazaars* already incorporated the key elements that characterize what we today understand as a market, such as a legal framework, institutions to enforce the rules, auctioning mechanisms, systems of payment, instruments of lending and borrowing, pledging of collateral, and agents. The code of Hammurabi, enacted some 3,750 years ago, further facilitated the development of commerce and investing. Centuries later, Ancient Rome counted with two forums, organized in areas reserved to specific products, each area being a guild or *corpus* (from where the term corporation is derived).

It did not take long before traders recognized that technology could be used to produce better transactions. Starting with the invention of computing devices such as the Sumerian abacus (4,700 years ago), and followed by the adoption of the Hindu-Arabic numeral system (1,300 years ago), and recording systems such as the ledger and double-entry bookkeeping (500 years ago), technology has always played a critical role in supporting traders and financial institutions. Communication technologies facilitated the creation of fast, global markets, where investors exchanged legal rights rather than the physical possession of an asset or commodity.

The past 50 years have witnessed the increasingly relevant role played by computers in financial markets and institutions: the automation of the back office in the 1970s, the development of middle office analytics in the 1980s, and the proliferation of statistical arbitrage trading systems in the 1990s. In the 2000s, high-frequency trading replaced human specialists with algorithms, increasing market efficiency and reducing the cost of liquidity.

The latest example of this endless modernization is the development of financial machine learning (FinML) algorithms. As important as the previous instances of modernization were, one particular characteristic sets FinML apart, even in historical terms. Previous technologies focused on ancillary aspects of the exchange process, such as speeding up calculations, facilitating memory storage and retrieval, or transmitting information. In contrast, FinML aims at automating decision-making, stepping into a role long thought to be the exclusive realm of market wizards.

Some of the best-performing fund managers in history happen to be systematic, and FinML has the potential of widening their advantage. In contrast, traditional fund managers have struggled to add value for the past two decades. In a highly competitive environment, it has become increasingly difficult for traditional managers to digest oceans of data fast enough before the opportunity disappears. As computers become more powerful, algorithms solve more complex tasks, and datasets continue to grow and expand, new technologies allow us to capture opportunities that were previously beyond our grasp. Whereas the pool for traditional alpha strategies is shrinking, the pool for technology-driven alpha is expanding.

This book could not have arrived at a better time. It is imperative that academic institutions adapt and modernize their graduate programs to meet the demands of the investment industry. Traditional syllabi set students for unemployment or underemployment. Today, financial analysts are still not being trained to process terabytes of data, in search of empirical evidence to support their claims. This does not necessarily mean that all financial analysts should become developers. However, financial analysts must learn to make evidence-based decisions, where storytelling is replaced with testable hypotheses. The classical statistical tools (e.g., econometrics) taught in university programs are too simplistic to model the complexity inherent to financial datasets, many of which are unstructured and non-numeric.

Moreover, the transition from standard machine learning to FinML is far from automatic. One cannot take an algorithm that is successful in driving cars or recognizing faces, and expect it to pick outperforming stocks. Billions of animals can recognize faces, and hundreds of millions of humans can drive cars. The fact that very few individuals excel at investing is indicative that this is a particularly difficult problem, and a reason to develop the subject of FinML independently from the area of general AI. FinML cannot be an exercise in data mining, and must integrate our knowledge of how economic systems work.

A number of peculiarities make investing a challenging question for both humans and machines. Markets evolve every day, and mechanisms we thought we understood will cease to work, as a consequence of changes in regulation, policies, or human behavior. For example, the market's response to surprises in the monthly non-farm payrolls release has changed over time. Over a short period of time, those changes seem undetectable, even though over a long period of time they are dramatic. FinML algorithms that detect and adapt smoothly to those subtle changes can be very valuable to investors.

Some fatalist voices have presented an apocalyptic vision of a near future in which machines replace most of the workforce, or widen the wealth gap even further. And yet, history offers us plenty of examples where mechanization led to prosperity. Ford's factory workers were paid more, not less, when their factories adopted the production chain. One aspect that makes the systematization of investing particularly intriguing is that it will disrupt highly paid jobs, which contrasts with the outcome of the mechanization of manufacturing in the 1980s. These individuals will generally have the leeway needed to acquire the new skills needed and evolve with the demands of the Information Age.

As with any disruptive technology, FinML offers challenges to those who resist it, and opportunities to those who embrace it. At the same time, investors must realize that FinML has become a buzzword term, which can and has been abused. All too often we will hear people promote as FinML dubious techniques that are not founded in sound science, or purely theoretical constructs that bear no resemblance with reality. Scientific laboratories have used machine learning for decades, and today machine learning plays a critical role in most scientific fields. Investors must learn to differentiate firms that utilize FinML as a marketing tool from those firms who use it as a tool for scientific discovery.

For institutional investors, FinML is a welcome development. We are excited at the opportunities offered by these technologies, as they modernize our financial markets and help our industry serve society better.

Marcos López de Prado
Abu Dhabi Investment Authority and Cornell University

Introduction

GERMÁN G. CREAMER ⓘ, GARY KAZANTSEV ⓘ and TOMASO ASTE ⓘ

1. Introduction

During the last decade we have witnessed a rapid expansion of artificial intelligence (AI) applications and use of machine learning (ML) algorithms in an increasingly broad range of problems in finance. This development is fueled by a unique confluence of factors: an exponentially growing computational capacity that is available for enterprises, and similarly exponential growth in the amount of machine-readable data, along with improvements in the state of the art which allow ML and AI applications that were impractical ten or twenty years ago.

There is an ambitious feeling emerging across industry and academia that some cognitive processes can be automated via ML and AI, radically expanding opportunities for automation especially in finance and the services industry. However, finance is very different from other domains, such as medical diagnosis, where ML and AI have been developed and successfully deployed. ML and AI require large and reliable training data sets to make machines 'learn' their models. But all financial data are not alike. We can characterize financial information as big data because of its large volume (financial time series data easily scales into petabytes), velocity (much of financial data is high-frequency), and variety (numerical, categorical, text, images, etc.). This data exhibits complex behavior: nonstationarity, nonlinear interactions, heteroscedasticity, and biases. The research goal in this domain is to find in this data relevant patterns that could be used for investment, risk management or trading decisions. Time series analysis and traditional statistics can facilitate the process of understanding, modeling, and forecasting the behavior of financial assets. Present day developments of ML and AI algorithms provide novel approaches and perspectives such as feature selection in high dimensional data that mixes large structured and unstructured datasets, and incorporates a large number of linear and nonlinear features. Some of these new perspectives are reported in this special issue.

Financial systems can provide an excellent opportunity for ML and AI researchers to develop and test new algorithms due to the availability of datasets and the persistent demand for novel solutions to complex new questions. Many financial problems do not require a forecast of a continuous variable, as they can be formulated as classification problems. For instance, a trader may only need to anticipate the market direction within a certain probable range rather than with a direct forecast of returns. This perspective influenced many researchers during the 1990s and early 2000s, leading them to apply ML algorithms to problems of algorithmic trading and market microstructure. Among the most common algorithms used were neural networks (Trippi and DeSieno 1992, Choi et al. 1995), traditional convex models such as support vector machines (Tay and Cao 2001), reinforcement learning (Moody and Saffell 2001, Bates et al. 2003, Dempster and Leemans 2006, Nevmyvaka et al. 2006), boosting (Creamer and Freund 2010) and genetic algorithms (Allen and Karjalainen 1999, Dempster et al. 2001). The main areas of application for many of these algorithms have been the equity markets, futures, and foreign exchange (Chaboud et al. 2014). It is difficult to estimate the true extent of the application of these methods in the industry, as publication of results has been sparse and limited in scope. We hope this special issue will highlight the new trend of an expanding and diversifying collaboration between researchers in academia and industry. This kind of cooperation cannot help but move the industry forward with interactive communication and dialogue regarding the current state of the art.

Recently, the range of ML and AI applications in finance has been extended to other markets. Some of the papers in derivative pricing using ML algorithms are oriented to the replication of the Black-Scholes (BS) model for pricing derivative instruments (Hutchinson et al. 1994, Amilon 2003). They fill a critical gap in the literature as they help to price derivatives using a data-driven approach without satisfying all the assumptions of the BS model. There are still many unsolved questions, such as finding an optimal model for the volatility smile. Other new developments by AI researchers include developing artificial agents for automated investment recommendation and portfolio optimization systems (Decker *et al.* 1996, Seo *et al.* 2004, Creamer 2015). These models have enabled the current generation of robo-advisors (Baker and Dellaert 2018) such as 'Warren' from Kensho, an AI startup acquired by Standard and Poor's, that recommend portfolio allocations based on the client's characteristics and market trends. In parallel, many large organizations have also explored the use of ML and AI methods for customer management, primarily to target new customers, anticipate their consumption patterns, define customer segmentation, develop recommendation systems for products, and reduce the attrition rate, thereby offering new incentives and products to clients with a high propensity to leave. This line of research has led to the highly competitive and profitable area of digital marketing (Domingos and Richardson 2001, Hill *et al.* 2006, Leskovec *et al.* 2006, Richardson and Domingos 2006).

Financial and risk management is another major area of application for ML algorithms. Ireland and Dempster (1988) and Dempster and Ireland (1989) proposed an innovative neural network approach to control and enhance a stochastic debt portfolio optimization model. Most of the other early risk management models were oriented to develop credit score systems using decision trees or other interpretable models that segmented the customers according to their risk level and demographic characteristics. These models were developed in-house and complemented the well-known Fair Isaac Corporation (FICO) score or other risk indicators provided by the large risk information providers. The application to other areas of risk in financial institutions was limited because of the restrictions imposed by the regulators and the methods that were acceptable by the early Basel accords. After the credit crisis of 2008 and thanks to the flexibility of Basel III, many new methods combining ML and social network analysis have been explored to evaluate systemic risk (Angelini *et al.* 2008, Koyuncugil and Ozgulbas 2012, Bao and Datta 2014, Birch and Aste 2014, O'Halloran *et al.* 2015, Fraiberger 2016, Manela and Moreira 2017, Van Liebergen 2017, Hanley and Hoberg Forthcoming, Glasserman and Mamaysky 2019) as well as alternative calculations of Value-at-Risk and its components: credit, market and operational risk. In the last few years, mainstream econometricians and finance researchers have also incorporated the use of ML methods to solve problems of asset pricing and financial forecasting. Some of the most important topics of research are the development of new factor analysis models that extend the original Fama-French approach and incorporate a diverse and extensive set of features for asset pricing models.

The combination of all these different applications in risk management, algorithmic trading, financial forecasting, asset pricing, portfolio optimization, customer management, and digital marketing, among other areas, has led to the current wave of FinTech/RegTech innovation. A plethora of startups are currently developing new solutions using ML and AI algorithms that have more flexibility and efficiency than many traditional large institutions (Financial Conduct Authority 2015, Institute of International Finance 2015, Arner *et al.* 2017, Basel Committee on Banking Supervision 2017, Financial Stability Board 2017, Philippon 2017, Rohner and Uhl 2018). Because of these changes, many financial institutions have created their own FinTech companies or units. They are embracing the use of ML and AI algorithms to find new solutions for problems of finance.

2. New perspectives

This special issue brings together papers that review some of the above financial topics, address unresolved questions, and propose new methods using innovative ML and AI perspectives. Additionally, all the papers include an empirical dimension that can help practitioners to explore new approaches to optimize their financial decisions. The current issue contains papers that address the following areas of the problem domain:

(i) Forecasting:
  (a) Universal model: A practical question for forecasting and the development of trading strategies is to build either a model for every stock or a universal model constructed with data from a large number of stocks. Sirignano and Cont use a large-scale Deep Learning model applied to a high-frequency database for U.S. equities to uncover nonparametric evidence for the existence of a universal and stationary relationship between price formation and order flow. This universal model outperforms asset-specific models.
  (b) Prediction markets: The wisdom of the crowd has received increasing interest in the last few years as it has shown predictive value in the case of elections, recommendation systems, etc. Bottazzi and Giachini predict the use of the crowd in financial markets finding that prices do not converge to the true probabilities in a repeated prediction market model based on fractional Kelly traders with heterogeneous beliefs. However, the average price of the crowd approximates the true probability with lower information loss than any individual belief.
  (c) Liquidity: The capacity to anticipate the liquidity demand and supply of the limit order book is vital for the exchanges as they want to provide enough liquidity to the market, and for the traders to find new liquidity-driven strategies. Chua and Chen deal with this problem approximating the liquidity demand and supply in the limit order book through a Vector Functional AutoRegressive framework.
  (d) Market cycle: A significant challenge for macro and financial economists is to anticipate substantial market changes. Procacci and Aste propose an unsupervised algorithm, Inverse Covariance Clustering, to cluster multivariate time series into different market states in a consistent temporal way. In their approach each market state is defined by a correlation network, characterizing the interdependencies between assets in each cluster. Their experiments accurately predict bull and bear market periods of the constituents of the Russell 1000 index.

(e) Stock price forecast: Matsushima uses a convolutional neural network with order-based inputs to forecast the price trend of the Tokyo Stock Exchange. A distinctive aspect of this model is its capacity to learn features of the order book.Following the tradition of the early papers that forecast the price direction with technical indicators, and ML algorithms, Chen and Ge predict the Hong Kong stock market price direction using the Attention mechanism in a Long-Short Term Memory (LSTM) network. The Attention mechanism allows the neural network to focus on the most critical inputs leading to an improvement of the tuning process and the final prediction in comparison to a simple LSTM model.

(ii) Microstructure: A significant challenge for microstructure literature is the simulation of market microstructure features such as order imbalance or mean reversion as they can undergo significant change among the different financial products. Ju and Kim develop a neural network model using the limit order book and path dependent features to examine the lead-lag relationship between the spot and futures markets for the Korea Exchange. The model is capable of learning market microstructure features such as spread-volatility correlation, order imbalance and mean reversion.

(iii) Causality: The default method of evaluating causality in the econometrics and finance literature is the Granger causality test. Creamer and Lee propose and assess a multivariate distance nonlinear causality test using the partial distance correlation in a time series framework. The test can detect nonlinear lagged relationships between time series, and when integrated with ML methods, can improve their forecasting power.

(iv) Option Pricing and volatility smile: A key research topic in option pricing literature is the volatility smile. In this respect, Halperin proposes an Inverse Reinforcement Learning algorithm based only on prices and traders actions, but not rewards. This algorithm is an extension of prior work, which describes a 'QLBS' model, combining Q-learning with the Black-Scholes model to reduce the option pricing and hedging problem to a rebalancing problem of a replicating portfolio of an option made of cash and stock. Halperin also indicates how the QLBS model can price a portfolio of options and provide a data-driven solution to the BS' volatility smile problem.

(v) Testing investment strategies: A major practical problem for the investment community is the generation of overly optimistic, although unrealistic, investment strategies due to multiple testing. Lopez de Prado and Lewis evaluate this problem and propose an unsupervised learning algorithm that determines the number of effectively uncorrelated trials required for filtering out false investment strategies

In closing, as financial econometrics developed to find new solutions for financial problems, ML and AI also grew to solve problems in specific domains. Considering the significant effort that researchers in the financial industry and academia invested in ML and AI, and the dynamic and 'big data' nature of the financial markets, we expect that future innovative development in this area may also come from finance. We hope that this special issue contributes to this new AI and financial ML literature and provides an opportunity to develop novel algorithms and test them on finance problems.

We thank the authors who have contributed to this special issue; the referees who have helped to select and improve the quality of the papers; Gregory Prastacos, Ionut Florescu, Dragos Bozdog and Stevens Institute of Technology for the institutional assistance; Patrick Jardine and Gail Hartley for their editorial advice, and Michael Dempster and Jim Gatheral -the Editors-in-Chief- for their support and encouragement in the development of this special issue.

Disclosure statement

No potential conflict of interest was reported by the authors.

ORCID

Germán G. Creamer ⓘ http://orcid.org/0000-0002-3159-5153
Gary Kazantsev ⓘ http://orcid.org/0000-0003-0166-4338
Tomaso Aste ⓘ http://orcid.org/0000-0002-4219-0215

References

Allen, F. and Karjalainen, R., Using genetic algorithms to find technical trading rules. *J. Financ. Econ.*, 1999, **51**, 245–271.

Amilon, H., A neural network versus Black Scholes: A comparison of pricing and hedging performances. *J. Forecast.*, 2003, **22**, 317–335.

Angelini, E., di Tollo, G. and Roli, A., A neural network approach for credit risk evaluation. *Q. Rev. Econ. Finance*, 2008, **4**, 733–755.

Arner, D., Barberis, J. and Buckley, R., FinTech, RegTech and the reconceptualization of financial regulation. *Nw. J. Int'l L. & Bus.*, 2017, **37**, 371–413.

Baker, T. and Dellaert, B., Regulating Robo advice across the financial services industry. *Iowa Law Rev.*, 2018, **103**, 713.

Bao, Y. and Datta, A., Simultaneously discovering and quantifying risk types from textual risk disclosures. *Manage. Sci.*, 2014, **60**, 1371–1391.

Basel Committee on Banking Supervision, Sound practices: Implications of Fintech developments for banks and bank supervisors. Technical report, Bank for International Settlements, 2017 Working Paper.

Bates, R., Dempster, M. and Romahi, Y., Evolutionary reinforcement learning in FX order book and order flow analysis. In *Proceedings of the IEEE International Conference on Computational Intelligence for Financial Engineering*, Hong Kong, March 20–23, 2003, pp. 355–362, 2003 (IEEE: Hong Kong).

Birch, A. and Aste, T., Systemic losses due to counterparty risk in a stylized banking system. *J. Stat. Phys.*, 2014, **156**, 998–1024.

Chaboud, A., Chiquoine, B., Hjalmarsson, E. and Vega, C., Rise of the machines: Algorithmic trading in the foreign exchange market. *J. Finance*, 2014, **69**, 2045–2084.

Choi, J., Lee, M. and Rhee, M., Trading S&P500 stock index futures using a neural network. In *Proceedings of the 3rd Annual International Conference on Artificial Intelligence Applications on Wall Street*, pp. 63–72, 1995 (New York).

Creamer, G., Can a corporate network and news sentiment improve portfolio optimization using the Black Litterman model? *Quant. Finance*, 2015, **15**, 1405–1416.

Creamer, G. and Freund, Y., Automated trading with boosting and expert weighting. *Quant. Finance*, 2010, **10**, 401–420.

Decker, K., Sycara, K. and Zeng, D., Designing a multi-agent portfolio management system. In *Proceedings of the Proceedings of the AAAI Workshop on Internet Information Systems*, 1996 (AAI Press: Menlo Park, CA).

Dempster, M. and Ireland, A., Object-oriented model integration in MIDAS. In *Proceedings of the Proceedings of the Twenty-Second Annual Hawaii International Conference on System Sciences, Vol. III: Decision Support and Knowledge Based Systems*, January 3–6, 1989, pp. 612–620, 1989 (Kailua-Kona, HI).

Dempster, M. and Leemans, V., An automated FX trading system using adaptive reinforcement learning. *Expert Syst. Appl.: Special Issue Financ. Eng.*, 2006, **30**, 534–552.

Dempster, M., Payne, T., Romahi, Y. and Thompson, G., Computational learning techniques for intraday FX trading using popular technical indicators. *IEEE Trans. Neural Netw.*, 2001, **12**, 744–754.

Domingos, P. and Richardson, M., Mining the network value of customers. In *Proceedings of the KDD '01: Proceedings Seventh ACM SIGKDD International Conference on Knowledge Discovery and Data Mining*, San Francisco, CA, pp. 57–66, 2001 (ACM: New York, NY).

Financial Conduct Authority, Call for input: Supporting the development and adoption of RegTech. Technical report, Financial Conduct Authority, 2015 Working Paper.

Financial Stability Board, Artificial intelligence and machine learning financial services. Technical report, Financial Stability Board, 2017 Working Paper.

Fraiberger, S., News sentiment and cross-country fluctuations. In *Proceedings of the Proceedings of 2016 EMNLP Workshop on Natural Language Processing and Computational Social Science*, November, 2016 (Austin, TX).

Glasserman, P. and Mamaysky, H., Does unusual news forecast market stress? *J. Financ. Quant. Anal.*, 2019, 1–38. doi:10.1017/S0022109019000127

Hanley, K. and Hoberg, G., Dynamic interpretation of emerging systemic risks. *Rev. Financ. Stud.*, forthcoming.

Hill, S., Provost, F. and Volinsky, C., Network-based marketing: Identifying likely adopters via consumer networks. *Stat. Sci.*, 2006, **21**, 256–276.

Hutchinson, J., Lo, A. and Poggio, T., A nonparametric approach to pricing and hedging derivative securities via learning networks. *J. Financ.*, 1994, **49**, 851–889.

Institute of International Finance, Regtech: Exploring solutions for regulatory challenges. Technical report, Institute of International Finance, 2015 Working Paper.

Ireland, A. and Dempster, M., A financial expert decision support system. In *Mathematical Models for Decision Support*, edited by G. Mitra, H. Greenberg, F. Lootsma, M. Rijkaert and H. Zimmermann, Vol. 48 NATO ASI Series (Series F: Computer and Systems Sciences), pp. 415–440, 1988 (Springer: Berlin, Heidelberg).

Koyuncugil, A. and Ozgulbas, N., Financial early warning system model and data mining application for risk detection. *Expert Syst. Appl.*, 2012, **39**, 6238–6253.

Leskovec, J., Adamic, L. and Huberman, B., The dynamics of viral marketing. In *Proceedings of the EC '06: Proceedings 7th ACM Conference on Electronic Commerce*, Ann Arbor, MI, pp. 228–237, 2006 (ACM: New York, NY).

Manela, A. and Moreira, A., News implied volatility and disaster concerns. *J. Financ. Econ.*, 2017, **123**, 137–162.

Moody, J. and Saffell, M., Learning to trade via direct reinforcement. *IEEE Trans. Neural Netw.*, 2001, **12**, 875–889.

Nevmyvaka, Y., Feng, Y. and Kearns, M., Reinforcement learning for optimized trade execution. In *Proceedings of the Proceedings of the 23rd International Conference on Machine Learning*, ICML 2006, Pittsburgh, PA, pp. 673–680, 2006 (ACM: New York, NY).

O'Halloran, S., Maskey, S., McAllister, G., Park, D. and Chen, K., Big data and the regulation of financial markets. In *Proceedings of the IEEE/ACM International conference on Advances in Social Networks Analysis and Mining*, August, 2015 (Paris).

Philippon, T., The Fintech opportunity. Technical report, Bank for International Settlements, 2017 Working Paper No. 655.

Richardson, M. and Domingos, P., Markov logic networks. *Mach. Learn.*, 2006, **62**, 107–136.

Rohner, P. and Uhl, M., Robo-Advisors vs. traditional investment advisors: An unequal game. *J. Wealth Manage.*, 2018, **21**, 44–50.

Seo, Y., Giampapa, J. and Sycara, K., Financial news analysis for intelligent portfolio management. Technical report CMU-RI-TR-04-04, Robotics Institute, Carnegie Mellon University, 2004.

Tay, F. and Cao, L., Application of support vector machines in financial time series forecasting. *Omega*, 2001, **29**, 309–317.

Trippi, R. and DeSieno, D., Trading equity index futures with a neural network. *J. Portfolio Manage.*, 1992, **19**, 27–33.

Van Liebergen, B., Machine learning: A revolution in risk management and compliance? *CAPCO Inst. J. Financ. Transform.*, 2017, **45**, 60–67.

Universal features of price formation in financial markets: perspectives from deep learning

JUSTIN SIRIGNANO and RAMA CONT

(*Received 21 July 2018; accepted 6 May 2019; published online 9 July 2019*)

Using a large-scale Deep Learning approach applied to a high-frequency database containing billions of market quotes and transactions for US equities, we uncover nonparametric evidence for the existence of a *universal* and *stationary* relation between order flow history and the direction of price moves. The universal price formation model exhibits a remarkably stable out-of-sample accuracy across a wide range of stocks and time periods. Interestingly, these results also hold for stocks which are not part of the training sample, showing that the relations captured by the model are universal and not asset-specific.

The universal model—trained on data from all stocks—outperforms asset-specific models trained on time series of any given stock. This weighs in favor of pooling together financial data from various stocks, rather than designing asset- or sector-specific models, as is currently commonly done. Standard data normalizations based on volatility, price level or average spread, or partitioning the training data into sectors or categories such as large/small tick stocks, do not improve training results. On the other hand, inclusion of price and order flow history over many past observations improves forecast accuracy, indicating that there is path-dependence in price dynamics.

1. Price formation: how markets react to fluctuations in supply and demand

The computerization of financial markets and the availability of detailed electronic records of order flow and price dynamics in financial markets over the last decade has unleashed TeraBytes of high-frequency data on transactions, order flow and order book dynamics in listed markets, which provide us with a detailed view of the high-frequency dynamics of supply, demand and price in these markets (Cont 2011). These data may be put to use to explore the nature of the price formation mechanism which describes how market prices react to fluctuations in supply and demand. At a high level, a 'price formation mechanism' is a map which represents the relationship between the market price and variables such as price history and order flow:

$$\text{Price } (t + \Delta t) = F \,(\text{Price history } (0 \ldots t), \text{ Order Flow}$$
$$\times \,(0 \ldots t), \text{Other Information}) = F(X_t, \epsilon_t),$$

where X_t is a set of state variables (e.g. lagged values of price, volatility, and order flow), endowed with some dynamics, and ϵ_t is a random 'noise' or innovation term representing the arrival of new information and other effects not captured entirely by the state variables. Market microstructure models, stochastic models and machine learning price prediction models can all be viewed as different ways of representing this map F.

One question, which has been implicit in the literature, is the degree to which this map F is *universal* (i.e. independent of the specific asset being considered). The generic, as opposed to asset-specific, formulation of market microstructure models seems to implicitly assume such a universality. Empirical evidence on the universality of certain stylized facts (Cont 2001) and scaling relations (Mandelbrot *et al.* 1997, Benzaquen *et al.* 2016, Kyle and Obizhaeva 2016, Patzelt and Bouchaud 2017, Toth *et al.* 2017, Andersen *et al.* 2018) seems to support the universality hypothesis. Creamer and Freund (2007) recommended training models via a universal approach in order to capture the diversity of different companies. Yet, the practice of statistical modeling of financial time series has remained asset-specific: when building a model for the returns of a given asset, market practitioners and econometricians typically use data from the same asset. For example, a model for Microsoft shares would be estimated using only time series of Microsoft share prices and would not use data from other stocks.

Furthermore, the data used for estimation is often limited to a recent time window, reflecting the belief that financial data can be 'non-stationary' and prone to regime changes which may render older data less relevant for prediction.

Due to such considerations, models considered in financial econometrics, trading and risk management applications are asset-specific and their parameters are (re)estimated over time using a time window of recent data. Such a model for an asset i may be expressed in the form

$$\text{Price}_i(t + \Delta t) = F(X_{0:t}^i, \epsilon_t \mid \theta_i(t)),$$

where the model parameter $\theta_i(t)$ is estimated using recent data on price and other state variables related to asset i. As a result, data sets are fragmented across assets and time and, even in the high-frequency realm, the size of data sets used for model estimation and training are orders of magnitude smaller than those encountered in other fields where Big Data analytics have been successfully applied. This is one of the reasons why, except in a few instances (Sirignano et al. 2016, Kolanovic and Krishnamachari 2017, Dixon 2018a, 2018b, Sirignano 2019), large-scale machine learning methods such as Deep Learning (Goodfellow et al. 2017) have not yet been deployed for quantitative modeling in finance.

On the other hand, if the relation between these variables were *universal* and *stationary*, i.e. if the parameter $\theta_i(t)$ varies *neither* with the asset i nor with time t, then one could potentially pool data across different assets and time periods and use a much richer data set to estimate/train the model. For instance, data on a flash crash episode in one asset market could provide insights into how the price of another asset would react to severe imbalances in order flow, whether or not such an episode has occurred in its history. This idea, known as *transfer learning*, has been used with great success in applications such as image and text recognition.

In this work, we provide evidence for the existence of such a universal, stationary relation between order flow and market price fluctuations, using a nonparametric approach based on Deep Learning. Deep learning can estimate nonlinear relations between variables using 'deep' multilayer neural networks which are trained on large data sets using 'supervised learning' methods (Bengio et al. 2015).

Using a deep neural network architecture trained on a high-frequency database containing billions of electronic market transactions and quotes for US equities, we uncover nonparametric evidence for the existence of a *universal* and *stationary* price formation mechanism relating the dynamics of supply and demand for a stock, as revealed through the order book, to subsequent variations in its market price. We assess the model by testing its out-of-sample predictions for the direction of price moves given the history of price and order flow, across a wide range of stocks and time periods. The universal price

formation model exhibits a remarkably stable out-of-sample prediction accuracy across time and across a wide range of stocks from different sectors. Interestingly, these results also hold for stocks which are not part of the training sample, showing that the relations captured by the model are universal and not asset-specific. We observe that the neural network thus trained outperforms linear models, pointing to the presence of nonlinear relationships between order flow and price changes.

Our paper provides quantitative evidence for the existence of a universal price formation mechanism in financial markets. The universal nature of the price formation mechanism is reflected by the fact that a model trained on data from all stocks outperforms, in terms of out-of-sample prediction accuracy, stock-specific linear and nonlinear models trained on time series of any given stock. This shows that the universal nature of price formation weighs in favor of pooling together financial data from various stocks, rather than designing stock- or sector-specific models as commonly done. Also, we observe that standard data transformations such as normalizations based on volatility or average spread, or partitioning the training data into sectors or categories such as large/small tick stocks, do not improve training results. On the other hand, inclusion of price and order flow history over many past observations improves forecasting performance, showing evidence of path-dependence in price dynamics.

Remarkably, the universal model is able to extrapolate, or *generalize*, to stocks not within the training set. The universal model is able to perform well on completely new stocks whose historical data the model was never trained on. This shows that the universal model captures features of the price formation mechanism which are robust across stocks and sectors and implies the possibility of using transfer learning for training price prediction models. This feature is quite interesting for applications in finance where missing data problems and newly issued securities often complicate model estimation.

Outline: Section 2 describes the dataset and the supervised learning approach used to extract information about the price formation mechanism. Section 3 provides evidence for the existence of a universal and stationary relationship linking order flow and price history to price variations. Section 4 summarizes our main findings and discusses some implications.

2. Data-driven modeling of price formation via deep learning

Applications such as image, text, and speech recognition have been revolutionized by the advent of 'Deep Learning'—the use of multilayer ('deep') neural networks trained on large data sets to uncover complex nonlinear relations between high-dimensional inputs ('features') and outputs (LeCun et al. 2015).

At an abstract level, a deep neural network represents a functional relation $y = f(x; \theta)$ between a high-dimensional input vector x and an output y through iterations ('layers') consisting of weighted sums followed by the application of nonlinear 'activation' functions. Each iteration corresponds to a 'hidden layer' and a deep neural network can have many hidden layers. The network weights are the parameters θ for the model. Neural networks can be used as 'universal approximators' for complex nonlinear relationships (Hornik *et al.* 1989), by appropriately choosing the weights in each layer.

In practice, the network weights are estimated by optimizing a regularized cost function reflecting in-sample discrepancy between the network output and desired outputs. This optimization is computationally intensive due to the large number of parameters (possibly millions) and the large amount of data. Stochastic gradient descent algorithms (e.g. RMSprop or ADAM) are used for training neural networks, and training is parallelized on Graphics Processing Units (GPUs).

We apply this approach to learn the relation between supply and demand on an electronic exchange—captured in the history of the order book for each stock—and the subsequent variation of the market price. Our data set is a high-frequency record of all orders, transactions and order cancellations for approximately 1000 stocks traded on the NASDAQ between January 1, 2014 and March 31, 2017.†

Electronic buy and sell orders are continuously submitted, cancelled and executed through the exchange's *order book*. A 'limit order' is a buy or sell order for a stock at a certain price and will appear in the order book at that price and remain there until cancelled or executed. The 'limit order book' is a snapshot of all outstanding limit orders and thus represents the visible supply and demand for the stock (see figure 1). In US stock markets, orders can be submitted at prices occurring at multiples of 1 cent. The 'best ask price' is the lowest sell order and the 'best bid price' is the highest bid price. The best ask price and best bid price are the prices at which the stock can be immediately bought or sold. The 'mid price' is the average of the best ask price and best bid price. The order book evolves over time as new orders are submitted, existing orders are cancelled, and trades are executed.

In electronic markets such as the NASDAQ, new orders may arrive at high frequency—sometimes every microsecond—and order books of certain stocks can update millions of times per day. This leads to TeraBytes of data, which we put to use to build a *data-driven model* of the price formation process.

Our deep learning model is a recurrent neural network with Long Short-Term Memory (LSTM) units (Gers *et al.* 2000) whose architecture is schematically represented in figure 2. LSTM networks can learn nonlinear representations of historical data, which it uses for predictions. Each LSTM unit has an internal state which maintains a nonlinear representation of all past data. This internal state is updated as new data arrives. Our network has 3 layers of LSTM units followed by a final fully-connected layer of rectified linear units (ReLUs). A probability distribution for the next price move is produced by applying a softmax activation function. LSTM units are specially designed to efficiently encode temporal

† Historical order book data was reconstructed from NASDAQ Level III data using the LOBSTER data engine (Huang and Polak 2011).

	Size	Price
	200	$80.03
Asks	0	$80.02
	400	$80.01
	1100	$80.00
	1000	$79.99
	500	$79.98
Bids	50	$79.97
	400	$79.96

Figure 1. The limit order book represents a snapshot of the supply and demand for a stock on an electronic exchange. The 'ask' side represents sell orders and the 'bid' side, buy orders. The size represents the number of shares available for sale/purchase at a given price. The difference between the lowest sell price (ask) and the highest buy price (bid) is the 'spread' (in this example, 1 cent).

sequences of data. Deep LSTM networks have found great success in speech and text recognition applications (Gers *et al.* 2000, Goodfellow *et al.* 2017).

We train the network to forecast the next price move from a vector of state variables, which encode the history of the order book over many observation lags. The index t represents the number of price changes. At a high level, the LSTM network is of the form

$$(Y_t, h_t) = f(X_t, h_{t-1}; \theta). \tag{0}$$

Y_t is the prediction for the next price move, X_t is the state of the order book at time t, h_t is the internal state of the deep learning model, representing information extracted from the *history* of X up to t, and θ designates the model parameters, which correspond to the weights in the neural network. At each time point t the model uses the current value of state variables X_t (i.e. the current order book) and the nonlinear representation of all previous data h_{t-1}, which summarizes relevant features of the history of order flow, to predict the next price move. In principle, this allows for arbitrary history-dependence: the history of the state variables $X_{0:t}$ may affect the evolution of the system, in particular price dynamics, at all future times $T \geq t$ in a nonlinear way. Alternative modeling approaches typically do not allow the flexibility of blending nonlinearity and history-dependence in this manner.

The (high-dimensional) parameter θ is estimated by minimizing a regularized negative log-likelihood objective function using stochastic gradient descent. The parameter θ is assumed to be constant across time and thus affects the output at all times in a recursive manner. A stochastic gradient descent step at time t requires calculating the sensitivity of the output to θ, via a chain rule, back through the previous times $t - 1, t - 2, \ldots$ (commonly referred to as 'backpropagation through time'). In theory, backpropagation should occur back to time 0. In practice, we limit the dependence on past data to a window of length T: $t - 1, t - 2, \ldots, t - T$.

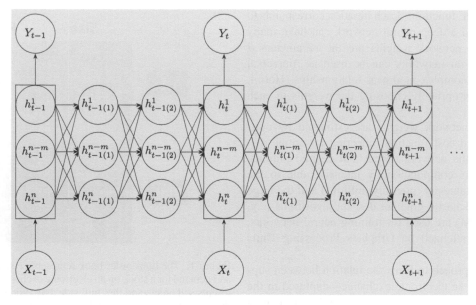

Figure 2. Architecture of a recurrent neural network.

In Section 3.4, we examine the dependence of the results on the choice of the window length T and evidence for memory effects.

The resulting LSTM network involves up to hundreds of thousands of parameters. This is relatively small compared to networks used for instance in image or speech recognition, but it is huge compared to econometric models traditionally used in finance. Previous literature has been almost entirely devoted to stochastic models with a very small number of parameters. It is commonly believed that financial data is far too noisy to build such large models without overfitting. As we will show, our results suggest that this is not necessarily the case, provided a flexible non-parametric framework is used for modeling dependencies.

Given the size of the data and the large number of network parameters to be learned, significant computational resources are required both for pre-processing the data and training the network. Training of deep neural networks can be highly parallelized on GPUs. Each GPU has thousands of cores, and training is typically $10\times$ faster on a GPU than a standard CPU. The NASDAQ data was filtered to create training and test sets. This data processing is parallelized over approximately 500 compute nodes. Training of asset-specific models was also parallelized, with each stock assigned to a single GPU node. 500 GPU nodes are used in total to train the stock-specific models.

These asset-specific models, trained on the data related to a single stock, were then compared to a 'universal model' trained on the combined data from all the stocks in the dataset. Data from various stocks were pooled together for this purposes without any specific normalization.

Due to the large amount of data, we distributed the training of the universal model across 25 GPU nodes using asynchronous stochastic gradient descent (figure 3). Each node loads a batch of data (selected at random from all stocks in the dataset), computes gradients of the model on the GPU, and then updates the model. Updates occur *asynchronously*, meaning node j updates the model without waiting for nodes $i \neq j$ to finish their computations.

3. Results

We split the universe of stocks into two groups of roughly 500 stocks; training is done on transactions and quotes for stocks from the first group. We distinguish:

- stock-specific models, trained using data on all transactions and quotes for a specific stock.
- the 'universal model', trained using data on all transactions and quotes for **all stocks** in the training set.

All models are trained for predicting the direction of the *next price move*. Specifically, if $\tau_1, \tau_2, \ldots$ are the times at which the mid-price P_t changes, we estimate $\mathbb{P}[P_{\tau_{k+1}} - P_{\tau_k} > 0 | X_{\tau_{0:k}}]$ and $\mathbb{P}[P_{\tau_{k+1}} - P_{\tau_k} < 0 | X_{\tau_{0:k}}]$ where X_t is the state of the limit order book at time t. The models therefore predict whether the next price move is up or down. The events are irregularly spaced in time. The time interval $\tau_{k+1} - \tau_k$ between price moves can vary considerably from a fraction of a second to seconds.

We measure the forecast accuracy of a model for a given stock via the proportion of observations for which it correctly predicts the direction of the next price move. This can be estimated using the empirical estimator

$$A_i = \frac{\begin{array}{c}\text{Number of price changes where model correctly}\\ \text{predicts price direction for stock } i\end{array}}{\text{Total number of price changes}} \times 100\%.$$

All results are *out-of-sample*: the accuracy is evaluated on time periods outside of the training set. Model accuracy is reported via the cross-sectional distribution of the accuracy score A_i across stocks in the testing sample, and models are compared by comparing their accuracy scores.

Our results provide evidence of short-term predictability of (mid-)price movements when order flow is observed. Models can achieve an accuracy significantly higher than 50%

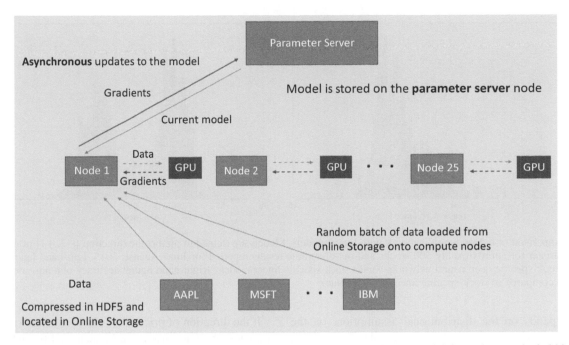

Figure 3. Asynchronous stochastic gradient descent for training the neural network. The dataset, which is too large to be held in the nodes' memories, is stored on the Online Storage system. Batches of data are randomly selected from all stocks and sent to the GPU nodes. Gradients are calculated on the GPUs and then the model is asynchronously updated.

for short-term prediction of mid-price movements using order flow data. Determining whether this predictability leads to profitable trading strategies requires a careful analysis of transaction costs, taking into account factors such as latency, a detailed study of which is beyond the scope of this paper.

In addition, we evaluate the accuracy of the universal model for stocks *outside* the training set. Importantly, this means we assess forecast accuracy for stock *i* using a model which is trained *without* any data on stock *i*. This tests whether the universal model can generalize to completely new stocks.

Typically, the out-of-sample dataset is a 3-month time period and the training set is a 17-month time period. (Therefore, the test set is approximately 15% of the dataset.) In the context of high-frequency data, 3 months corresponds to hundreds of millions of observations and therefore provides a rigorous test of model performance.

The main findings of our data-driven approach may be summarized as follows:

- **Nonlinearity**: Data-driven models trained using deep learning substantially outperform linear models in terms of forecasting accuracy (Section 3.1).
- **Universality**: The model uncovers universal features that are common across all stocks (Section 3.2). These features generalize well: they are also observed to hold for stocks which are not part of the training sample.
- **Stationarity**: The model performance in terms of price forecasting accuracy is remarkably stable across time, even a year out of sample. This shows evidence for the existence of a *stationary* relationship between order flow and price changes (Section 3.3), which is stable over long time periods.

- **Path-dependence and long-range dependence**: Inclusion of price and order flow history is shown to substantially increase the forecast accuracy. This provides evidence that price dynamics depend not only on the current or recent state of the limit order book but on its *history*, possibly over long time scales (Section 3.4).

Our results show that there is far more common structure across data from different financial instruments than previously thought. Providing a suitably flexible model is used which allows for nonlinearity and history-dependence, data from various assets may be pooled together to yield a data set large enough for deep learning.

3.1. Deep learning versus linear models

Linear state space models, such as Vector Autoregressive (VAR) models, have been widely used in the modeling of high-frequency data and in empirical market microstructure research (Hasbrouck 2007) and provide a natural benchmark for evaluating the performance of a forecast. Linear models are easy to estimate and capture in a simple way the trends, linear correlations and autocorrelations in the state variables.

The results in figure 4 show that the deep learning models substantially outperform linear models. (To provide context, an increase of even 1% in accuracy is considered a significant improvement in high-frequency modeling.)

The linear (VAR) model may be formulated as follows: at each observation we update a vector of *linear* features h_t and then use a probit model for the conditional probability of an upward price move given the state variables:

$$h_t = Ah_{t-1} + BX_t,$$
$$Y_t = \mathbb{P}(\Delta P_t > 0 | X_t, h_t) = G(CX_t + Dh_t), \qquad (-1)$$

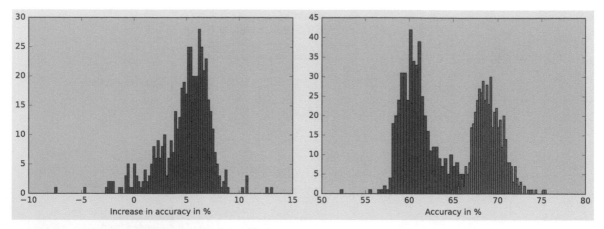

Figure 4. Comparison of a deep neural network with linear models. Models are trained to predict the direction $\{-1, +1\}$ of next mid-price move. Comparison for approximately 500 stocks and out-of-sample results reported for June–August, 2015. Left-hand figure: increase in accuracy of stock-specific deep neural networks versus stock-specific linear models. Right-hand figure: accuracy of a universal deep neural network (red) compared to stock-specific linear models (blue).

where G depends on the distributional assumptions on the innovations in the linear model. For example, if we use a logistic distribution for the innovations in the linear model, then the probability distribution of the next price move is given by a logistic function applied to a linear function of the current order book and linear features:

$$\mathbb{P}(\Delta P_t > 0 | X_t, h_t) = \frac{1}{1 + \exp(CX_t + Dh_t)} \quad (0)$$

We compare the neural network against a linear model for approximately 500 stocks. To compare models we report the difference in accuracy scores across the same test data set. Let

- L_i be the accuracy of the stock-specific linear model g_{θ_i} for asset i estimated on data only from stock i,
- $\hat{A}_i$ be the accuracy of the stock-specific deep learning model f_{θ_i} trained on data only from stock i, and
- A_i be the accuracy for asset i of the *universal* deep learning model f_θ trained on a pooled data set of all quotes and transactions for all stocks.

The left plot in figure 4 reports the cross-sectional distribution for the increase in accuracy $\hat{A}_i - L_i$ when moving from the stock-specific linear model to the stock-specific deep learning model. We observe a substantial increase in accuracy, between 5% and 10% for most stocks, when incorporating nonlinear effects using the neural networks.

The right plot in figure 4 displays histograms of A_i (red) and L_i (blue). We clearly observe that moving from a stock-specific linear model to the universal nonlinear model trained on all stocks substantially improves the forecasting accuracy by around 10%.

The deep neural network outperforms the linear model since it is able to estimate nonlinear relationships between the price dynamics and the order book, which represents the visible supply and demand for the stock. This is consistent with an abundant empirical and econometric literature documenting nonlinear effects in financial time series, but the large magnitude of this improvement can be attributed to the flexibility of the neural network in representing nonlinearities.

If the direction of price moves is not symmetric in the data set, above 50% accuracy can be achieved by simply predicting the most frequent direction of price moves. However, this feature is easily captured by the linear model we use as a benchmark. Figure 4 shows however that the deep learning forecast performs significantly better than the benchmark linear model, which indicates that the accuracy is not explainable by an imbalance or trend: the deep learning model is able to learn relationships between the order book and price beyond the information contained in the distribution of price moves.

More specifically, sensitivity analysis of our data-driven model uncovers stable nonlinear relations between state variables and price moves, i.e. *nonlinear features* which are useful for forecasting.

Figure 5 presents an examples of such a feature: the relation between the depth on the bid and ask sides of the order book and the probability of a price decrease. Such relations have been studied in queueing models of limit order book dynamics (Cont *et al.* 2010, Cont and de Larrard 2013). In particular, it was shown in Cont and de Larrard (2013) that when the order flow is symmetric then there exists a 'universal' relation—not dependent on model parameters—between bid depth, ask depth and the probability of a price decrease at the next price move. However, the derivations in these models hinge on various statistical assumptions which may or may not hold and the universality of such relations remained to be empirically verified.

Our analysis shows that there is indeed evidence for such a universal relation, across a wide range of assets and time periods. Figure 5 (left) displays the probability of a price decrease as a function of the depth (the number of shares) at the best bid/ask price. The larger the best ask size, the more likely the next price prove will be downwards. The probability is approximately constant along the center diagonal where the bid/ask imbalance is zero. However, as observed in queueing models (Cont *et al.* 2010, Cont and de Larrard 2013, Figueroa-Lopez and Chavez-Casillas 2017), even under simplifying assumptions, the relation between this probability and various measures of the bid/ask imbalance is not linear. Furthermore, such queueing models typically focus on the influence of depth at the top of the order book and it is more difficult to

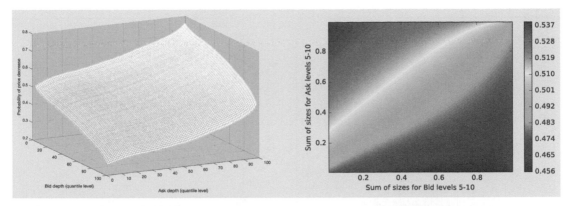

Figure 5. Left: relation between depth at the bid, depth at the ask and the probability of a price decrease. The *x*-axis and *y*-axis display the quantile level corresponding to the observed bid and ask depth. Right: Contour plot displaying the influence of levels deeper in the order book (5–10) on the probability of a price decrease.

Table 1. Absolute change in the probability of a price increase following to a 10% increase in queue size at a given depth in the limit order book. The final column is a 10% increase in size for all levels $5, \ldots, 10$.

Level	1	2	3	4	5–10
Sensitivity	1.7%	0.4%	0.2 %	0.2%	0.4%

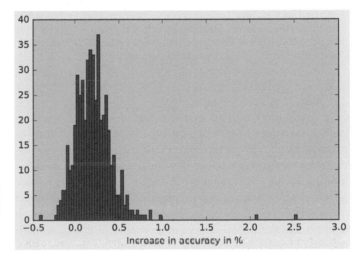

Figure 6. Comparison of two universal models. The first model is trained using 10 levels of bid and ask sizes. The second model is trained using only 4 levels of bid and ask sizes. Models are trained to predict direction $\{+1, -1\}$ of next mid-price move. Comparison for 489 stocks and out-of-sample results reported for June–August, 2015.

extract information from deeper levels of the order book. The right contour plot in figure 5 displays the influence of limit orders deeper in the order book (here: total size aggregated across levels 5–10) on the probability of a price decrease. We see that the influence is less than the depth at the top of the book, as illustrated by the tighter range of predicted probabilities, but still significant.

Unlike previous empirical work which has often been limited to analyzing the link between price movement and the depth at the top of the order book, we have examined all levels of the order book for which there is a non-zero queue size. It is thus interesting to examine whether the learning algorithm ends up by selecting a subset of the levels as being more relevant for price forecasting. Table 1 shows the sensitivity of the probability of an (upward) price move to a unit change in a one level of the order book, as a function of the distance to the mid-price. As observed in Cont *et al.* (2014), the first level has a stronger impact on price dynamics, but deeper levels also seem to contain information relevant for forecasting. Figure 6 supports this hypothesis, showing that a model trained using 10 levels of the order book outperforms a model trained, say using 4 levels of the order book.

3.2. Universality across assets

A striking aspect of our results is the stability across stocks of the features uncovered by the deep learning model, and its ability to extrapolate ('generalize') to stocks which it was not trained on. This may be illustrated by comparing forecasting accuracy of stock-specific models, trained only on data of a given stock, to a universal model trained on a pooled data set of 500 stocks, a much larger but extremely heterogeneous

data set. As shown in figure 7, which plots $A_i - \hat{A}_i$, the universal model consistently outperforms the stock-specific models. This indicates there are common features, relevant to forecasting, across all stocks. Features extracted from data on stock A may be relevant to forecasting of price moves for stock B.

We also test whether this increase out-of-sample in accuracy is statistically significant i.e. whether it cannot be purely a result of estimation error. Given the large size of the data sets involved, we find that, for all stocks in our sample,

- the universal deep learning model outperforms the stock-specific deep learning model at 99.99% confidence level.
- the stock-specific deep learning model outperforms the linear model at 99.99% confidence level.

Given the heterogeneity of the data, one might imagine that time series from different stocks should be first normalized (by average daily volume, average price or volatility, etc.) before pooling them. Surprisingly, this appears *not* to be the

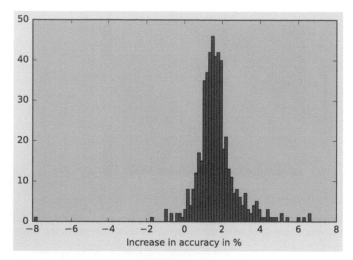

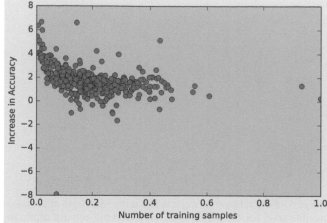

Figure 7. Out-of-sample forecasting accuracy of the universal model compared with stock-specific models. Both are deep neural networks with three LSTM layers followed by a ReLU layer. All layers have 50 units. Models are trained to predict the direction of the next move. Comparison across 489 stocks, June–August, 2015.

Figure 8. Increase in out-of-sample forecast accuracy (in %) of the universal model compared to stock-specific model, as a function of size of training set for stock-specific model (normalized by total sample size, $N = 24.1$ million). Models are trained to predict the direction of next price move. Comparison across 500 stocks, June–August, 2015.

case: we have observed that standard data transformations such as normalizations based on average volume, volatility or average spread, or partitioning the training data into sectors or categories such as large/small tick stocks do not improve training results. For example, a deep learning model trained on small tick stocks does not outperform the universal model in terms of forecasting price moves for small tick stocks. It appears that the model arrives at its own data-driven normalization of inputs based on statistical features of the data rather than ad hoc criteria.

The source of the universal model's outperformance is well-demonstrated by figure 8. The universal model most strongly outperforms the stock-specific models on stocks with less data. The stock-specific model is more exposed to overfitting due to the smaller dataset while the universal model is able to *generalize* by interpolating across the rich scenario space of the pooled data set and therefore is less exposed to overfitting. So, the existence of these common features seems to argue for pooling the data from different stocks, notwithstanding their heterogeneity, leading to a much richer and larger set of training scenarios. Using 1 year of the pooled data set is roughly equivalent to using 500 years (!) of data for training a single-stock model and the richness of the scenario space is actually *enhanced* by the diversity and heterogeneity of behavior across stocks.

Due to the large amount of data, very large universal models can be estimated without overfitting. Figure 9 shows the increase in accuracy for a universal model with 150 units per layer (which amounts to several hundred thousand parameters) versus a universal model with 50 units per layer.

Remarkably, the universal model is even able to *generalize* to stocks which were not part of the training dataset: if the model is only trained on data from stocks $\{1, \ldots, N\}$, its forecast accuracy is similar for stock $N + 1$. This implies that the universal model is capturing features in the relation between order flow and price variations which are common to all stocks. Table 2 illustrates the forecast accuracy of a universal

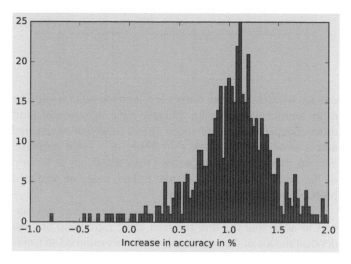

Figure 9. Comparison of two universal models: a 150 unit per layer model versus 50 unit per layer model. Models are trained to predict direction $\{-1, +1\}$ of next mid-price move. Out-of-sample prediction accuracy for direction of next price move, across approximately 500 stocks (June–August, 2015).

model trained *only* on stocks $1 - 464$ (for January 2014–May 2015), and tested on stocks $465 - 489$ (for June–August 2015). This universal model outperforms stock-specific models for stocks $465 - 489$, even though the universal model has never seen data from these stocks in the training set. The universal model trained only on stocks $1 - 464$ performs roughly the same for stocks $465 - 489$ as the universal model trained on the entire dataset of stocks $1 - 489$. Results are reported in table 2.

Figure 10 displays the accuracy of the universal model for 500 completely new stocks, which are not part of the training sample. The universal model achieves a high accuracy on these new stocks, demonstrating that it is able to generalize to assets that are not included in the training data. This is especially relevant for applications, where missing

Table 2. Comparison of universal model trained on stocks 1–464 versus (1) stock-specific models for stocks 465–489 and (2) universal model trained on all stocks 1–489. Models are trained to predict direction of next mid-price move. Second column shows the fraction of stocks where the universal model trained only on stocks 1–464 outperforms models (1) and (2). The third column shows the average increase in accuracy of the universal model trained on stocks 1–464 versus models (1) and (2). Comparison for stocks 465–489 and out-of-sample results reported for June–August, 2015. The training time period is January 2014–May 2015.

Model	Comparison	Average increase in accuracy
Stock-specific	25/25	1.45%
Universal model trained on stocks 1–489	4/25	− 0.15%

Table 3. Out-of-sample forecast accuracy of deep learning models trained on entire training set (19 months) vs. deep learning models trained for shorter time periods immediately preceding the test period, across 50 stocks Aug 2015. Models are trained to predict the direction of next price move. Second column shows the fraction of stocks where the 19th month model outperforms models trained on shorter time periods. The third column shows the average increase in accuracy across all stocks.

Size of training set	% of stocks for which 19-month training outperforms short-term training	Average increase in accuracy for 19-month model
1 month	100%	7.2%
3 months	100%	3.7%
6 months	100%	1.6%

data issues, stock splits, new listings and corporate events constantly modify the universe of stocks.

3.3. Stationarity

The relationships uncovered by the deep learning model are not only stable across stocks but also stationary in time. This is illustrated by examining how forecast accuracy behaves when the training period and test period are separated in time.

Figure 10 shows the accuracy of the universal model on 500 stocks which were not part of the training sample. The left histogram displays the accuracy in June–August, 2015, shortly after the training period (January 2014–May 2015), while the right plot displays the cross-sectional distribution of accuracy for the *same* model in January–March, 2017, *18 months after the training period*. Interestingly, even one year after the training period, the forecasting accuracy is stable, without *any* adjustments.

Such stability contrasts with the common practice of 'recalibrating' models based on a moving window of recent data

due to perceived non-stationarity. If the data were non-stationary, accuracy would decrease with the time span separating the training set and the prediction period and it would be better to train models only on recent periods immediately before the test set. However, we observe that this is not the case: Table 3 reports forecast results for models trained over periods extending up to 1, 3, 6, and 19 months before the test set. Model accuracy consistently increases as the length of the training set is increased. The message is simple: use all available data, rather than an arbitrarily chosen time window.

Note that these results are *not* incompatible with the data itself being non-stationary. The stability we refer to is the stability of the *relation* between the inputs (order flow and price history) and outputs (forecasts). If the inputs themselves are non-stationary, the output will be non-stationary but that does not contradict our point in any way.

3.4. Path-dependence

Statistical modeling of financial time series has been dominated by *Markovian* models which, for reasons of analytical tractability, assume that the evolution of the price and other

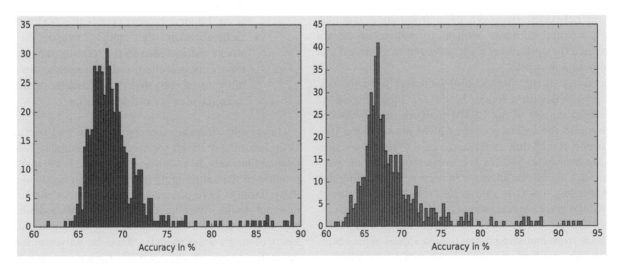

Figure 10. Performance on 500 new stocks which the model has never seen before. Left: out-of-sample accuracy reported for June–August, 2015. Right: out-of-sample accuracy reported for January–March, 2017. Universal model trained on data from January 2014–May 2015.

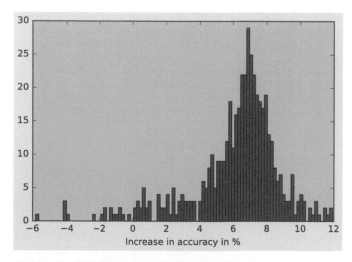

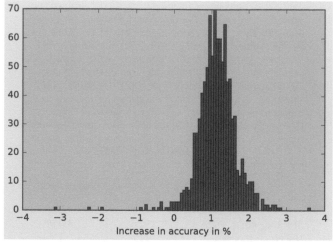

Figure 11. Comparison of out-of-sample forecast accuracy of a LSTM network with a feedforward neural network trained to forecast the direction of next price move based on the current state of the limit order book. Cross-sectional results for 500 stocks for test period June–August, 2015.

Figure 12. Out-of-sample increase in accuracy when using a 5000-step sequence versus a 100-step sequence, across 1000 stocks. Test period: June–August 2015.

state variables only depends on their current value and there is no added value to including their history beyond one lag. There is a trove of empirical evidence going against this hypothesis, and pointing to long-range dependence in financial time series (Mandelbrot *et al.* 1997, Bouchaud *et al.* 2004, Lillo and Farmer 2004, Bacry *et al.* 2008, Taranto *et al.* 2014). Our results are consistent with these findings: we find that the *history* of the limit order book contains significant additional information beyond that contained in its current state.

Figure 11 shows the increase in accuracy when using an LSTM network, which is a function of the history of the order book, as compared with a feedforward neural network, which is only a function of the most recent observation (a Markovian model). The LSTM network, which incorporates temporal dependence, significantly outperforms the Markovian model. We have also tested to determine whether feedforward neural networks with larger numbers of hidden units can reduce the performance gap between the feedforward and recurrent neural networks. However, even using more complex feedforward neural networks with more parameters are not able to reduce the performance gap between feedforward and recurrent neural networks.

The accuracy of the forecast also increases when the network is provided with a longer history as input. Figure 12 displays the accuracy of the LSTM network on a 5000-step sequence minus the accuracy of the LSTM network on a 100-step sequence. Recall that a step $\Delta_k = \tau_{k+1} - \tau_k$ is on average 1.7 s in the dataset so 5000 lags corresponds to 2 h on average. There is a significant increase in accuracy, indicating that the deep learning model is able to find relationships between order flow and price change events over long time periods.

Our results show that there is significant gain in model performance from including many lagged values of the observations in the input of the neural network, a signature of significant—and exploitable—temporal dependence in order book dynamics.

4. Discussion

Using a Deep Learning approach applied to a large dataset of billions of orders and transactions for 1000 US stocks, we have uncovered evidence of a *universal price formation mechanism* relating history of the order book for a stock to the (next) price variation for that stock. More importantly, we are able to *learn* this mechanism through supervised training of a deep neural network on a high-frequency time series of the limit order book. The resulting model displays several interesting features:

- Universality: the model is stable across stocks and sectors, and the model trained on all stocks outperforms stock-specific models, even for stocks not in the training sample, showing that features captured are not stock-specific.
- Stationarity: model performance is stable across time, even a year out of sample.
- Evidence of 'long memory' in price formation: including order flow history as input, even up to several hours, improves prediction performance.
- Generalization: the model extrapolates well to stocks not included in the training sample. This is especially useful since it demonstrates its applicability to recently listed instruments or those with incomplete or short data histories.

Our results illustrate the applicability and usefulness of Deep Learning methods for modeling of intraday behavior of financial markets. In addition to the fundamental insights they provide on the nature of price formation in financial markets, these findings have practical implications for model estimation and design. Training a single universal model is simpler and more straightforward than training and maintaining thousands of single-asset models. Since the universal model can generalize to new stocks—without training on their historical data—it can also be applied to newly issued stocks or stocks with missing data or shorter data histories.

Acknowledgements

The authors thank seminar participants at the London Quant Summit 2018, NYC Quant Summit 2018, the London Quantitative Finance Seminar, University of Colorado Boulder, JP Morgan, Freiburg Institute for Advanced Study, ETH Zurich, the SwissQuote Conference on Machine Learning in Finance 2018 and Princeton University for their comments. Computations for this paper were performed using a Blue Waters supercomputer grant 'Distributed Learning with Neural Networks'.

Disclosure statement

No potential conflict of interest was reported by the authors.

References

Andersen, T., Bondarenko, O., Obizhaeva, A. and Kyle, P., Intraday trading invariance in the E-Mini S&P 500 futures market. Working Paper, Social Science Research Network, 2018.

Bacry, E., Kozhemyak, A. and Muzy, J., Continuous cascade models for asset returns. *J. Econ. Dyn. Control*, 2008, **32**(1), 156–199.

Bengio, Y., LeCun, Y. and Hinton, G., Deep learning. *Nature*, 2015, **521**, 436–444.

Benzaquen, M., Donier, J. and Bouchaud, J.P., Unravelling the trading invariance hypothesis. *Market Microstruct. Liq.*, 2016, **2**, 1650009.

Bouchaud, J., Gefen, Y., Potters, M. and Wyart, M., Fluctuations and response in financial markets: The subtle nature of 'random' price changes. *Quant. Finance*, 2004, **4**(2), 176–190.

Cont, R., Empirical properties of asset returns: Stylized facts and statistical issues. *Quant. Finance*, 2001, **1**(2), 223–236.

Cont, R., Statistical modeling of high frequency financial data: Facts, models and challenges. *IEEE Sig. Process.*, 2011, **28**, 16–25.

Cont, R. and de Larrard, A., Price dynamics in a Markovian limit order market. *SIAM J. Financial Math.*, 2013, **4**(1), 1–25.

Cont, R., Kukanov, A. and Stoikov, S., The price impact of order book events. *J. Financial Econom.*, 2014, **12**(1), 47–88.

Cont, R., Stoikov, S. and Talreja, R., A stochastic model for order book dynamics. *Oper. Res.*, 2010, **58**(3), 549–563.

Creamer, S. and Freund, Y., Automated trading with boosting and expert weighting. *Quant. Finance*, 2007, **10**(4), 401–420.

Dixon, M., Sequence classification of the limit order book using recurrent neural networks. *J. Comput. Sci.*, 2018a, **24**(1), 277–286.

Dixon, M., A high frequency trade execution model for supervised learning. *High Freq.*, 2018b, **1**(1), 32–52.

Figueroa-Lopez, J. and Chavez-Casillas, J., One-level limit order book model with memory and variable spread. *Stoch. Process. Their. Appl.*, 2017, **127**, 2447–2481.

Gers, Felix A., Schmidhuber, Jürgen and Cummins, Fred, Learning to forget: Continual prediction with LSTM. *Neural Comput.*, 2000, **12**(10), 2451–2471.

Goodfellow, I., Bengio, Y. and Courville, A., *Deep Learning*, 2017 (MIT Press: Cambridge, MA).

Hasbrouck, J., *Empirical Market Microstructure: The Institutions, Economics, and Econometrics of Securities Trading*, 2007 (Oxford University Press: Oxford).

Huang, R. and Polak, T., LOBSTER: Limit Order Book Reconstruction System, Technical documentation, 2011.

Hornik, K., Stinchcombe, M. and White, H., Multilayer feedforward networks are universal approximators. *Neural Netw.*, 1989, **2**(5), 359–366.

Kolanovic, M. and Krishnamachari, R.T., Big data and AI strategies: Machine learning and alternative data approach to investing. J.P. Morgan Global Quantitative & Derivatives Strategy Report, 2017.

Kyle, A.S. and Obizhaeva, A.A., Market microstructure invariance: Empirical hypotheses. *Econometrica*, 2016, **84**(4), 1345–1404.

LeCun, Y., Bengio, Y. and Hinton, G., Deep Learning. *Nature*, 2015, **521**(7553), 436.

Lillo, F. and Farmer, J., The long memory of the efficient market. *Stud. Nonlinear Dyn. Econom.*, 2004, **8**(3).

Mandelbrot, B., Calvet, L. and Fisher, A., The multifractal model of asset returns. Cowles Foundation Discussion Paper No. 1164, 1997.

Patzelt, F. and Bouchaud, J.P., Universal scaling and nonlinearity of aggregate price impact in financial markets. *Phys. Rev. E*, 2017, **97**(1), 012304.

Sirignano, J.A., Deep learning for limit order books. *Quant. Finance*, 2019, **19**(4), 549–570.

Sirignano, J., Sadhwani, A., Chen, L. and Giesecke, K., Deep learning for mortgage risk. arXiv:1607.02470, 2016.

Taranto, D.E., Bormetti, G. and Lillo, F., The adaptive nature of liquidity taking in limit order books. *J. Stat. Mech.: Theory Exp.*, 2014, **6**(3), P06002.

Toth, B., Eisler, Z. and Bouchaud, J., The short-term price impact of trades is universal. *Market Microstruct. Liq.*, 2017, **3**(2), 1850002.

Far from the madding crowd: collective wisdom in prediction markets

GIULIO BOTTAZZI ⓘ and DANIELE GIACHINI ⓘ

(*Received 9 May 2018; accepted 6 May 2019; published online 9 July 2019*)

We investigate market selection and bet pricing in a repeated prediction market model. We derive the conditions for long-run survival of more than one agent (the crowd) and quantify the information content of prevailing prices in the case of fractional Kelly traders with heterogeneous beliefs. It turns out that, apart some non-generic situations, prices do not converge, neither almost surely nor on average, to true probabilities, nor are they always nearer to the truth than the beliefs of all surviving agents. This implies that, in general, prediction market prices are not maximum likelihood estimators of the true probabilities. However, when more than one agent survives, the average price emerging from a prediction market approximates the true probability with lower information loss than any individual belief.

Far from the madding crowd's ignoble strife
Their sober wishes never learn'd to stray.
Elegy Written in a Country Churchyard
Thomas Gray

1. Introduction

In his 2004 best-seller book ' The Wisdom of Crowds' James Surowiecki provides many examples and anecdotes of how, by aggregating the beliefs of independently deciding individuals, one may get rather accurate predictions about uncertain events. When different opinions are collected and aggregated, a sort of *collective intelligence* seems to emerge, letting the crowd be wiser than any of its members. In economics, Surowiecki's idea can be traced back to the classical article by Hayek (1945), who advanced the thesis that a decentralized economy is successful in aggregating the large amount of sparse pieces of information through prices. That is, the price that comes out from the market interaction of agents with heterogeneous and incomplete information condenses all the relevant knowledge and provides a means by which agents can make right decisions.

The informative role of markets has a broad relevance, but it is probably epitomized in the so-called prediction markets. These are markets where bets on binary events are exchanged.† The Iowa Electronic Market (IEM), operated by the University of Iowa, is the most prominent example: in that market people can bet on events like Presidential Elections or Congressional Control by means of future contracts that pay 1 dollar if the event is realized and 0 otherwise. In this frame, it is common to interpret the price of the bet as the probability the crowd assigns to the realization of the event. Exactly because of their ability to provide accurate evaluations of the likelihood of uncertain events, prediction markets recently received the support of famous economists (Arrow *et al.* 2008).

The present paper studies prediction markets in which traders bet on repeatedly occurring events.‡ These models share similarities with other financial market models and have

---

† See Wolfers and Zitzewitz (2004) for a discussion of prediction markets. More generally, trading in some financial instruments is basically equivalent to betting on the outcome of an uncertain event. For instance, the price of Credit Default Swaps is generally recognized as a prediction about the probability of default of the underlying bond issuer.
‡ The case of one-shot prediction markets has also been addressed by the literature, see e.g. Gjerstad (2005), Wolfers and Zitzewitz (2006), Manski (2006), He and Treich (2017).

the advantage that the objective probability of occurrence represents a natural benchmark for evaluating the correctness of market price and agents' beliefs. Specifically, Beygelzimer *et al.* (2012) find that, under the assumption that agents bet according to the Kelly criterion (Kelly 1956), the market price adapts to the success probability at optimal rate (i.e. in a Bayesian fashion) and provides a prediction that is only slightly worse than that of the most accurate agent. Kets *et al.* (2014) go further and, using an argument similar to that applied by Blume and Easley (1992) to Arrow security models, show that with Kelly investors only the agents with the most accurate beliefs survive in the long run and, consequently, market prices converge there. By means of numerical studies, they also analyze markets populated by either myopic CRRA utility maximizers or fractional Kelly traders.† They argue that in those economies more than one agent may survive in the long-run and, when this happens, the expected price matches the success probability, in particular when agents are parsimonious and bet only a small fraction of their wealth.

There is a natural connection between the competition of portfolios rules in prediction markets and the aggregation of probabilistic models by machine learning techniques. In fact, several model combination methods used in machine learning (such as product of expert and mixture of expert) can be obtained as prediction market equilibrium prices (Storkey 2011). This connection can be actually exploited in practice: according to Storkey *et al.* (2012), the price emerging from a market populated by agents (i.e. prediction models) with heterogeneous and myopic isoelastic utility functions can outperform state-of-the-art single and aggregate classifiers (Storkey *et al.* 2012). The core of the connection between market interaction and model selection resides in the process of re-allocation of individual wealth generated by the trading activity of agents with heterogeneous predictions. This wealth allocation dynamics provides a powerful training tool to weight the different predictions (Barbu and Lay 2012) and, while standard methods (e.g. boosting) aggregate homogeneous models, an artificial prediction market can be used to combine different probabilistic classifiers (Storkey 2011). Studying the interaction of heterogeneous betting functions, Barbu and Lay (2012) claim that the artificial prediction market wealth update maximizes the likelihood by gradient ascent. Such a result is exact when betting functions are of the fractional Kelly type (they call it 'constant function'), while it holds in an approximate way for different betting rules. By means of experimental comparison, they also show that artificial prediction markets can outperform random forest (Breiman 2001) and adaboost (Freund and Schapire 1996) in classification problems. Along the same lines, Hu and Storkey (2014) model agents in terms of risk measures and show that market dynamics provide a global optimization algorithm.

In this paper we investigate the asymptotic properties of repeated prediction markets, providing an analysis valuable both for those interested in financial market dynamics and those interested in artificial market predictors. We model agents in terms of fractional Kelly bettors. In this way, as well as complementing previous results in the literature, we are considering agents whose behavior resembles risk aversion and, at the same time, implement a form of mixture of experts linearly combining their own opinion with the market one (Beygelzimer *et al.* 2012). We provide simple conditions to evaluate long-run strategy survival and dominance (Bottazzi and Dindo 2014, 2015). These can be used to assess from the outset whether the market selects the probabilistic model (beliefs) of one agent over the other or converges to a mixture of the two. We show that a difference between the expected price and the success probability generally emerges and is persistent, so that the average price is neither a consistent nor an unbiased estimator of the success probability. In fact, it turns out that there are generic situations in which the average prevailing price is further away from the truth than the belief of one of the traders, even if it approximates the truth with lower information loss than the belief of any agent in the market. This corrects the claim in Barbu and Lay (2012) about prediction markets performing maximum likelihood estimation. We use the results of Bottazzi and Giachini (2017) to argue that such a statement holds only in the limit of agents that, in mixing models, discard their own and give full weight to aggregate predictions. We also show that when taking an arithmetic average of agents' predictions provides an unbiased estimation of success probability, the prediction market price is generically biased and inconsistent. Thus, when a simple average of probabilistic models (like in random forest) is the best choice for aggregation, artificial markets provide an inferior prediction. Finally, we adapt the argument of Dindo and Massari (2017) to show that the results we derive generally apply to the case of any number of fractional Kelly traders. Again, this corrects the previous claim by Kets *et al.* (2014) that the inclusion of more fractional Kelly traders may change the emerging properties of the market.

2. The model

Consider a repeated prediction market (as in Kets *et al.* 2014) populated by N agents who repeatedly bet on a binary event. Agents can choose to gamble on the occurrence of the event or against it. The amount of wealth which is not bet is considered invested in a riskless security on which, without loss of generality, we assume no interest is payed. The total amount bet is redistributed among the winners proportionally to the amount they have bet, that is, according to the procedure commonly know as *parimutuel*. The risky bet is based on an independent Bernoulli trial s_t with success probability π_*, unknown to the agents, $s_t = 1$ meaning that at time t the event occurred and $s_t = 0$ that it did not. At every time t, every agent i has to decide the fraction of wealth $b_{i,t} \in [0, 1]$ bet on the uncertain outcome and the side of the bet, $\sigma_{i,t} \in \{0, 1\}$. The fraction of wealth $1 - b_{i,t}$, considered invested in a riskless security, carries over to the next time step. Let $w_{i,t}$ denote the wealth

---

† The fractional Kelly rule is a generalization of Kelly betting and consists in investing in each asset proportionally to a linear combination of the individual belief and the market price, see MacLean *et al.* (1992, 2004, 2005). It can be derived from intertemporal expected log-utility maximization under the assumption that agents naively learn from prices (Dindo and Massari 2017).

of agent i at time t, then given the parimutuel procedure, the evolution of individual wealth reads

$$w_{i,t} = (1 - b_{i,t})w_{i,t-1} + \delta_{s_t,\sigma_{i,t}}\, w_{i,t-1} b_{i,t} \frac{\sum_{j=1}^{N} b_{j,t} w_{j,t-1}}{\sum_{j=1}^{N} \delta_{s_t,\sigma_{j,t}} b_{j,t} w_{j,t-1}},$$ (1)

where $\delta_{a,b}$ stands for the Kronecker delta: it is equal to 1 if $a = b$ and 0 otherwise. The parimutuel procedure simply redistributes the wealth among bettors, but does not change its total amount so that, without loss of generality, we can assume $\sum_{i=1}^{N} w_{i,t} = 1$ at any t.

For our analysis it is better to rewrite the model as a discrete time economy in which two Arrow securities are exchanged: the first security pays 1 if the event occur and zero otherwise, the second does the opposite. Let $p_t = \sum_{j=1}^{N} \delta_{1,\sigma_{j,t}} b_{j,t} w_{j,t-1} / \sum_{j=1}^{N} b_{j,t} w_{j,t-1}$. This quantity is the fraction of the amount bet on the occurrence of the event over the total amount bet, thus $p_t \in [0, 1]$. It can be thought as the 'price' of the first Arrow security. The price of the second Arrow security is, consequently, $1 - p_t$. Equation (1) becomes

$$w_{i,t} = \begin{cases} \dfrac{(1 - b_{i,t})p_t + b_{i,t}}{p_t}\, w_{i,t-1} & \text{if } s_t = 1 \text{ and } \sigma_{i,t} = 1, \\[2mm] \dfrac{(1 - b_{i,t})(1 - p_t)}{1 - p_t}\, w_{i,t-1} & \text{if } s_t = 0 \text{ and } \sigma_{i,t} = 1, \\[2mm] \dfrac{(1 - b_{i,t})p_t}{p_t}\, w_{i,t-1} & \text{if } s_t = 1 \text{ and } \sigma_{i,t} = 0, \\[2mm] \dfrac{(1 - b_{i,t})(1 - p_t) + b_{i,t}}{1 - p_t}\, w_{i,t-1} & \text{if } s_t = 0 \text{ and } \sigma_{i,t} = 0. \end{cases}$$

Now, define the investment function $\alpha_{i,t} = (1 - b_{i,t})p_t + \sigma_{i,t} b_{i,t}$ so that, by definition, $\alpha_{i,t} \in [0, 1]$. Then the individual wealth evolution becomes

$$w_{i,t} = \begin{cases} \dfrac{\alpha_{i,t}}{p_t}\, w_{i,t-1} & \text{if } s_t = 1, \\[2mm] \dfrac{1 - \alpha_{i,t}}{1 - p_t}\, w_{i,t-1} & \text{if } s_t = 0. \end{cases}$$ (2)

Thus, the evolution of wealth is equivalent to that of an agent investing a fraction $\alpha_{i,t}$ of his wealth in the first Arrow security and the remaining fraction $1 - \alpha_{i,t}$ in the second, with the price of the securities set by the market clearing condition†

$$p_t = \sum_{i=1}^{N} \alpha_{i,t} w_{i,t-1}.$$ (3)

Following the literature on repeated betting (Gjerstad 2005, Kets et al. 2014) we assume that each agent possesses an individual constant belief π_i, in general different from the truth π_*, about the probability of occurrence of

the event and invests according to a fractional Kelly rule

$$\alpha_{i,t} = \alpha_i(p_t) = c_i \pi_i + (1 - c_i)p_t,$$ (4)

with $c_i \in (0, 1]$. This investment rule is a generalization of the Kelly rule and is defined as a linear combination of the individual belief and the market price (MacLean et al. 1992, 2004, 2005, 2010, MacLean and Ziemba 1999, Ziemba 2003, Thorp 2011). The mixing parameter c_i describes the agent's risk averse behavior (MacLean et al. 2010): a c_i close to 1 means that agent i is wagering almost all her wealth in the risky bet, while a c_i close to 0 means that the agent is keeping her wealth safe by investing mainly in the riskless security. Following Beygelzimer et al. (2012), fractional Kelly betting can be also interpreted as a mixture of experts approach, in which the agent i gives weight c_i to her own prediction and weight $1 - c_i$ to the market prediction.

3. Pairwise comparison

Let us focus on the two-agent model, $N = 2$. As we will see in a moment, the notion of 'crowd' and 'wisdom', which are the core of the present analysis, can be effectively discussed also in this simple case. Given the conservation of aggregate wealth, with two agents the dynamics of the system is one dimensional and we simplify the notation setting $w_t = w_{1,t}$, such that $w_{2,t} = 1 - w_t$. We consider investment rules as in (4) and without loss of generality we assume $\pi_1 < \pi_2$. Thus, in terms of (w_t, p_t), the dynamics of the economy is described by the following‡

$$w_t = \begin{cases} \dfrac{c_1 \pi_1 + (1 - c_1)p_t}{p_t}\, w_{t-1} & \text{if } s_t = 1 \\[2mm] \dfrac{1 - c_1 \pi_1 - (1 - c_1)p_t}{1 - p_t}\, w_{t-1} & \text{if } s_t = 0 \end{cases}$$ (5)

together with the market clearing condition

$$p_t = \frac{c_1 \pi_1 w_{t-1} + c_2 \pi_2 (1 - w_{t-1})}{c_1 w_{t-1} + c_2 (1 - w_{t-1})}.$$ (6)

We say that agent 1 dominates (or, equivalently, agent 2 vanishes) if

$$\lim_{t \to \infty} w_t = 1 \text{ almost surely (a.s.)},$$ (7)

that agent 2 dominates (or, equivalently, agent 1 vanishes) if

$$\lim_{t \to \infty} w_t = 0 \text{ a.s.}$$ (8)

and that both agents survive if

$$\limsup_{t \to \infty} w_t > 0 \text{ a.s.} \; \wedge \; \liminf_{t \to \infty} w_t < 1 \text{ a.s.}.$$ (9)

We identify the persistent existence of a crowd with the asymptotic survival of both agents.§

---

† This change of variables clarifies that the analytic results in Kets et al. (2014) are in fact identical to those derived in Blume and Easley (1992). For related contributions in the same setting see also Plott and Chen (2002), Einbinder (2006), Ottaviani and Sorensen (2009), Blume and Easley (2009).

‡ Under these assumptions, the model matches exactly the example provided in Bottazzi and Dindo (2014), Section 2.
§ We use (7) and (9) for consistency with Bottazzi and Dindo (2014). In the present simplified framework one can equivalently define

3.1. Reconsidering the crowd

Since the repeated prediction market considered here is a particular short-lived assets market, we can exploit the analysis put forward in Bottazzi and Dindo (2014) to investigate its long-run dynamics, providing an analytically background for, and extending, the numerical results in Kets *et al.* (2014). First of all, notice that $p_t \in [\pi_1, \pi_2]$ and that $p = \pi_i$ with $i = 1, 2$ are deterministic fixed points of the dynamics. That is, if $p_t = \pi_i$, then it will be $p_\tau = \pi_i$ for any $\tau > t$. In the language of Bottazzi and Dindo (2014), these are two Market Selection Equilibria (MSE). The discussion of this section relies on how the system behaves in the proximity of these two MSE.

From (5) the conditional expected drift of the log-difference of the individual wealth is equal to the difference of the relative entropy of the two strategies

$$\mu(p_t) = \mathrm{E}\left[\log \frac{w_t}{w_{t-1}} - \log \frac{1-w_t}{1-w_{t-1}} \bigg| p_t\right]$$

$$= \pi_* \log \frac{\alpha_1(p_t)}{\alpha_2(p_t)} + (1-\pi_*) \log \frac{1-\alpha_1(p_t)}{1-\alpha_2(p_t)}$$

$$= I_{\pi_*}(\alpha_2(p_t)) - I_{\pi_*}(\alpha_1(p_t)), \qquad (10)$$

where $I_{\pi_*}(x) = \pi_* \log \pi_*/x + (1-\pi_*) \log(1-\pi_*)/(1-x)$.†
A necessary condition for the dominance of agent i is that the MSE $p = \pi_i$ is stable, or in other terms that if the price is at some point sufficiently near to π_i, then it will almost surely converge there and agent i will ultimately own all wealth. Bottazzi and Dindo (2014) prove that if $I_{\pi_*}(\alpha_1(\pi_1)) < I_{\pi_*}(\alpha_2(\pi_1))$ then the MSE in which agent 1 dominates ($w_1 = 1$) is asymptotically stable, while if $I_{\pi_*}(\alpha_1(\pi_1)) > I_{\pi_*}(\alpha_2(\pi_1))$ it is unstable. It works analogously for the MSE in which agent 2 dominates ($w_1 = 0$): just switch 1 and 2 in the previous inequalities. While in a generic stochastic dynamical system local results do not translate into global predictions, in the present model, using the results in Bottazzi and Dindo (2015), one can prove the following.

PROPOSITION 3.1 *Given the system defined in* (5) *and* (6), *and with the definition in* (10), *one has*

   (i) *if the MSE $p = \pi_1$ is stable ($\mu(\pi_1) > 0$) then the MSE $p = \pi_2$ is unstable ($\mu(\pi_2) > 0$), agent 1 dominates, agent 2 vanishes and $p_t \to \pi_1$ almost surely,*

   (ii) *if the MSE $p = \pi_2$ is stable ($\mu(\pi_2) < 0$) then the MSE $p = \pi_1$ is unstable ($\mu(\pi_1) < 0$), agent 2 dominates, agent 1 vanishes and $p_t \to \pi_2$ almost surely,*

   (iii) *if both MSE are unstable ($\mu(\pi_1) \leq 0$ and $\mu(\pi_2) \geq 0$) then both agents survive, $\limsup_{t\to\infty} p_t = \pi_2$ and $\liminf_{t\to\infty} p_t = \pi_1$ almost surely.*

Proof See Appendix 1. ∎

---

dominance and survival requiring that $\lim_{t\to\infty} \mathrm{E}[w_t] = 1$ and $\lim_{t\to\infty} \mathrm{E}[w_t] > 0$, respectively, as in Kets *et al.* (2014).
† The wealth of the strategy with zero relative entropy, the one of a Kelly trader ($c = 1$) with correct beliefs, never decreases in expectation. This is the optimal strategy for an agent, irrespective of what the other agents do, but it unrealistically requires the precise knowledge of the probability π_*.

The previous proposition derives global predictions about the asymptotic dynamics of the system from the local stability analysis of MSE. Hence, the conditions we provide offer a simple procedure to establish from the outset whether the market will asymptotically select one of agents' probabilistic models or propose a combination of the two. Notice also that the proposition rules out the possibility that both MSE are asymptotically stable: it is not possible that the market selects either one model or the other depending on the particular sequence of events realized.‡ This result is particularly important when artificial markets are used for machine learning, since a model aggregation procedure that presents such path dependency would be unreliable.

The situation can be easily appreciated with a graphical analysis. Consider the left panel of figure 1. The inclined lines represent the two strategies α_1 and α_2 as function of price. Their intersections with the diagonal (dashed line) represents the two MSE, $p = \pi_1$ and $p = \pi_2$, while the horizontal line is the true probability, $\pi_* = 0.5$. In this case the Euclidean distance is proportional to the 'information' distance measured using the relative entropy. We can conclude thus that the MSE $p = \pi_1$ is stable while the MSE $p = \pi_2$ is unstable. More generally, for all realized prices in $[\pi_1, \pi_2]$, strategy α_1 is always nearer to the truth than strategy α_2. As a consequence, along any trajectory, the expected growth rate of the wealth of agent 1 is positive. On the right panel the situation is the opposite. Here the beliefs of both agents are below the truth, and it is the wealth of agent 2 that constantly increases on average. In fact the MSE in which agent 2 dominates is the only stable MSE. These two situations are in fact rather generic: when both π_1 and π_2 are greater or lower than π_*, the agent with the belief nearest to the truth always dominates, irrespective of the value of the mixing coefficients c_1 and c_2.

The case $\pi_1 < \pi_* < \pi_2$ is more interesting: this is the only case in which the last condition of Proposition 3.1 can be fulfilled. In other terms a persistent crowd requires not only a certain degree of divergence of opinions, but also the contemporaneous presence of a 'pessimist' and an 'optimist' belief. Consider the situation in figure 2 where the belief of agent 1 is the closest to the truth. Notice that the MSE $p = \pi_2$ is always unstable: when the price is near to π_2, the strategy of the wealthiest agent, agent 2, is always further away from the truth than the strategy of agent 1. Conversely, the stability of the MSE $p = \pi_1$ depends on the value of c_2: for large values of c_2 (left panel) it is asymptotically stable, while for low values of c_2 (right panel) it is unstable. There exists a value of c_2, call it $\bar{c}_2$, such that the distance between π_1 and π_* and the distance between $\alpha_2(\pi_1)$ and π_* are the same. Then, if $c_2 < \bar{c}_2$ the MSE $p = \pi_1$ is unstable and both agents survive, while if $c_2 > \bar{c}_2$ it is asymptotically stable and agent 1 dominates. In the case in which the belief of agent 2 is the closest to the truth, the reverse holds.

In conclusion, agents can both survive only if the wealth share of each agent grows, in expectation, when the other

---

‡ This is not a general property of this kind of market models, though. It is the case here because agents adopt fractional Kelly rules. What might happen with myopic CRRA strategies, for instance, is discussed in Bottazzi and Dindo (2013) and Bottazzi and Giachini (2018).

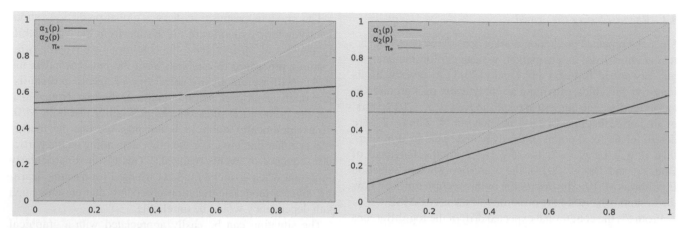

Figure 1. Local stability. **Left panel**: $\pi_* = 0.5$, $\pi_1 = 0.6$, $c_1 = 0.9$, $\pi_2 = 0.8$ and $c_2 = 0.3$. **Right panel**: $\pi_* = 0.5$, $\pi_1 = 0.2$, $c_1 = 0.5$, $\pi_2 = 0.4$ and $c_2 = 0.8$.

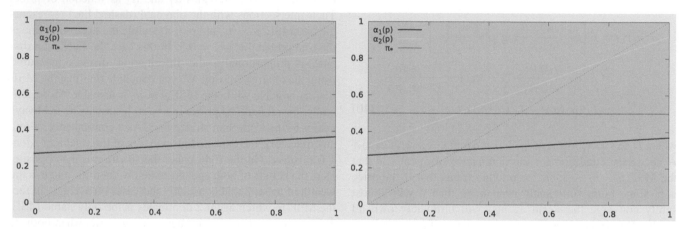

Figure 2. Local stability. In both the plots we set $\pi_* = 0.5$, $\pi_1 = 0.3$, $\pi_2 = 0.8$, $c_1 = 0.9$. **Left**: $c_2 = 0.9$. **Right**: $c_2 = 0.4$.

agent is the wealthiest. This consideration entails another seemingly counter-intuitive consideration: when the prevailing market price is near to one agent's belief, that agent, on average, loses wealth in favor of the opponent. The presence of the mixing coefficient in the fractional Kelly rule makes this possible. When agent 1 dominates the market, agent 2 invests according to a strategy that mixes his belief with the belief of the other agent, producing a result that can have a lower relative entropy with respect to the success probability than the belief of agent 1. It is immediate to see that this may be the case only when the 'mixing' coefficient of the agent with the worst belief is small enough (c.f. figure 2).† Figure 3 shows the combinations of beliefs that allow for the survival of both agents in the case $c_1 = c_2 = c$. These combinations cover a substantial part of the parameter space and their area is greater the lower the value of c. One can interpret these conclusions as saying that, not knowing the true probability, the agent with the lowest c has *ex-ante* the highest chances to survive. Hence, consistently with what done in Kets *et al.* (2014), and to avoid favoring, so to speak, one agent over the other, in what follows we will assume $c_1 = c_2 = c$.

---

† Conversely, the agent's mixing parameter does not affect the ability of a trader to dominate the market. However, as MacLean *et al.* (1992) argue, there is a trade-off between risk and expected growth. Nonetheless here we are interested in asymptotic outcomes, thus, assuming that we are in a situation in which an agent dominates, the fact that her c is small only implies that her wealth will converge to 1 slower than a case in which her c is large.

3.2. Reconsidering the wisdom

In their analysis the contributions mentioned in Section 1 ascribe two possible degrees of wisdom to prediction markets (Beygelzimer *et al.* 2012, Kets *et al.* 2014). The prevailing price could replicate (almost) exactly the true value of the asset, a sort of 'strong' wisdom, or it could be just more precise than (almost) any individual evaluation, a sort of 'weak' wisdom. Moreover, when repeated markets are considered, the question that arises is whether these properties are (almost) always satisfied or, conversely, satisfied only on average. To investigate these issues we find useful to introduce the following formal definitions.

DEFINITION 1 Let $E_t[p]$ stand for the unconditional price average computed after the initial transient of t periods

$$E_t[p] = \lim_{T \to \infty} \frac{1}{T} \sum_{\tau=t}^{t+T-1} p_\tau,$$

then when $t \to \infty$

(i) a prediction market is *almost surely strongly wise* if $\text{Prob}\{p_t = \pi_*\} \to 1$;

(ii) a prediction market is *almost surely weakly wise* if $\text{Prob}\{|p_t - \pi_*| < |\pi_i - \pi_*|\} \to 1$ for any agent i;

(iii) a prediction market is *on average strongly wise* if $E_t[p] \to \pi_*$;

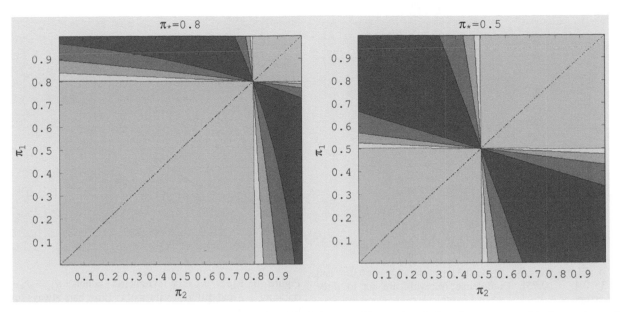

Figure 3. Combinations of beliefs that let both agents survive. Shaded areas of increasing dark color correspond to increasing values of $c_1 = c_2 = c$: the lightest is 0.01, then 0.1, 0.25 and 0.5 which is the darkest. Every shaded area contains those darker than itself.

(iv) a prediction market is on *average weakly wise* if $|E_t[p] - \pi_*| < |\pi_i - \pi_*|$ for any agent i.

By expressing the above properties asymptotically, we allow for a possible initial transient phase and focus on the long-run dynamics of the system. Investigating properties $1-4$ is also informative of the performance of prediction markets in estimating the success probability, especially in terms of consistency and unbiasedness.

According to Proposition 3.1, in the long-run either one of the two agents dominates or both survive. In the first case the price converges to the belief of the dominating agent. If this belief is not correct, the market does not show any wisdom as defined above. Thus, in what follows we constrain the analysis to the region of the parameters space in which both agents survive, that is in which the conditions of point *iii* in Proposition 3.1 are satisfied. In this case price fluctuates between π_1 and π_2 and the asymptotic probability that the prevailing price is equal to the success probability is zero, irrespective of agents' belief and the mixing parameter they adopt.† One has the following.

COROLLARY 3.2 *In the economy with two fractional Kelly traders as defined in (5) and (6), when both traders survive, the market is never almost surely strongly wise while it is almost surely weakly wise if and only if $\pi_* - \pi_1 = \pi_2 - \pi_*$.*

Consider now two beliefs π_1 and π_2 whose relative entropy with respect to the success probability is opposite to their Euclidean distance, that is such that $I_{\pi_*}(\pi_1) > I_{\pi_*}(\pi_2)$ but $\pi_* - \pi_1 < \pi_2 - \pi_*$. Due to the convexity of the relative entropy function this is possible and generic. Let $\tilde{c}$ be the value of the mixing parameter for which $\mu(\pi_2) = 0$. Then, when $c > \tilde{c}$, agents 2 dominates and it is $\lim_{t\to\infty} E_t[p] = \pi_2$. Conversely if $c < \tilde{c}$ both agents survive. However, for a continuity argument, if c is sufficiently near to $\tilde{c}$, the expected price will be near to π_2, thus not only different from π_*, but

also farther away from π_* than π_1.‡ We can then conclude the following.

COROLLARY 3.3 *In the economy with two fractionally Kelly traders as defined in (5) and (6), there generically exist individual beliefs and mixing coefficients for which the market is neither on average strongly wise nor on average weakly wise.*

Since this conclusion seems to contradict the finding in Kets *et al.* (2014), we repeat their numerical experiment to analyze the source of disagreement. We set $\pi_1 = 0.3$, $\pi_2 = 0.8$, $c = 0.01$ and for each value of $\pi_* \in \{0.35, 0.4, \ldots, 0.75\}$ we set the initial price equal to π_*. We iterate the stochastic map generated by (5) and (6) for a number of steps high enough for the price history to distribute according to the invariant distribution of the process. The procedure is independently repeated for $N = 10^6$ times and from the N independent runs the average and standard deviation are computed. Figure 4 (dark line) reports the difference of the final price averaged over the N replications and the true value π_*, together with $\sim 99\%$ confidence intervals obtained adding and subtracting from the difference three times the standard deviation over $\sqrt{N}$. The hypothesis that the crowd is on average strongly wise is rejected for a large set of π_* values. The difference with respect to the results presented in Kets *et al.* (2014) lies in the computation of confidence intervals. In Kets *et al.* (2014) the authors compute 10^3 time averages over the last 10^4 observations of runs consisting of 10^5 periods. They estimate the expected price as the average across the 10^3 time averages, while they use the 5th and the 95th percentiles of the time averages' empirical distribution as confidence interval. The price dynamics is however strongly autocorrelated and this can cause biases in the estimation of the time averages which result in too wide confidence intervals.

---

† Following the same reasoning, it is easy to show that this also applies to the more general case when $c_1 \neq c_2$.

‡ As a specific example, take $\pi_* = 0.2$, $\pi_1 = 0.1$, $\pi_2 = 0.32$ and $c = 0.96$. Numerical simulations show that in this case it is $E[p] = 0.3191 \pm 0.00003$.

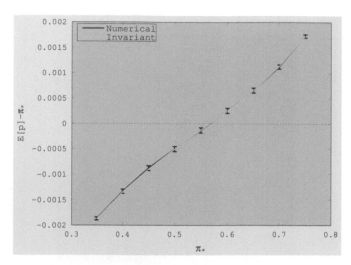

Figure 4. $E[p] - \pi_*$ for $\pi_1 = 0.3$, $\pi_2 = 0.8$, $c = 0.01$ and $\pi_* \in \{0.35, 0.4, \ldots, 0.75\}$. Confidence intervals are set to three standard errors.

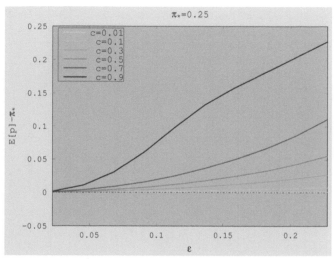

Figure 5. $E[p] - \pi_*$ for symmetric beliefs $\pi_1 = \pi_* - \varepsilon$ and $\pi_2 = \pi_* + \varepsilon$ and different values of c. Error bars always lower than 0.001 are not reported.

As a robustness check, in figure 4 we also report the difference between the true value and the expected price obtained using the Fokker–Planck approximation of the invariant distribution of agents relative wealth derived in Bottazzi and Giachini (2017). As can be seen, the result obtained through the Fokker–Planck approximation is never significantly different from the numerical simulations and provides robust evidence of the discrepancy between the average price and the true probability. Moreover, since the Fokker–Planck solution approximates the invariant distribution, we can conclude that the average price is not only a biased estimator of π_*, but, in general, it is also inconsistent. That is, this lack of wisdom is not a matter of how long one averages the price: even letting the number of observations become arbitrary large, the bias does not disappear.

Looking at prediction market from a machine learning perspective, our results amend the statement of Barbu and Lay (2012): showing the presence of an asymptotic bias implies that prediction market cannot generically perform maximum likelihood estimation. This does not imply, however, that artificial markets might outperform other aggregation procedures. But their advantage is not generic. For instance, considering agents with beliefs on average correct, it is not enough to ensure that the average price is correct. Thus, when aggregation by arithmetic average, like in random forest, is the best choice, prediction market can propose an inferior mixture. This point is made clear in figure 5 where we plot the deviation of the average price from the true probability π_* in the case of beliefs with symmetric values around the truth, $\pi_1 = \pi_* - \varepsilon$ and $\pi_2 = \pi_* + \varepsilon$. Values are obtained following the same numerical procedure applied for figure 4. If $\epsilon > 0$ the deviation is never zero, but it decreases with c.

In general, it would be useful to assess how far from the true values the price tends to be. A natural way to do it is to compare the bias with the magnitude of price fluctuations, by considering the ratio $(E[p] - \pi_*)/\sigma(p)$. If this ratio is small, the estimate obtained by taking the price average is better then just picking one realized price at random. Figure 6 shows

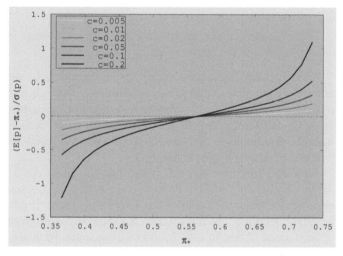

Figure 6. $(E[p] - \pi_*)/\sigma(p)$ for $\pi_1 = 0.3$, $\pi_2 = 0.8$, $\pi_* \in (0.35, 0.75)$ and different values of c.

the values of $(E[p] - \pi_*)/\sigma(p)$ for $\pi_* \in (0.35, 0.75)$ and different values of c computed using the approximate invariant distribution of Bottazzi and Giachini (2017). Notice that for all the c considered, it is $E[p] = \pi_*$ for $\pi_* \simeq 0.5656$ which is close, but not equal, to the point, $\pi_* \simeq 0.5609$, in which the relative entropy of agents' beliefs with respect to the truth is equal. Not only $E[p] - \pi_*$ decreases with c, but with lower values of c, also the ratio $(E[p] - \pi_*)/\sigma(p)$ becomes smaller. This is consistent with the conjecture that $\lim_{c \to 0} E[p] = \pi_*$ put forward in Kets et al. (2014) and proved in Bottazzi and Giachini (2017). Actually Bottazzi and Giachini (2017) prove a stronger result: $\lim_{c \to 0}(\lim_{t \to \infty} p_t) = \pi_*$, which implies the following.

PROPOSITION 3.4 *In the economy with two fractionally Kelly traders as defined in (5) and (6), if both agents survive, then in the limit of c going to zero the market is almost surely strongly wise.*

Proof See Bottazzi and Giachini (2017). ∎

Thus, in the limit of agents giving full weight to market prediction, the price becomes an unbiased and consistent estimator of π_*. This also explains the divergence between our results and the statement in Barbu and Lay (2012) about markets performing maximum likelihood estimation: the small enough mixing coefficient they consider† is, generically, zero. On this point, one could argue that for machine learning purposes setting c to almost zero should not be an issue. However, looking at equation (5), one immediately notices the drawback in computational terms of such a choice: wealth increments become infinitesimally small and, consequently, the transient phase extremely long. A trade-off between goodness of estimates and computation time cannot be avoided.‡

Notice how in figure 6 the bias goes in the direction of the agent that is, in terms of relative entropy, the closest to the truth. Indeed one generally finds that approximating the true probability with the average price induces a loss of information which is lower than the loss one would obtain by using the belief of any agent. In this sense, the market results informationally efficient. Formally one has the following.

PROPOSITION 3.5 *In the economy with two fractionally Kelly traders as defined in (5) and (6), if both agents survive, then $I_{\pi_*}(\mathrm{E}[p]) \leq I_{\pi_*}(\pi_i)$ with $i = 1,2$.*

Proof See Appendix 2. ∎

Summarizing, in a repeated prediction market, where more than one agent manages to survive in the long-run, the bet price does not converge almost surely to the true probability and there exists generic cases in which it fluctuates away from the truth more than the best belief in the market. At the same time, the average price, even if it does not provide a consistent and unbiased estimator of the true probability, approximates the true probability with a lower information loss than any individual belief. Moreover, the price bias disappears when agents bet (almost) nothing.

4. More than two agents

The analysis so far concerned the seemingly special case of just two traders. Although this small number might appear peculiar, we have seen that also in this simple case, we are able to discuss, measure and explain the presence of wisdom in prevailing market prices. The aim of this section is to show that when more agents are considered, the asymptotic dynamics of the market are in fact not expected to change because, in the long run, only those agents with beliefs nearest to the truth in the optimist and pessimist group will survive.

Assume $N > 2$ agents are trading in the market, with individual beliefs $\pi_1 < \ldots < \pi_k < \pi_* < \pi_{k+1} < \ldots < \pi_N$. Thus agent k and $k+1$ have the most correct beliefs, and we denote all other agents as having 'external beliefs'. In particular, agent 1 and N are characterized by somehow extreme beliefs,

and are those farthest from the truth. Consider $j < k$ and notice that

$$I_{\pi_*}(\alpha_k(\pi_j)) = I_{\pi_*}(c\pi_k + (1-c)\pi_j) \leq cI_{\pi_*}(\pi_k) + (1-c)I_{\pi_*}(\pi_j) < I_{\pi_*}(\pi_j),$$

which means that when an agent in $\{1, \ldots, k-1\}$ owns almost all wealth, agent k grows more than him. As a consequence, none of these agents will ever dominate. An identical argument shows that also the agents in $\{k+2, \ldots, N\}$ never dominate.

But will agents with external beliefs survive in the long run? Let us see what might happen for different values of the mixing parameter c. When this value is sufficiently large, for $j < k$ it is

$$I_{\pi_*}(\alpha_k(p)) \sim I_{\pi_*}(\pi_k) < I_{\pi_*}(\pi_j) \sim I_{\pi_*}(\alpha_j(p)), \forall p$$

so that, according to (10), $\lim_{t \to \infty} w_t^k / w_t^j = +\infty$ almost surely and agent j vanishes. Following the same argument, it is $\lim_{t \to \infty} w_{k+1,t} / w_{j,t} = +\infty$ for $j > k+1$. Thus, all agents different from k and $k+1$, that is those with external beliefs, vanish when c is sufficiently large.

Analogously, when the value of the mixing parameter is small, $c \sim 0$, we expect the price to converge in distribution to the true value π_* so that

$$\mathrm{E}\left[I_{\pi_*}(\alpha_i(p))\right] \to I_{\pi_*}(\alpha_i(\pi_*)).$$

Thus, the strategy of agent k will have a lower entropy than the strategy of agent j for any $j < k$ and the strategy of agent $k+1$ will have a lower entropy than the strategy of agent j for any $j > k+1$. Thus, also in the case of a sufficiently small c, agents with external beliefs vanish in the long run. In general we have the following (see also Dindo and Massari 2017).

PROPOSITION 4.1 *In the economy with $N > 2$ fractional Kelly traders with beliefs $\pi_1 < \ldots < \pi_k < \pi_* < \pi_{k+1} < \ldots < \pi_N$, any agent $j \in \{1, \ldots, k-1, k+2, \ldots, N\}$ vanishes.*

Proof See Appendix 3. ∎

Since this is in contrast with what reported in Kets *et al.* (2014), we repeat their exercise. We consider a market with three agents and compute their asymptotic average wealth following the same numerical methodology used to obtain the dark line in figure 4. Results are reported in figure 7. In the left panel, the market share of the agent with the external belief always vanishes so that, asymptotically, only at most two agents survive, irrespectively of the true probability. On the right panel, the wealth share of the agent with extra marginal belief is zero also when the value of c is small. The difference with respect to what previously reported in Kets *et al.* (2014) is probably again due to the inconsistent procedure they adopt and to the increased length of our simulations. The finding is significant, however, as it establishes the generality of the results obtained through the analysis of the two-agent case.

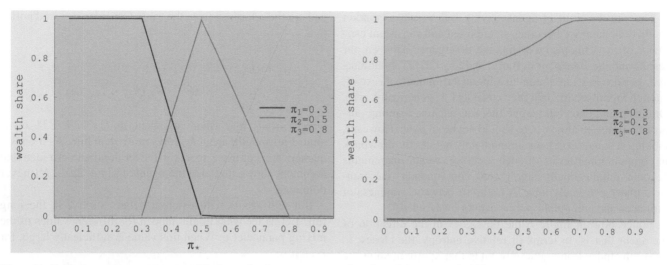

Figure 7. **Left:** Asymptotic average wealth shares for three agents as a function of the true probability π_* with $c = 0.01$. Error bars always lower than 0.001 are not reported. **Right:** Asymptotic average wealth shares for three agents for different values of c with $\pi_* = 0.6$. Error bars always lower than 0.001 are not reported.

5. Conclusion

We presented a simple model in which two fractional Kelly traders repeatedly bet on a uncertain binary outcome, occurring with fixed and unknown probability. If agents' beliefs about the probability of success are one bigger and one lower then the truth, and if they bet a sufficiently small fraction of their wealth, then they both survive and none ends up winning all the money. This is the effect of the fractional Kelly betting, which mixes *a priori* beliefs with contemporary prices, and leads to a situation in which the wealthiest agent is, persistently, the one who gains less (or loses more). Some previous contributions, both in the financial economics and machine learning literature, suggest that, in this case, the market becomes 'wise', in the sense that the price history emerging from agents' interaction carries more information about the true probability than the individual beliefs of the agents. We define several possible types of wisdom and investigate whether and to which extent prediction markets are actually characterized by them. Our results are mixed. On the one hand we show that, in general, the price does not converge, neither almost surely nor in expectation, to the true unknown probability. Moreover, there are situations in which the average prevailing price is farther away from the true probability than the individual belief of one trader. On the other hand, we find that the price average approximates the true probability with lower information loss than any belief in the market and, as showed by Bottazzi and Giachini (2017), when agents bet an infinitesimal amount of their wealth the price reveals the truth.

Looking at prediction markets from a machine learning perspective, our analysis extends previous studies on the asymptotic properties of the aggregated probabilistic classifier represented by the emerging price. We show that prediction markets do not provide in general a consistent and unbiased estimation of the success probability. In fact, in those cases in which a simple average of individual models is the best choice for aggregation, the price provides an inferior predictor. Nonetheless, in terms of relative entropy, the prediction

offered by market prices is better, on average, than any individual probabilistic evaluation. Unbiasedness and consistency are achieved in the limit of agents giving full weight to prices in their investing rule, even if this happens at the expenses of an extremely long training phase.

Since those results have been derived in the case of two fractional Kelly traders, the question that remains is how general they can be. With respect of having more than two traders of that sort, we conclude that in this case there are essentially no differences, because at most two agents may survive in the long run. With respect to the inclusion of other kind of strategies or probabilistic models, the question remains open. It must be stressed, however, that previous results by Blume and Easley (2009) make clear that no possible wisdom can generically emerge when intertemporal expected utility maximizing agents are considered. On the other hand, Jahedpari *et al.* (2017) study artificial prediction markets populated by adaptive strategies and, like in our case, find the emergence of some degree of collective wisdom. Through a series of experiments on several datasets, they show that artificial prediction markets outperform alternatives from the literature on prediction with expert advice (Cesa-Bianchi and Lugosi 2006). In some sense, it is precisely because fractional Kelly betting is non-optimal under agents' beliefs that a crowd can persist and, because of that, prediction markets can show some sort of wisdom. A key element characterizing the behavior of our agents is their inability to learn the probability of success. We found this assumption in the previous literature on repeated prediction markets and we decided to keep it. From an economic point of view, this is done in search of a higher realism. Indeed, if we endow the agents with the ability to perfectly learn the truth, not only the realized prices will converge there, but the crowd essentially disappears as agents become asymptotically identical. To say it in the machine learning language, having individual models already able to learn the truth makes aggregation useless. Since the progressive convergence of opinions is clearly something that we do not observe in real markets, we can deduce that real traders are not able to learn the truth, whatever it might be. We decided to shape our agents on their example. Conversely, the question of what happens when agents are capable of some sort of imperfect learning, or if the price fixing mechanism differs from Walrasian market clearing (as in Frongillo *et al.* 2012), is interesting and will be the subject of future research.

Acknowledgments

If there is any good idea in this paper, it probably emerged in some discussion with Pietro Dindo. In any case, we retain the exclusive paternity of all the bad ones. We thank Filippo Massari and Remco Zwinkels for useful suggestions.

Disclosure statement

No potential conflict of interest was reported by the authors.

Funding

We gratefully acknowledge the funding from the European Union's Horizon 2020 research and innovation program under grant agreement No 640772—DOLFINS.

ORCID

G. Bottazzi ⓘ http://orcid.org/0000-0003-2565-4732
D. Giachini ⓘ http://orcid.org/0000-0002-0001-5240

References

Arrow, K.J., Forsythe, R., Gorham, M., Hahn, R., Hanson, R., Ledyard, J.O., Levmore, S., Litan, R., Milgrom, P., Nelson, F.D., Neumann, G.R., Ottaviani, M., Schelling, T.C., Shiller, R.J., Smith, V.L., Snowberg, E., Sunstein, C.R., Tetlock, P.C., Tetlock, P.E., Varian, H.R., Wolfers, J. and Zitzewitz, E., The promise of prediction markets. *Science*, 2008, **320**, 877–878.

Barbu, A. and Lay, N., An introduction to artificial prediction markets for classification. *J. Mach. Learn. Res.*, 2012, **13**, 2177–2204.

Beygelzimer, A., Langford, J. and Pennock, D.M., Learning performance of prediction markets with Kelly bettors. Proceedings of the 11th International Conference on Autonomous Agents and Multiagent Systems-Volume 3, pp. 1317–1318, 2012.

Blume, L. and Easley, D., Evolution and market behavior. *J. Econ. Theory.*, 1992, **58**, 9–40.

Blume, L. and Easley, D., The market organism: Long-run survival in markets with heterogenous traders. *J. Econ. Dyn. Control*, 2009, **33**, 1023–1035.

Bottazzi, G. and Dindo, P., Selection in asset markets: The good, the bad, and the unknown. *J. Evolut. Econ.*, 2013, **23**, 641–661.

Bottazzi, G. and Dindo, P., Evolution and market behavior with endogenous investment rules. *J. Econ. Dyn. Control*, 2014, **48**, 121–146.

Bottazzi, G. and Dindo, P., Drift criteria for persistence of discrete stochastic processes on the line. Technical report, Laboratory of Economics and Management (LEM), Sant'Anna School of Advanced Studies, Pisa, Italy, 2015.

Bottazzi, G. and Giachini, D., Wealth and price distribution by diffusive approximation in a repeated prediction market. *Phys. A Stat. Mech. Appl.*, 2017, **471**, 473–479.

Bottazzi, G. and Giachini, D., New results on betting strategies, market selection, and the role of luck. LEM Papers Series 2018/08, Laboratory of Economics and Management (LEM), Sant'Anna School of Advanced Studies, Pisa, Italy, 2018.

Breiman, L., Random forests. *Mach. Learn.*, 2001, **45**, 5–32.

Cesa-Bianchi, N. and Lugosi, G., *Prediction, Learning, and Games*, 2006 (Cambridge University Press: Cambridge).

Dindo, P. and Massari, F., The wisdom of the crowd in dynamic economies. Working Paper 2017–17, Department of Economics, Cà Foscari University of Venice, 2017.

Einbinder, M., Information markets: Using market predictions to make administrative decisions. *Va. Law. Rev.*, 2006, **92**, 149–186.

Freund, Y. and Schapire, R.E., Experiments with a new boosting algorithm. Proceedings of the Icml, Vol. 96, pp. 148–156, 1996.

Frongillo, R.M., Penna, N.D. and Reid, M.D., Interpreting prediction markets: A stochastic approach. Proceedings of the 25th International Conference on Neural Information Processing Systems-Volume 2, pp. 3266–3274, 2012.

Gjerstad, S., Risk aversion, beliefs, and prediction market equilibrium. Technical report, Economic Science Laboratory, University of Arizona, 2005.

Hayek, F.A., The use of knowledge in society. *Amer. Econ. Review*, 1945, **35**, 519–530.

He, X.Z. and Treich, N., Prediction market prices under risk aversion and heterogeneous beliefs. *J. Math. Econ.*, 2017, **70**, 105–114.

Hu, J. and Storkey, A., Multi-period trading prediction markets with connections to machine learning. Proceedings of the 31st International Conference on International Conference on Machine Learning-Volume 32, pp. 1765–1773, 2014.

Jahedpari, F., Rahwan, T., Hashemi, S., Michalak, T.P., De Vos, M., Padget, J. and Woon, W.L., Online prediction via continuous artificial prediction markets. *IEEE. Intell. Syst.*, 2017, **32**, 61–68.

Kelly, J., A new interpretation of information rates. *Bell Syst. Tech. J.*, 1956, **35**, 917–926.

Kets, W., Pennock, D.M., Sethi, R. and Shah, N., Betting strategies, market selection, and the wisdom of crowds. Proceedings of the 28th AAAI Conference on Artificial Intelligence, pp. 735–741, 2014.

MacLean, L.C. and Ziemba, W.T., Growth versus security tradeoffs in dynamic investment analysis. *Ann. Oper. Res.*, 1999, **85**, 193–225.

MacLean, L., Ziemba, W.T. and Blazenko, G., Growth versus security in dynamic investment analysis. *Manage. Sci.*, 1992, **38**, 1562–1585.

MacLean, L.C., Sanegre, R., Zhao, Y. and Ziemba, W.T., Capital growth with security. *J. Econ. Dyn. Control*, 2004, **28**, 937–954.

MacLean, L.C., Ziemba, W.T. and Li, Y., Time to wealth goals in capital accumulation. *Quant. Finance*, 2005, **5**, 343–355.

MacLean, L., Thorp, E. and Ziemba, W., Good and bad properties of the Kelly criterion. *Risk*, 2010, **20**, 1–11.

Manski, C.F., Interpreting the predictions of prediction markets. *Econ. Lett.*, 2006, **91**, 425–429.

Ottaviani, M. and Sorensen, P.N., Aggregation of information and beliefs: Asset pricing lessons from prediction markets. Discussion Papers 09–14, Department of Economics, University of Copenhagen, 2009.

Plott, C.R. and Chen, K.Y., Information aggregation mechanisms: Concept, design and implementation for a sales forecasting problem. Working Paper 1131, California Institute of Technology, 2002.

Storkey, A., Machine learning markets. Proceedings of the 14th International Conference on Artificial Intelligence and Statistics, pp. 716–724, 2011.

Storkey, A.J., Millin, J.J. and Geras, K.J., Isoelastic agents and wealth updates in machine learning markets. Proceedings of the 29th International Conference on Machine Learning, pp. 1019–1026, 2012.

Surowiecki, J., *The Wisdom of Crowds*, 2004 (Anchor: New York).

Thorp, E.O., The Kelly criterion in blackjack sports betting, and the stock market. The Kelly Capital Growth Investment Criterion: Theory and Practice, pp. 789–832, 2011, World Scientific.

Wolfers, J. and Zitzewitz, E., Prediction markets. *J. Econ. Perspect.*, 2004, **18**, 107–126.

Wolfers, J. and Zitzewitz, E., Interpreting prediction market prices as probabilities. Working Paper 12200, National Bureau of Economic Research, 2006.

Ziemba, W.T., *The Stochastic Programming Approach to Asset, Liability, and Wealth Management*, 2003 (Research Foundation of AIMR, Scorpion: Charlottesville).

Appendices

Appendix 1. Proof of Proposition 3.1

Let us define

$$\Delta_{\pi_*}(\pi_1 \| \pi_2) = \pi_* \log \frac{\pi_1}{\pi_2} + (1 - \pi_*) \log \frac{1 - \pi_1}{1 - \pi_2}.$$

Using the strict concavity of the logarithmic function it is immediate to see that $\mu(\pi_1) < c_2 \Delta_{\pi_*}(\pi_1 \| \pi_2)$ and $\mu(\pi_2) > c_1 \Delta_{\pi_*}(\pi_1 \| \pi_2)$.

Then $\mu(\pi_1) > 0$ implies $\Delta_{\pi_*}(\pi_1 \| \pi_2) > 0$ and, in turn, $\mu(\pi_2) > 0$. Analogously, $\mu(\pi_2) < 0$ implies $\Delta_{\pi_*}(\pi_1 \| \pi_2) < 0$ and $\mu(\pi_1) < 0$.

Consider the dynamics of the ratio of individual wealth $z_t = \log w_t / (1 - w_t)$. If $\pi_1 < p_t < \pi_2$, then $z_t - z_{t-1} < 0$ if $s_t = 1$ and $z_t - z_{t-1} > 0$ if $s_t = 0$. This excludes the possibility of a finite deterministic fixed point or of deterministic drift for z_t. Moreover, since

$$\log \frac{\pi_1}{\pi_2} \le z_t - z_{t-1} \le \log \frac{1 - \pi_1}{1 - \pi_2},$$

the process z_t has bounded increments. Finally notice that

$$\lim_{z \to +\infty} \mathrm{E}[z_t - z_{t-1} | z_{t-1} = z] = \mu(\pi_2)$$

and

$$\lim_{z \to -\infty} \mathrm{E}[z_t - z_{t-1} | z_{t-1} = z] = \mu(\pi_1).$$

Then if $\mu(\pi_1) > 0$ and $\mu(\pi_2) > 0$, according to Bottazzi and Dindo (2015, Theorem 3.1), z_t diverges to $+\infty$ a.s. and the first statement of the proposition follows.

If $\mu(\pi_2) < 0$ and $\mu(\pi_1) < 0$, according to Bottazzi and Dindo (2015, Corollary 3.1), z_t diverges to $-\infty$ a.s. and the second statement of the proposition follows.

Finally if $\mu(\pi_2) > 0$ and $\mu(\pi_1) < 0$, according to Bottazzi and Dindo (2015, Theorem 2.2), the process of z_t is persistent. Since z_t

increases with probability $1 - \pi_*$ and decreases with probability π_*, one has that, as long as $\pi_* \in (0, 1)$, it is $\limsup_{t \to \infty} z_t = +\infty$ and $\liminf_{t \to \infty} z_t = -\infty$ a.s., so that the third statement follows.

Appendix 2. Proof of Proposition 3.5

Without loss of generality consider the wealth of the first agent. If both agents survive it must be $\mathrm{E}[\log(w_t / w_{t-1})] = 0$, which implies

$$
\begin{aligned}
c\mathrm{E}\left[I_{\pi_*}(p) - I_{\pi_*}(\pi_1)\right] &= c\mathrm{E}\left[\pi_* \log \frac{\pi_1}{p} + (1 - \pi_*) \log \frac{1 - \pi_1}{1 - p}\right] \\
&\le \mathrm{E}\left[\pi_* \log\left(c\frac{\pi_1}{p} + 1 - c\right) + (1 - \pi_*) \log \right. \\
&\quad \left. \times \left(c\frac{1 - \pi_1}{1 - p} + 1 - c\right)\right] = 0,
\end{aligned}
$$

so that

$$\mathrm{E}\left[I_{\pi_*}(p)\right] \le I_{\pi_*}(\pi_1).$$

Moreover, from the convexity of the relative entropy and the Jensen's inequality, it is

$$I_{\pi_*}(\mathrm{E}[p]) \le \mathrm{E}\left[I_{\pi_*}(p)\right],$$

which proves the assertion.

Appendix 3. Proof of Proposition 4.1

Notice that for $t \to \infty$ it is $\mathrm{E}[\log(w_{i,t} / w_{i,t-1})] \le 0$ for any $i \in \{1, \ldots, N\}$, where the equality holds for every surviving agent while the strict inequality holds for all the vanishing agents. Following the argument of Dindo and Massari (2017), one can always write $\pi_i = \lambda_j \pi_j + (1 - \lambda_j)\pi_*$ with $\lambda_j \in (0, 1)$ and either $i = k, j \in \{1, \ldots, k-1\}$ or $i = k+1, j \in \{k+2, \ldots, N\}$.

Recalling that $\mathrm{E}[\log w_{i,t} / w_{i,t-1}] = \mathrm{E}[I_{\pi_*}(p_t) - I_{\pi_*}(\alpha_{i,t})]$, by Jensen's inequality and the strict convexity of $I_{\pi_*}(\cdot)$, one has

$$\mathrm{E}[\log(w_{i,t} / w_{i,t-1})] - \mathrm{E}[\log(w_{j,t} / w_{j,t-1})] > (1 - \lambda_j)$$
$$\mathrm{E}[I_{\pi_*}(\alpha_{j,t}) - (1 - c)I_{\pi_*}(p_t)].$$

It follows

$$\mathrm{E}[\log(w_{j,t} / w_{j,t-1})] < \frac{1}{\lambda_j} \mathrm{E}[\log(w_{i,t} / w_{i,t-1})],$$

which directly implies the statement.

Forecasting limit order book liquidity supply–demand curves with functional autoregressive dynamics

YING CHEN, WEE SONG CHUA and WOLFGANG KARL HÄRDLE

(*Received 28 March 2018; accepted 6 May 2019; published online 9 July 2019*)

We develop a dynamic model to simultaneously characterize the liquidity demand and supply in a limit order book. The joint dynamics are modeled in a unified Vector Functional AutoRegressive (VFAR) framework. We derive a closed-form maximum likelihood estimator under sieves and establish asymptotic consistency of the proposed method under mild conditions. We find the VFAR model presents strong interpretability and accurate out-of-sample forecasts. In application to limit order book records of 12 stocks in the NASDAQ, traded from 2 January 2015 to 6 March 2015, the VFAR model yields R^2 values as high as 98.5% for in-sample estimation and 98.2% in out-of-sample forecast experiments. It produces accurate 5-, 25- and 50-min forecasts, with RMSE as low as 0.09–0.58 and MAPE as low as 0.3–4.5%. The predictive power stably reduces trading cost in the order splitting strategies and achieves excess gains of 31 basis points on average.

1. Introduction

Liquidation of large orders has attracted much attention from researchers and practitioners. Markets address the large order liquidation problem in one of three ways: call auctions, dealer markets and limit order books, see Foucault *et al.* (2005). Among them, Limit Order Book (LOB) has emerged as the main source for liquidity and exhibits a growing importance worldwide. LOB records investors' orders on both the bid and ask sides with price and volume constraints. With a limit order, investors can improve the execution price, either buying or selling, according to their choice, but the execution

is not immediate as a market order, nor guaranteed. Harris (1990) defines three components of liquidity as being: (1) tightness such as bid–ask spread at the best price level; (2) depth measured by quantities, e.g. eXchange Liquidity Measure (XLM); and (3) resilience referring to the recovery for deviations of spreads from their competitive level. As such, LOB contains the comprehensive information on market liquidity, not only a single-valued liquidity measurement at the best bid–ask price level, but also the queuing liquidities at deeper levels in the book. In this paper, we develop a dynamic model to simultaneously characterize the liquidity demand and supply in the LOB. The objectives are to understand the joint dynamics of liquidity at multiple levels and on both the

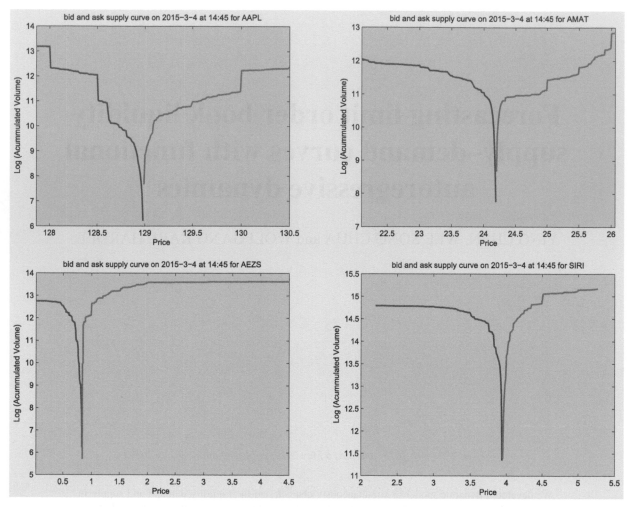

Figure 1. AAPL, AMAT, AEZS, and SIRI liquidity demand and supply curves at an arbitrarily selected time point. In our study, AAPL has the largest market value; AEZS has the smallest value and the smallest bid–ask spread on average; SIRI is the most active stock; and AMAT is the relatively less active stock among the rest.

bid and ask sides of the LOB, and explore the applicability of a dynamic model in the order splitting strategy.

Liquidity in the LOB can be well represented by a pair of demand and supply curves that are defined as the (log) accumulated volumes on the quoted prices. The demand curve corresponds to the bid side and the supply is associated with the ask side. As an illustration, figure 1 displays the liquidity curves of four stocks: Apple Inc. (AAPL); Applied Materials, Inc. (AMAT); AEterna Zentaris Inc. (AEZS); and Sirius XM Holdings Inc. (SIRI), based on the snapshots of book on 4 March 2015 at 14:45:00. Each pair of demand and supply curves forms a V-shape that is monotonically decreasing on the bid side and monotonically increasing on the ask side. The gap at the center represents the bid–ask spread, i.e. the *market tightness* at the best price level. Moreover, the *market depth* is reflected by the gradients of the liquidity curves. More precisely, the steeper the curves are, the less price impact there is for large orders, and thus the more liquidity is ready to be supplied or consumed in the market. Liquidity is concentrated on relatively few quoted prices near the best bid and ask prices, while the tails are relatively flat. This flattening out of the tail, or the gentle gradient in the tails, implies low liquidity. A buy or sell of large volumes at the extreme prices will trigger a drastic change in the price and thus increase trading cost. The

dynamic dependence of the series on the liquidity demand and supply curves naturally inherits the *market resilience*, the third component of liquidity.

Liquidity is serially dependent, i.e. the current value of liquidity depends on its own past values. Though with limited information, the popular single-valued liquidity measures are found to be serially dependent; e.g. bid–ask spread (see Benston and Hagerman 1974, Stoll 1978, Fleming and Remolona 1999) and XLM (see Cooper *et al.* 1985, Gomber *et al.* 2015). These findings motivate as a first proxy the adoption of autoregressive models for liquidity in the LOB. Groß–Klußmann and Hautsch (2013) propose a long memory autoregressive conditional Poisson model for the quoted bid–ask spreads. Huberman and Halka (2001) evidence the serial dependence of bid–ask spread and market depth in an autoregressive framework. Härdle *et al.* (2015) propose a local adaptive multiplicative error model to forecast the high-frequency series of 1-min cumulative trading volumes of several NASDAQ blue chip stocks. Chordia *et al.* (2005) document in a vector autoregressive model the cross-sectional dependence among the liquidity measures of bid–ask spread, market depth and order flow, and other statistics of volatility and returns in the stock and bond markets, where the liquidity measures depend on both their own past values and the

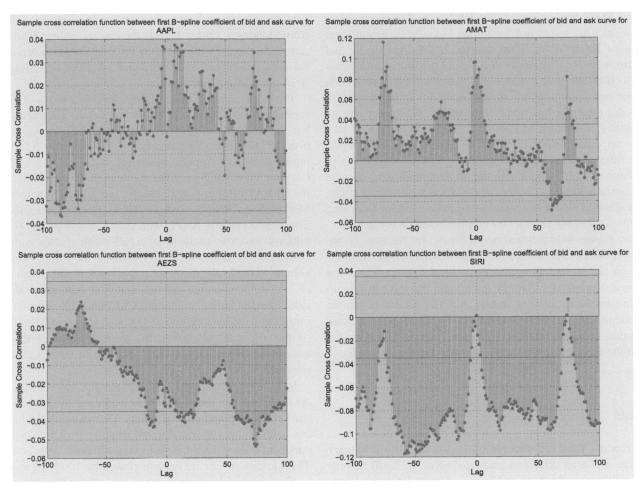

Figure 2. Sample cross-correlation function between first B-spline coefficient of the bid and ask curve for AAPL, AMAT, AEZS, and SIRI.

historical values of the other measures. Härdle *et al.* (2012) empirically analyze the seasonally-adjusted liquidity supply curves in the LOB using a dynamic semiparametric factor model, where the extracted factors of the curves are modeled in the Vector Error Correction (VEC) framework.

It is worth noting that there also exists serial cross-dependence in the bivariate series of liquidity demand and supply. The impact of public information on limit orders result in similar changes on both bid and ask sides, and can cause investors to switch from one side to the other. Thus it introduces lead–lag cross-dependence in both sides of liquidity. The joint serial cross-dependence suggests richer dynamics should be utilized in liquidity analysis. Building on this idea, we develop a Vector Functional AutoRegressive (VFAR) model to describe the joint dynamics of the bivariate series—liquidity demand and supply curves on the bid and ask sides of an electronic open LOB—simultaneously in a unified framework. While there is in general co-integration or a common trend in demand and supply when both variables are scalar time series, the model features the dependence of the series of curves, which is stable over time. Figure 2 displays the sample cross-correlations between the fundamental representatives of the demand and supply curves of the four stocks (the 'first B-spline coefficients' of the bid and ask curves). This first proxy shows that there are significant lead–lag cross-dependencies between the demand and supply curves, but the patterns deviate far from the persistence of a unit root.

In the VFAR model, we derive a closed-form maximum likelihood estimator under a sieve and establish the asymptotic consistency of the method. We investigate the finite sample performance of the proposed model along with the LOB records of 12 stocks traded in NASDAQ from 2 January 2015 to 6 March 2015, where the stocks are carefully selected to represent various types with different market capitalization and liquidity. We find the VFAR presents a strong predictability in liquidity, producing R^2 values as high as 98.5 % for in-sample estimation and 98.2 % in out-of-sample forecast experiments. Moreover, it yields accurate 5-, 25- and 50-min forecasts, with RMSE as low as 0.09–0.58 and MAPE as low as 0.3 –4.5%. Finally, the predictive power stably reduces trading cost in the order splitting strategies and achieves excess gains of 31 basis points on average.

We would like to highlight the difference between our study and the existing ones in the literature. Above all, we develop a dynamic model to estimate and forecast liquidity demand and supply curves simultaneously and demonstrate the application in order splitting execution. Härdle *et al.* (2012) implement a dynamic semiparametric factor model for liquidity curves, but the extracted factors are handled separately on each side, although it is possible to capture the joint evolution of bid and ask sides. Secondly, we develop the FAR modeling for multiple functional time series, where the continuous curves are modeled in a convolutional VFAR that is stationary. Whereas in the functional time series literature,

Bosq (2000) has proposed the FAR model for univariate functional time series and developed Yule–Walker estimation (see also Besse *et al.* 2000, Guillas 2001, Antoniadis and Sapatinas 2003, Chaudhuri *et al.* 2016). Mourid and Bensmain (2006) propose a maximum likelihood estimation with Fourier expansions, as far as we know this is the first work to model multiple functional time series. We investigate its theoretical properties, and within a maximum likelihood estimator approach based on *B*-spline expansions, we provide more flexibility in fitting beyond the Fourier expansion in Chen and Li (2017). Although the implementation focuses on the bivariate liquidity demand and supply curves in our study, the developed model is general and can be used for analyzing multiple functional time series in other research areas.

This paper is structured as follows. In Section 2, we describe the LOB data. Section 3 introduces the VFAR modeling in detail including the estimation approach and the theoretical properties. Section 4 presents the modeling setup and in-sample estimation results, reports the out-of-sample forecast results and demonstrates the application to an order execution strategy. Section 5 provides concluding remarks. All of the theoretical proofs are contained in the Appendix.

2. Data

We consider the LOB records of 12 stocks from 2 January 2015 to 6 March 2015 (44 trading days). The LOB records contain the quoted prices and volumes up to 100 price levels on each side of ask and bid. All the quotes are timestamped with decimal precision up to nanoseconds ($= 10^{-9}$ s). In total, the (buy or sell) order book contains 400 values from the best ask price, best ask volume, best bid price, and best bid volume until the 100-th best ask (bid) price and corresponding volume. The data was obtained from LOBSTER through the Research Data Center of the Collaborative Research Center 649 (https://sfb649.wiwi.hu-berlin.de/fedc/). Note that the records of the 12 stocks in LOBSTER only contain the information in the National Association of Securities Dealers Automated Quotations (NASDAQ) stock market. NASDAQ is a continuous auction trading platform where the normal

continuous trading hours are between 9:30 am to 4:00 pm from Monday to Friday. During the normal trading, if an order cannot be executed immediately or completely, the remaining volumes are queued in the bid and ask sides according to a strict price-time priority order.

The stocks correspond to high variations in terms of market capitalization, liquidity tightness and depth. They are Apple Inc. (AAPL), Microsoft Corporation (MSFT), Intel Corporation (INTC), Cisco Systems, Inc. (CSCO), Sirius XM Holdings Inc. (SIRI), Applied Materials, Inc. (AMAT), Comcast Corporation (CMCSA), AEterna Zentaris Inc. (AEZS), eBay Inc. (EBAY), Micron Technology, Inc. (MU), Whole Foods Market, Inc. (WFM), and Starbucks Corporation (SBUX). The largest stock is AAPL with market value of USD737.41 billions, and the smallest is AEZS with market value of USD35.38 millions. When considering the 5-min queueing volume in the LOB, the most active stock is SIRI, with value of 3.73 millions on the bid side and 7.61 millions on the ask side. The lest active stocks are CMCSA with value of 0.02 millions on the bid side and SBUX with value of 0.03 millions on the ask side. Moreover, the average value of the bid–ask spread varies from 0.0062 (AEZS) to 0.0213 (SBUX), see table 1.

In data pre-processing, we remove the first 15 min after opening and the last 5 min before closing to eliminate the market opening and closing effect. The accumulated bid and ask volumes are log-transformed when constructing liquidity curves to reduce the impact of extraordinarily large volumes. The liquidity curves are smoothed over the 100 price levels of LOB on each side using *B*-spline basis functions. Moreover, to remove the impact of microstructure noise, the sampling frequency is set to be 5 min for a good strike between bias and variance, see AitSahalia *et al.* (2005), Zhang *et al.* (2005), and Härdle *et al.* (2018). As such, there are 75 pairs of bid and ask liquidity curves on each day for each stock. Over the whole sample period of 44 trading days, it amounts to 3300 pairs of bid and ask supply curves for each stock.

The liquidity curves exhibit significant serial dependence over time. As an illustration, figure 3 shows the sample cross-correlations between the log-accumulated volumes at best bid and ask prices for four representative stocks including AAPL with the largest market value, AEZS with the smallest value

Table 1. Summary statistics on liquidity measures for the 12 stocks traded in NASDAQ.

Ticker symbol	Mean spread (USD)	Bid vol		Ask vol	
		Min	Max	Min	Max
AAPL	0.0125	52,267	710,020	61,305	1,298,696
MSFT	0.0101	90,344	928,319	122,377	621,471
INTC	0.0102	158,900	557,251	146,959	1,142,641
CSCO	0.0101	134,790	1,316,058	266,455	4,458,672
SIRI	0.0101	1,266,528	3,725,304	3,002,680	7,605,467
AMAT	0.0102	78,944	334,794	180,749	787,983
CMCSA	0.0106	23,668	128,916	40,638	146,724
AEZS	0.0062	145,635	767,785	472,689	1,158,740
EBAY	0.0110	42,060	160,572	52,813	415,033
MU	0.0107	95,907	497,910	102,357	595,200
WFM	0.0153	34,538	114,386	41,019	159,488
SBUX	0.0213	27,467	151,022	34,914	166,932

Note: Sampling frequency is 5 min.

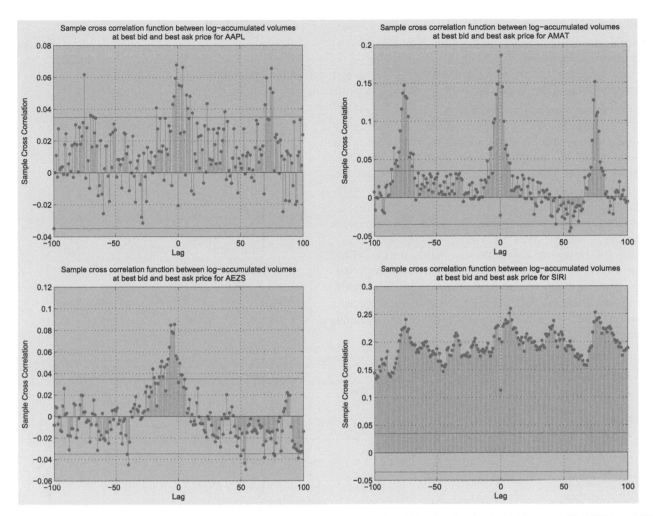

Figure 3. Sample cross-correlation function between log-accumulated volumes at best bid and ask price for AAPL, AMAT, AEZS, and SIRI.

and the smallest bid–ask spread on average, SIRI the most active stock, and AMAT the relatively mid active stock among the rest. While the simultaneous dependence between the bid and ask sides is insignificant or negatively correlated, there are significant positive serial correlations on the first lagged values of the opposite side and then decays for higher order. Similar features are observed in the other eight stocks, which are not displayed. The bid–ask cross-dependency motivates analyzing the liquidity demand and supply curves jointly.

In addition, the serial cross-dependence between the series of curves is reflected in figure 2, where the sample cross-correlations are computed based on the first B-spline coefficients of the bid and ask curves, which will be detailed later. It shows that there are significant lead–lag cross-dependence between the demand and supply curves, but the patterns deviate far from the persistence of unit root. We also perform the Johansen (1991) co-integration test to assess the null hypothesis of co-integration of bid and ask sides. The results support rejecting co-integration.

3. Vector functional autoregression

In this section, we present the Vector Functional AutoRegressive (VFAR) model that is to describe the joint serial cross-dependence of multiple series of continuous curves.

We show how to estimate the functional parameters of the bivariate liquidity demand and supply curves, with the help of B-spline expansions and sieve method. A closed-form estimator is presented and asymptotic consistency provided.

The liquidity curves are defined on the quoted price, denoted as τ, which is assumed to be exogenous. The quoted prices are observed on a dense tick grid, that is re-scaled separately for bid and ask sides into a continuous interval $[0, 1]$, with the minimum price as 0 and maximum price as 1. Denote by $X_t^{(a)}(\tau)$ and $X_t^{(b)}(\tau)$ the liquidity supply and demand curves on the ask (a) side and the bid (b) side at $t = 1, \ldots, n$. The curves are realizations of a functional stochastic process in the space $C_{[0,1]}$ of real continuous functions on $[0, 1]$. In other words, each pair of the liquidity curves is one functional object. Over time, the curves form bivariate time series of n functional objects, each on the bid and ask sides. In our study, the curves are obtained by smoothing over the discrete log-accumulated volumes against the quoted prices at every time point.

To handle the joint dynamics of the two continuous liquidity curves, we propose a Vector Functional AutoRegressive (VFAR) model of order p:

$$\begin{bmatrix} X_t^{(a)} - \mu_a \\ X_t^{(b)} - \mu_b \end{bmatrix} = \sum_{k=1}^{p} \begin{bmatrix} \rho^{aa,k} & \rho^{ab,k} \\ \rho^{ba,k} & \rho^{bb,k} \end{bmatrix} \begin{bmatrix} X_{t-k}^{(a)} - \mu_a \\ X_{t-k}^{(b)} - \mu_b \end{bmatrix} + \begin{bmatrix} \varepsilon_t^{(a)} \\ \varepsilon_t^{(b)} \end{bmatrix},$$

(1)

where the operators $\rho^{aa,k}$, $\rho^{ab,k}$, $\rho^{ba,k}$, and $\rho^{bb,k}$ measure the serial cross-dependence among the liquidity demand and supply curves on their kth lagged values. The operators are bounded linear operator from $\mathcal{H}$ to $\mathcal{H}$, a real separable Hilbert space endowed with its Borel σ-algebra $B_{\mathcal{H}}$. The mean function is denoted as $(\mu_a(\tau), \mu_b(\tau))^\top \overset{\text{def}}{=} (\mathsf{E}[X_t^{(a)}(\tau)], \mathsf{E}[X_t^{(b)}(\tau)])^\top$. Under stationarity, both the serial cross-dependence and the mean are constant over time. The innovations $\{\varepsilon_t^{(a)}\}_{t=1}^n$ and $\{\varepsilon_t^{(b)}\}_{t=1}^n$ are strong $\mathcal{H}$-white noise, independently and identically distributed with zero mean and finite second moment, $0 < \mathsf{E}\|\varepsilon_1^{(a)}\|^2 = \cdots = \mathsf{E}\|\varepsilon_n^{(a)}\|^2 < \infty$ and $0 < \mathsf{E}\|\varepsilon_1^{(b)}\|^2 = \cdots = \mathsf{E}\|\varepsilon_n^{(b)}\|^2 < \infty$, where the norm $\| \cdot \|$ is induced from the inner product $\langle \cdot, \cdot \rangle$ of $\mathcal{H}$. The innovation processes $\varepsilon_t^{(a)}$ and $\varepsilon_t^{(b)}$ need not be cross-independent.

In the following, we derive the estimation for the VFAR model of order 1, which can be generalized for higher order. For the notational simplification, the superscript k is dropped. We consider the convolutional VFAR, where each operator ρ is represented by a convolution kernel Hilbert–Schmidt operator,

$$
\begin{aligned}
& X_t^{(a)}(\tau) - \mu_a(\tau) \\
&\quad = \int_0^1 \kappa_{ab}(\tau - s)\{X_{t-1}^{(b)}(s) - \mu_b(s)\}\,\mathrm{d}s \\
&\qquad + \int_0^1 \kappa_{aa}(\tau - s)\{X_{t-1}^{(a)}(s) - \mu_a(s)\}\,\mathrm{d}s + \varepsilon_t^{(a)}(\tau), \\
& X_t^{(b)}(\tau) - \mu_b(\tau) \\
&\quad = \int_0^1 \kappa_{bb}(\tau - s)\{X_{t-1}^{(b)}(s) - \mu_b(s)\}\,\mathrm{d}s \\
&\qquad + \int_0^1 \kappa_{ba}(\tau - s)\{X_{t-1}^{(a)}(s) - \mu_a(s)\}\,\mathrm{d}s + \varepsilon_t^{(b)}(\tau). \quad (2)
\end{aligned}
$$

The kernel function $\kappa_{xy} \in L^2([0, 1])$ and $\|\kappa_{xy}\|_2 < 1$ for $xy = aa$, ab, ba, and bb, where $\| \cdot \|_2$ denotes the L^2 norm in $C_{[0,1]}$. Note that a linear operator ρ on a Hilbert space $\mathcal{H}$ with norm $\| \cdot \|$ and inner product $\langle \cdot, \cdot \rangle$ is Hilbert–Schmidt if $\rho(\cdot) = \sum_j \lambda_j \langle \cdot, e_j \rangle f_j$, where $\{e_j\}$ and $\{f_j\}$ are orthonormal bases of $\mathcal{H}$ and $\{\lambda_j\}$ is a real sequence such that $\sum_j \lambda_j^2 < \infty$.

Expand the functional terms in (2) using the B-spline basis functions in $L^2([0, 1])$:

$$
B_{j,m}(\tau) = \frac{\tau - w_j}{w_{j+m-1} - w_j} B_{j,m-1}(\tau) + \frac{w_{j+m} - \tau}{w_{j+m} - w_{j+1}} B_{j+1,m-1}(\tau),
$$
$$
m \geq 2,
$$

where m is the order, $w_1 \leq \cdots \leq w_{J+m}$ denote the sequence of knots, and

$$
B_{j,1}(\tau) = \begin{cases} 1 & \text{if } w_j \leq \tau < w_{j+1}, \\ 0 & \text{otherwise}. \end{cases}
$$

Plug-in the B-spline expansions to the VFAR model (2), we obtain the relationship of the B-spline coefficients in the framework of VFAR:

$$
\begin{aligned}
d_{t,h}^a = p_h^a &+ d_h^a(\varepsilon_t^{(a)}) + \sum_{i=1}^\infty \\
&\times \left\{ \sum_{j=1}^\infty \left(\frac{w_{j+m} - w_{j+1}}{w_{j+m} - w_j} - \frac{w_{j+m+1} - w_{j+2}}{w_{j+m+1} - w_{j+1}} \right) c_j^{aa} - c_h^{aa} \right\} \\
&\times \frac{w_{i+m} - w_i}{m} d_{t-1,i}^a + \sum_{i=1}^\infty \\
&\times \left\{ \sum_{j=1}^\infty \left(\frac{w_{j+m} - w_{j+1}}{w_{j+m} - w_j} - \frac{w_{j+m+1} - w_{j+2}}{w_{j+m+1} - w_{j+1}} \right) c_j^{ab} - c_h^{ab} \right\} \\
&\times \frac{w_{i+m} - w_i}{m} d_{t-1,i}^b, \\
d_{t,h}^b = p_h^b &+ d_h^b(\varepsilon_t^{(b)}) + \sum_{i=1}^\infty \\
&\times \left\{ \sum_{j=1}^\infty \left(\frac{w_{j+m} - w_{j+1}}{w_{j+m} - w_j} - \frac{w_{j+m+1} - w_{j+2}}{w_{j+m+1} - w_{j+1}} \right) c_j^{bb} - c_h^{bb} \right\} \\
&\times \frac{w_{i+m} - w_i}{m} d_{t-1,i}^b + \sum_{i=1}^\infty \\
&\times \left\{ \sum_{j=1}^\infty \left(\frac{w_{j+m} - w_{j+1}}{w_{j+m} - w_j} - \frac{w_{j+m+1} - w_{j+2}}{w_{j+m+1} - w_{j+1}} \right) c_j^{ba} - c_h^{ba} \right\} \\
&\times \frac{w_{i+m} - w_i}{m} d_{t-1,i}^a, \quad (3)
\end{aligned}
$$

where $d_{t,j}^a$ and $d_{t,j}^b$ are the B-spline coefficients for the observed functional data $X_t^{(a)}$ and $X_t^{(b)}$, respectively; p_h^a are the coefficients associated with the expansion of the mean on the ask side $\mu_a(\tau) - \int_0^1 \kappa_{ab}(\tau - s)\mu_b(s)\,\mathrm{d}s - \int_0^1 \kappa_{aa}(\tau - s)\mu_a(s)\,\mathrm{d}s$ and p_h^b are the coefficients on the bid side for $\mu_b(\tau) - \int_0^1 \kappa_{bb}(\tau - s)\mu_b(s)\,\mathrm{d}s - \int_0^1 \kappa_{ba}(\tau - s)\mu_a(s)\,\mathrm{d}s$; $d_j^a(\varepsilon_t^{(a)})$ and $d_j^b(\varepsilon_t^{(b)})$ are the B-spline coefficients for the unknown innovations $\varepsilon_t^{(a)}$ and $\varepsilon_t^{(b)}$, respectively; and c_j^{aa}, c_j^{ab}, c_j^{ba}, and c_j^{bb} are the B-spline coefficients for the unknown kernel functions κ_{aa}, κ_{ab}, κ_{ba}, and κ_{bb}, respectively. As such, the original problem of estimating the functional parameters can now be equivalently solved by the estimation of the B-spline coefficients in (3).

Given a finite sample of the functional objects, it is however impossible to estimate the infinite coefficients in (3) for $i, j = 1, \ldots, \infty$. The estimation is conducted with the help of a sieve.

3.1. Maximum likelihood estimator under sieve

We introduce a sequence of subsets—named sieve for the parameter space Θ, which is denoted by $\{\Theta_{J_n}\}$ with $J_n \to +\infty$ as $n \to +\infty$, see e.g. Grenander (1981) on the theory of sieves. In other words, the dimension of the subset is allowed to increase with the sample size. We have $\Theta_{J_n} \subseteq \Theta_{J_n+1}$ and the union of subsets $\bigcup \Theta_{J_n}$ is dense in the parameter space.

The sieve is defined as follows:

$$
\Theta_{J_n} = \left\{ \kappa_{xy} \in L^2 \mid \kappa_{xy}(\tau) = \sum_{l=1}^{J_n} c_l^{xy} B_{l,m}(\tau), \tau \in [0,1], \right.
$$

$$
\left. \times \sum_{l=1}^{J_n} l^2 (c_l^{xy})^2 \le v J_n \right\}, \tag{4}
$$

where v is some known positive constant such that the constraint on c_l^{xy} can be satisfied generally without sacrifice of the growth rate of J_n. We will show the estimation in the finite subsets of the parameter space.

Under the sieve with J_n, Equation (3) can be represented in a form as follows:

$$
y_t = v + C y_{t-1} + u_t, \tag{5}
$$

where $y_t = (d_{t,1}^a, \ldots, d_{t,J_n}^a, d_{t,1}^b, \ldots, d_{t,J_n}^b)^\top$, $v = (p_1^a, \ldots, p_{J_n}^a, p_1^b, \ldots, p_{J_n}^b)^\top$, $u_t = (d_1^a(\varepsilon_t^{(a)}), \ldots, d_{J_n}^a(\varepsilon_t^{(a)}), d_1^b(\varepsilon_t^{(b)}), \ldots, d_{J_n}^b(\varepsilon_t^{(b)}))^\top$, and $C = \left[\begin{smallmatrix} R^{aa} R^{ab} \\ R^{ba} R^{bb} \end{smallmatrix} \right]$ with R^{xy} being a $J_n \times J_n$ matrix with elements $r_{h,i}^{xy} = \{ \sum_{j=1}^{J_n} ((w_{j+m} - w_{j+1})/(w_{j+m} - w_j) - (w_{j+m+1} - w_{j+2})(w_{j+m+1} - w_{j+1})) c_j^{xy} - c_h^{xy} \} ((w_{i+m} - w_i)/m)$, for $xy = aa, ab, ba,$ and bb.

We impose an assumption that the B-spline coefficients $d_j^a(\varepsilon_t^{(a)})$ and $d_j^b(\varepsilon_t^{(b)})$ are independently and identically Gaussian distributed with mean zero and constant variance $\sigma_{j,a}^2$ and $\sigma_{j,b}^2$, respectively. Following Geman and Hwang (1982), we define the likelihood function for (5) over the approximating subspace (4) of the original parameter space. The transition density is as follows:

$$
g\left(X_t^{(a)}, X_t^{(b)}, X_{t-1}^{(a)}, X_{t-1}^{(b)}, \rho^{aa}, \rho^{ab}, \rho^{ba}, \rho^{bb} \right)
$$

$$
= \frac{1}{(2\pi)^{Kn/2}} \left| I_n \otimes \Sigma_u \right|^{-1/2}
$$

$$
\times \exp \left\{ -\frac{1}{2} \left(\mathbf{y} - (Z^\top \otimes I_K) \boldsymbol{\beta} \right)^\top (I_n \otimes \Sigma_u^{-1}) \right.
$$

$$
\left. \left(\mathbf{y} - (Z^\top \otimes I_K) \boldsymbol{\beta} \right) \right\},
$$

where $\mathbf{y} = \mathrm{vec}(y_1, \ldots, y_n)$, $Z = \left[\begin{smallmatrix} 1 & \cdots & 1 \\ y_0 & \cdots & y_{n-1} \end{smallmatrix} \right]$, $\boldsymbol{\beta} = \mathrm{vec}(v, C)$, $\mathbf{u} = \mathrm{vec}(u_1, \ldots, u_n)$, $K = 2J_n$, I_n is an $n \times n$ identity matrix, and vec is the column stacking operator.

The Maximum Likelihood Estimators (MLEs) are obtained with closed-form:

$$
\widehat{\boldsymbol{\beta}} = \left\{ (ZZ^\top)^{-1} Z \otimes I_K \right\} \mathbf{y} \quad \text{orequivalently,}
$$

$$
\widehat{B} = (\widehat{v}, \widehat{C}) = YZ^\top (ZZ^\top)^{-1}, \tag{6}
$$

$$
\widehat{\Sigma_u} = \frac{1}{n} (Y - BZ)(Y - BZ)^\top,
$$

where the first column of $\widehat{B}$ in (6) contains the estimators of coefficients for the mean function $v = (p_1^a, \ldots, p_{J_n}^a, p_1^b, \ldots, p_{J_n}^b)^\top$. Let $\boldsymbol{\theta} = (\theta_1, \ldots, \theta_1, \theta_2, \ldots, \theta_2)$, with $\theta_1 = (c_1^{aa}, \ldots, c_{J_n}^{aa}, c_1^{ba}, \ldots, c_{J_n}^{ba})^\top$ and $\theta_2 = (c_1^{ab}, \ldots, c_{J_n}^{ab}, c_1^{bb}, \ldots, c_{J_n}^{bb})^\top$,

such that $\boldsymbol{\theta}$ contains J_n columns of θ_1 and J_n columns of θ_2. The estimator for c_j^{xy} for $xy = aa, ab, ba, bb$ is as follows:

$$
\widehat{\boldsymbol{\theta}} = Q^{-1} YZ^\top (ZZ^\top)^{-1} (\mathbf{0}_{2J_n \times 1}, I_{2J_n})^\top W,
$$

where $W = \mathrm{diag}(m/(w_{1+m} - w_1), \ldots, m/(w_{J_n+m} - w_{J_n}), m/(w_{1+m} - w_1), \ldots, m/(w_{J_n+m} - w_{J_n}))$, $Q = \left[\begin{smallmatrix} Q^1 & \mathbf{0}_{J_n \times J_n} \\ \mathbf{0}_{J_n \times J_n} & Q^1 \end{smallmatrix} \right]$, with Q^1 being a $J_n \times J_n$ matrix with elements in the jth diagonal equals $q_j - 1$ and the remaining elements in the jth column equals q_j, $q_j = (w_{j+m} - w_{j+1})/(w_{j+m} - w_j) - (w_{j+m+1} - w_{j+2})/(w_{j+m+1} - w_{j+1})$, and $\mathbf{0}$ is the zero matrix.

3.2. Asymptotic property

We establish the consistency property of the sieve estimators. Let $H(\rho, \psi)$ denote the conditional entropy between a set of operators $\rho = (\rho^{aa}, \rho^{ab}, \rho^{ba}, \rho^{bb})$ and a given set of operators ψ:

$$
H(\rho, \psi) = \mathsf{E}_\rho \left[\log g(X_t^{(a)}, X_t^{(b)}, X_{t-1}^{(a)}, X_{t-1}^{(b)}, \psi) \right].
$$

THEOREM 3.1 *Assume $\{\Theta_{J_n}\}$ is chosen such that conditions* **Con**1 *and* **Con**2 *in Appendix 3 are in force. Suppose that for each $\delta > 0$, we can find subsets $\Gamma_1, \Gamma_2, \ldots, \Gamma_{l_{J_n}}$ of Θ_{J_n}, $J_n = 1, 2, \ldots$ such that*

(i) *$D_{J_n} \subseteq \bigcup_{k=1}^{l_{J_n}} \Gamma_k$, where $D_{J_n} = \{\rho \in \Theta_{J_n} \mid H(\rho_{0|\Theta_{J_n}}, \rho) \le H(\rho_{0|\Theta_{J_n}}, \rho_{J_n}) - \delta\}$ for every $\delta > 0$ and every J_n.*

(ii) *$\sum_{n=1}^{+\infty} l_{J_n}(\varphi_{J_n})^n < +\infty$, where given l sets $\Gamma_1, \ldots, \Gamma_l$ in Θ_{J_n}, $\varphi_{J_n} = \sup_k \inf_{t \ge 0} \mathsf{E}_{\rho_{0|\Theta_{J_n}}} \exp\{t \log(g(X_t^{(a)}, X_t^{(b)}, X_{t-1}^{(a)}, X_{t-1}^{(b)}, \Gamma_k)/g(X_t^{(a)}, X_t^{(b)}, X_{t-1}^{(a)}, X_{t-1}^{(b)}, \rho_{J_n}))\}$.*

Then we have $\sup_{\widehat{\rho}_n \in M_{J_n}^n} \| \widehat{\rho}_n - \rho_{0|\Theta_{J_n}} \|_{\mathscr{S}} \to 0$ a.s.

The norm $\| \cdot \|_{\mathscr{S}}$ is a Hilbert–Schmidt norm for the convolution kernel operator and its Hilbert–Schmidt norm is $\| \rho \|_{\mathscr{S}} = (\sum_j \lambda_j^2)^{1/2}$. The use of Hilbert–Schmidt norm comes from the fact that it forms a class of operators embedded in the whole space of Hilbert–Schmidt operators and for any convolution kernel operator ρ, the Hilbert–Schmidt norm of ρ is equal to the L^2 norm of its kernel function, in particular, $\| \rho \|_{\mathscr{S}} = \| \kappa \|_2$.

Note that in Theorem 3.1, $g(X_t^{(a)}, X_t^{(b)}, X_{t-1}^{(a)}, X_{t-1}^{(b)}, \Gamma_k) = \sup_{\psi \in \Gamma_k} g(X_t^{(a)}, X_t^{(b)}, X_{t-1}^{(a)}, X_{t-1}^{(b)}, \psi)$. We define the set of all the MLEs on Θ_{J_n} given the sample size n as $M_{J_n}^n = \{\rho \in \Theta_{J_n} \mid \ell(X_1^{(a)}, \ldots, X_n^{(a)}, X_1^{(b)}, \ldots, X_n^{(b)}; \rho) = \sup_{\psi \in \Theta_{J_n}} \ell(X_1^{(a)}, \ldots, X_n^{(a)}, X_1^{(b)}, \ldots, X_n^{(b)}; \psi)\}$. Let ρ_0 denotes the true set of values for the set of parameters $(\rho_0^{aa}, \rho_0^{ab}, \rho_0^{ba}, \rho_0^{bb})$. We follow Mourid and Bensmain (2006) for the proof of Theorem 3.1 to show the convergence of the ML estimator to $\rho_{0|\Theta_{J_n}}$, the projections of the true operators on sieve, see Appendix 3 for details. Together with the convergence of $\rho_{0|\Theta_{J_n}}$ to the true set of operators ρ_0 as the sieve dimension grows, we prove that the ML estimator converges to the true set of operators ρ_0.

THEOREM 3.2 *If $J_n = \mathcal{O}(n^{1/3-\eta})$ for $\eta > 0$, then $\| \widehat{\kappa}_{J_n} - \kappa_{0|\Theta_{J_n}} \|_2 \to 0$ a.s. when $n \to +\infty$. $\widehat{\kappa}_{J_n} = (\widehat{\kappa}_{aa,J_n}, \widehat{\kappa}_{ab,J_n}, \widehat{\kappa}_{ba,J_n}, \widehat{\kappa}_{bb,J_n})$ is the set of sieve estimators on Θ_{J_n} and $\kappa_{0|\Theta_{J_n}} = (\kappa_{aa,0|\Theta_{J_n}}, \kappa_{ab,0|\Theta_{J_n}}, \kappa_{ba,0|\Theta_{J_n}}, \kappa_{bb,0|\Theta_{J_n}})$ is the projection of the set of true kernel functions κ_0 on Θ_{J_n}. $\| \widehat{\kappa}_{J_n} - \kappa_{0|\Theta_{J_n}} \|_2 \to$*

Table 2. R^2, RMSE, and MAPE for in-sample estimation of the 12 stocks.

Ticker symbol	VFAR			RW vs. VFAR		
	R^2 (%)	RMSE	MAPE (%)	R^2	RMSE	MAPE
AAPL	92.03	0.34	3.61	**0.97**	**1.18**	**1.05**
MSFT	95.19	0.18	0.95	**0.98**	**1.16**	**1.07**
INTC	94.79	0.19	0.92	**0.98**	**1.15**	**1.07**
CSCO	96.16	0.19	0.86	**0.99**	**1.13**	**1.06**
SIRI	98.29	0.09	0.29	**1.00**	**1.09**	**1.00**
AMAT	95.83	0.18	0.89	**0.99**	**1.15**	**1.09**
CMCSA	93.39	0.19	1.20	**0.97**	**1.18**	**1.13**
AEZS	98.48	0.42	2.18	**0.98**	**1.45**	**1.05**
EBAY	94.88	0.23	1.55	**0.98**	**1.15**	**1.06**
MU	95.14	0.26	1.17	**0.98**	**1.16**	**1.08**
WFM	95.52	0.20	1.57	**0.98**	**1.16**	**1.01**
SBUX	94.77	0.22	2.51	**0.98**	**1.17**	**1.05**

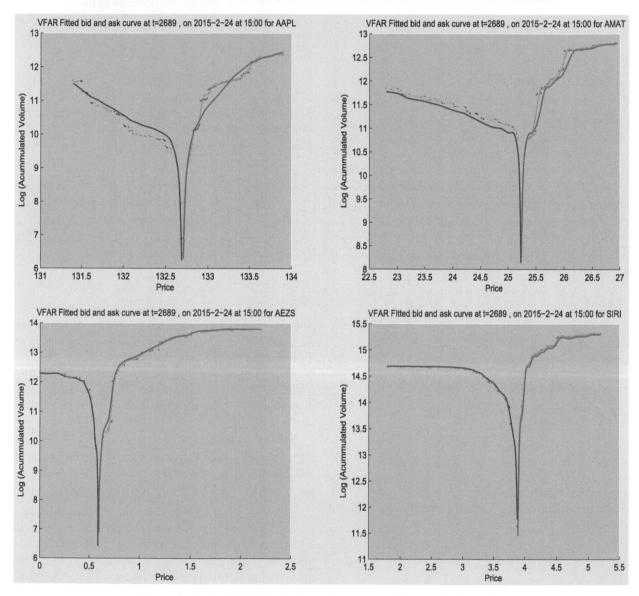

Figure 4. Estimated bid (and ask) supply curves vs. the actually observed.

0 *a.s. means that each* $\|\widehat{\kappa}_{xy,J_n} - \kappa_{xy,0|\Theta_{J_n}}\|_2 \to 0$ *a.s. for* $xy = aa, ab, ba, bb$.

By checking the conditions of Theorem 3.1, we can achieve the proof of Theorem 3.2. The proof is detailed in Appendix 4.

As $n, J_n \to \infty$, we have $\kappa_{0|\Theta_J} \to \kappa_0$ as $\kappa_{xy,0|\Theta_J}$ in $\kappa_{0|\Theta_J}$ is just the B-spline truncation of the corresponding true kernel $\kappa_{xy,0}$ in κ_0 on Θ_{J_n}. Finally we have the sieve estimator $\widehat{\kappa}_{J_n}$ converges to the true set of kernel functions κ_0.

4. Modeling liquidity demand and supply curves

We apply the convolutional VFAR model to study the joint dynamics of the liquidity demand and supply curves in the LOB. We investigate the in-sample and out-of-sample predictability based on the records of the 12 stocks with high variations over 44 trading days from date 2 January 2015 to 6 March 2015. We evaluate the accuracy of prediction and also demonstrate the application of the VFAR forecast in order execution strategy.

On each day, the liquidity demand and supply curves are obtained by using the B-spline expansions on the log-accumulated volumes. Throughout the analysis, we assumed prices are known exogenous variables. The equally spaced price percentiles are used as nodes and $J_n = 20$ is chosen in the sieve. The value of J_n is selected for giving on average the highest explanatory power over all the 12 stocks in our analysis. There are in total 20 coefficients on the bid side and another 20 on the ask side.

One may suspect co-integration between the bid and ask sides, though there is no empirical evidence on the existence of co-integration in figure 2, we also consider the Random Walk (RW) model as an alternative, where the liquidity curves are predicted by the most recent curves at the previous time point. The selection of random walk is also motivated by the fact the it provides a general good predictability and is hard to beat under market efficiency.

Three measures are used to evaluate the prediction performance. They are Root Mean Squared Error (RMSE), Mean Absolute Percentage Error (MAPE) for accuracy, and R^2 for the explanatory power:

$$
\text{RMSE} = \sqrt{\frac{\sum_{xy=a,b} \sum_{t=1}^{n} \sum_{\tau} \left\{ X_t^{(xy)}(\tau) - \widehat{X}_t^{(xy)}(\tau) \right\}^2}{\sum_{t-1}^{n} N_t}},
$$

$$
\text{MAPE} = \frac{\sum_{xy=a,b} \sum_{t=1}^{n} \sum_{\tau} \frac{\left| X_t^{(xy)}(\tau) - \widehat{X}_t^{(xy)}(\tau) \right|}{X_t^{(xy)}(\tau)}}{\sum_{t=1}^{n} N_t},
$$

$$
R^2 = 1 - \frac{\sum_{xy=a,b} \sum_{t=1}^{n} \sum_{\tau} \left\{ X_t^{(xy)}(\tau) - \widehat{X}_t^{(xy)}(\tau) \right\}^2}{\sum_{xy=a,b} \sum_{t=1}^{n} \sum_{\tau} \left\{ X_t^{(xy)}(\tau) - \bar{X} \right\}^2},
$$

(7)

where X is the actual value, $\widehat{X}$ denotes the estimate or forecast, and N_t is the total number of the observed price quotes on both sides of LOB at time point t. For each stock, we calculate these measures for the estimated/forecasted liquidity curves using the VFAR model and the alternative RW model, respectively.

4.1. In-sample estimation

We conduct the in-sample estimation over the whole time period of the 44 days. Table 2 reports the R^2, RMSE and MAPE of the estimated liquidity curves. It shows that VFAR provides high explanatory power for all the stocks, with R^2 ranging from 92 % (AAPL) to 98 % (AEZS), and superior prediction accuracy with RMSE smaller than 0.42 (AEZS)

and MAPE lower than 3.61 % (AAPL). We compare the performance of VFAR and the alternative RW model. On the right panel, the ratio of each measure is computed for the estimates based on the RW model against those on the VFAR model. The best relative performance is marked in bold-face. Without exception, the VFAR model is better than the alternative. In terms of R^2, VFAR outperforms by up to 3 % (AAPL the largest stock and CMCSA the least active stock). As for estimation accuracy, the relative performance reaches to 13 % in MAPE (CMCSA) and at least 9 % (SIRI, the most

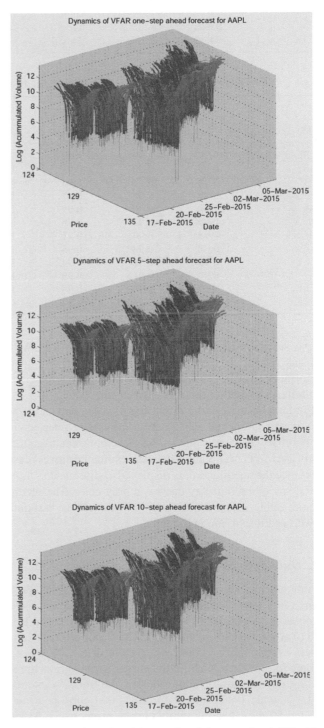

Figure 5. Dynamics of multi-step ahead forecast for AAPL. Top: 5-min ahead forecast; middle: 25-min ahead forecast; bottom: 50-min ahead forecast.

Table 3. R^2, RMSE, MAPE for multi-step ahead VFAR forecast of the 12 stocks.

Ticker symbol	R^2 (%)			RMSE			MAPE (%)		
	1-step	5-steps	10-steps	1-step	5-steps	10-steps	1-step	5-steps	10-steps
AAPL	91.13	85.64	83.74	0.37	0.48	0.51	3.61	4.21	4.49
MSFT	95.38	91.56	89.65	0.18	0.24	0.27	0.93	1.42	1.63
INTC	94.02	89.44	86.95	0.19	0.26	0.28	0.95	1.46	1.74
CSCO	96.67	93.07	90.35	0.21	0.31	0.36	0.88	1.44	1.76
SIRI	98.14	96.23	95.31	0.09	0.13	0.14	0.30	0.52	0.62
AMAT	95.47	92.17	89.99	0.19	0.25	0.29	1.00	1.47	1.72
CMCSA	92.80	89.22	88.09	0.20	0.24	0.25	1.15	1.56	1.69
AEZS	98.23	97.71	97.43	0.48	0.55	0.58	2.22	2.85	3.14
EBAY	94.64	91.54	89.74	0.23	0.29	0.32	1.31	1.79	2.03
MU	95.37	92.35	90.60	0.22	0.28	0.31	1.18	1.70	1.99
WFM	95.18	92.24	91.15	0.20	0.26	0.27	1.25	1.76	1.94
SBUX	94.49	91.82	90.63	0.23	0.28	0.30	1.81	2.27	2.48

Table 4. Ratio of R^2, RMSE, MAPE for multi-step ahead RW forecast to VFAR forecast of the 12 stocks.

Ticker symbol	R^2			RMSE			MAPE		
	1-step	5-steps	10-steps	1-step	5-steps	10-steps	1-step	5-steps	10-steps
AAPL	0.97	0.93	0.90	1.15	1.19	1.22	1.03	1.11	1.13
MSFT	0.99	0.98	0.97	1.10	1.12	1.14	0.97	0.98	1.02
INTC	0.98	0.96	0.94	1.12	1.16	1.19	1.02	1.05	1.07
CSCO	0.99	0.98	0.97	1.09	1.13	1.14	1.01	1.01	1.05
SIRI	1.00	0.99	0.99	1.04	1.10	1.09	0.90	0.90	0.90
AMAT	0.99	0.97	0.96	1.11	1.16	1.18	1.01	1.05	1.09
CMCSA	0.98	0.94	0.91	1.14	1.23	1.28	1.06	1.13	1.19
AEZS	0.98	0.98	0.98	1.36	1.40	1.39	1.05	1.12	1.12
EBAY	0.99	0.96	0.94	1.12	1.19	1.23	1.05	1.11	1.16
MU	0.98	0.96	0.95	1.15	1.20	1.22	1.08	1.12	1.15
WFM	0.99	0.96	0.94	1.13	1.23	1.29	1.05	1.12	1.20
SBUX	0.98	0.96	0.94	1.15	1.21	1.24	1.03	1.11	1.15

active stock) and up to 45 % (AEZS that has the smallest bid–ask spread on average) in RMSE. We find the superior performance of the VFAR is robust with respect to market capitalization, market tightness and depth.

Figure 4 visualizes the fitted liquidity demand and supply curves and the actual values at an arbitrarily selected date, 24 February 2015 at 3 pm, of the four representative stocks, AAPL, AMAT, AEZS and SIRI. The estimated curves reasonably trace the queuing orders displayed as discrete dots as well as the smoothed liquidity curves in gray color. The accuracy is quite stable, especially in the middle around the best quotes as well as the extreme in the tails.

4.2. Out-of-sample forecast

In this section, we analyze the model's forecasting performance in a realistic setup. In particular, a trader is assumed to observe the LOB at 5-min snapshots, with the information over the past 30 trading days. The trader can only submit orders every 5 min and thus asks for multi-step ahead out-of-sample forecasts for the liquidity curves, starting from the 31st trading day onwards. Among others, the trader is interested in 1-, 5- and 10-step ahead forecasts that correspond to 5-, 25- and 50-min ahead liquidity curves, respectively. As such, the first pair of the forecasted curves is for time $t = 2251$, based on the past 30 trading days of $30 \times 75 = 2250$ functional objects. Each time, he moves forward one period, i.e.

5 min and performs re-estimation and forecast until reaching the end of the sample at $t = 3300$.

Figure 5 gives graphical illustrations of the forecasted liquidity curves for AAPL with the VFAR model. The forecasts closely trace the realized liquidity curves. It is remarkable that the VFAR model is able to catch the dynamic movements of the liquidity curves over the period from 17 February to 06 March 2015 for different forecast horizon from 5- to 50-min.

Table 3 reports the RMSE, MAPE and predictive power of the liquidity curves forecast for the 12 stocks. Even if in the 'worst' case, the VFAR approach is able to achieve high R^2 ranging from 91.13 % (1-step AAPL) to 83.74 % (10-step AAPL), low RMSE of 0.48 (1-step AEZS) to 0.58 (10-step AEZS), and low MAPE of 3.61 % (1-step AAPL) to 4.49 % (10-step AAPL). The relative performance of the alternative RW model is summarized in table 4. Again, the VFAR model dominates the RW model across forecast horizons and forecast measures. Though the improvement in R^2 is weak, the advantage is obvious in terms of the forecast error reduction. In terms of RMSE, the VFAR model reaches about 4 % (1-step SIRI) in the worst case and 36 % (1-step AEZS) and 40 % (5-step AEZS) in the best case. On the other hand, the VFAR model does not always yield improvement in the MAPE comparison. However, the RW performs better than VFAR only in 5 out of 36 instances. In other cases, VFAR outperforms the RW by up to 20 %. The relative superior performance grows as the forecast horizon increases, indicating that the

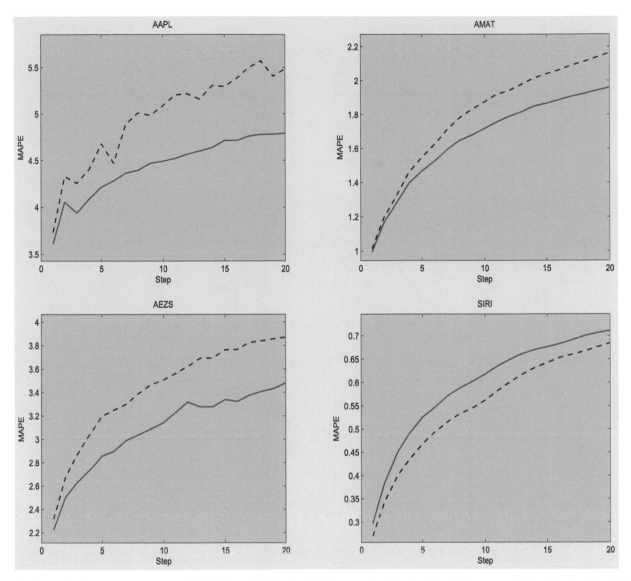

Figure 6. Mean absolute percentage errors (MAPEs) implied by the VFAR approach (blue) and the RW approach (black dashed) for different number of steps ahead forecasts, corresponding to 5–100 min.

utilization of cross-dependence in liquidity curves helps to improve out-of-sample prediction.

We also find that the strong predictability of the VFAR model is stable with respect to forecast horizons. Figure 6 displays the MAPEs for various multi-steps ahead forecasts ranging from 1 to 20 steps ahead for the four representative stocks AAPL, AMAT, AEZS, and SIRI. Except SIRI, the VFAR forecasts outperform the RW with lower MAPEs. As we forecast further into the future, the advantage of VFAR over RW increases for AAPL, AMAT and AEZS. As the most active stock considered in our data analysis, SIRI has weaker predictive power in the out-of-sample forecasting. It is the only asset for which MAPE is greater than the random walk specification alternative, although this difference shrinks as the steps forward increase. This weaker predictive power could be due to the fact that SIRI is the most active stock, and its dynamics is difficult to characterize, even by the VFAR.

To summarize, the proposed VFAR model is able to successfully predict the liquidity curves over various forecasting periods. These results can be applied to various financial and economics applications, and we will show next an application to order execution strategy as an example.

4.3. Application to order execution strategy

In this section, we show how to utilize the forecasting results in the previous section to a practical application on order execution. Assume that an investor decides to buy (sell) v number of shares over a course of a trading day, starting from 9:45 to 15:55. The volume v to be traded is chosen to be 5 or 10 times the average pending volume at the best bid (ask) price, yielding the following buy (sell) quantities in the respective two cases of (a) high and (b) very high liquidity demand:

(a) AAPL-4000 (4000); MSFT-26 000 (29 000); INTC-27 000 (31 000); CSCO-67 000 (53 000); SIRI-675 000 (654 000); AMAT-17 000 (18 000); CMCSA-7000 (8000); AEZS-12 000 (17 000); EBAY-6000 (6000); MU-8000 (8000); WFM-2000 (3000); SBUX-2000 (2000).

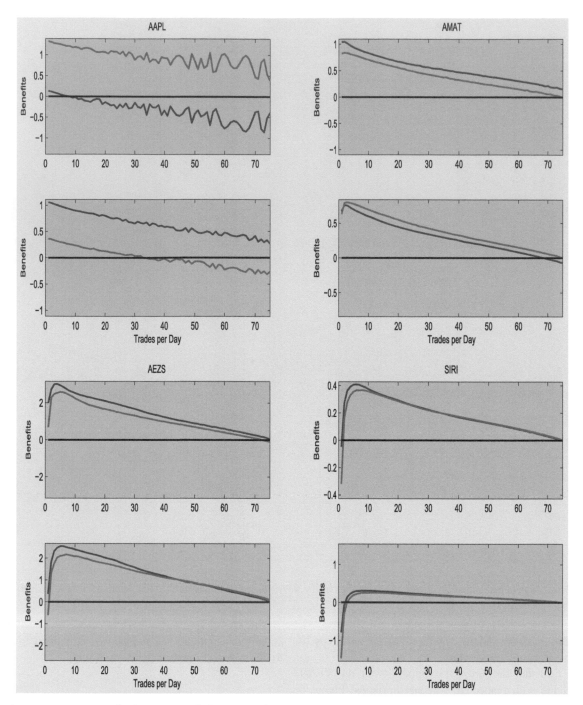

Figure 7. Average percentage gains by strategy (ii) in excess of the equal-splitting strategy (i) when buying (blue) and selling (red) shares based on m VFAR-predicted time points per day. For each stock, top: high liquidity demand corresponding to 5 times the average first level market depth; bottom: very high liquidity demand corresponding to 10 times the average first level market depth.

(b) AAPL-8000 (8000); MSFT-52 000 (58 000); INTC-54 000 (62 000); CSCO-134 000 (106 000); SIRI-1 350 000 (1 308 000); AMAT-34 000 (36 000); CMCSA-14 000 (16 000); AEZS-24 000 (34 000); EBAY-12 000 (12 000); MU-16 000 (16 000); WFM-4000 (6000); SBUX-4000 (4000).

Suppose that trading is only performed on a 5 min grid throughout the day corresponding to 75 possible trading time points, and investor can only make decision at 9:45 but not monitor the market anymore during the day. The forecasting horizon covers $h = 75$ periods on each trading day. The following are two execution strategies the investor can use:

(i) Splitting the buy (sell) order of size v equally in 5-min frequency over the trading day, resulting into 75 trades of size $v/75$ each; see Almgren and Chriss (2000).

(ii) Placing different orders at m (5-min interval) time points throughout the day where the VFAR predicted implied trading costs c of volume v are smallest. The volume is split over the m time points according to the relative proportion of expected trading costs, i.e. at time point i, $w_i \cdot v$ shares are traded, with $w_i = c_i / \sum_{j=1}^{m} c_j$ for $i = 1, \ldots, m$; see Härdle et al. (2012).

Note that strategy (i) is a special case of strategy (ii) with $m = 75$ and the volume v is equally split. For strategy (ii), if $m = 1$, it is the extreme case where the whole quantity is traded only once. The VFAR prediction of the trading costs involves predicting the whole bid and ask curve at each time point and compute the effective cost of trading using prevailing bid and ask quotes assumed to be known at the respective time points.

We implement these strategies to 14 forecasting days, from 17 February to 06 March 2015. Figure 7 shows the average percentage reduction in trading costs of strategy (ii) in excess of the equal-splitting strategy (i) for different values of $m \in [1, 75]$ for AAPL, AMAT, AEZS, and SIRI. Overall, we observe that strategic placement of orders according to VFAR predictions achieve excess gains of 31 basis points on average. Generally, the behavior of the curves is similar, increasing as m increases from 1, and converge to zero as m reaches the upper limit of 75. The pattern shows that making small number of large market orders is superior to an equal-splitting strategy, while for the extreme case where $m = 1$, there is lesser benefit or even loss since the transactions have to walk up the book too severely and cause large price impacts; and where $m = 75$, the relative benefit only results from the strategic non-equal weighting scheme. All in all, the VFAR model is successful in predicting times when the market is sufficiently deep to execute large orders.

5. Conclusion

Predictions of future liquidity supply and demand in the limit order book (LOB) help in analyzing optimal splitting strategies for large orders to reduce cost. To capture not only the volume around the best bid and ask price in the LOB, but also the pending volumes more deeply in the book, it becomes an ultra-high dimensional problem. Motivated by the significant cross-dependency of the bid and ask side of the market, we proposed a Vector Functional AutoRegressive (VFAR) model to estimate and forecast the liquidity supply and demand curves in the functional domain.

The model is applied to 12 stocks traded in the National Association of Securities Dealers Automated Quotations (NASDAQ) stock market. It is shown that the VFAR model gives R^2 values as high as 98.5 % for in-sample estimation. In out-of-sample forecast experiments, it produces accurate 5-, 25- and 50-min forecasts, with MAPE as low as 0.3 –4.5%. The predictive power of the VFAR model can be further used to improve order execution strategies at lower trading cost.

Our results contribute to the finance domain in helping both practitioners and academics to better understand the dynamics of available liquidity of a LOB and aiding to construct a forward-looking trading strategy. In the area of financial econometrics, we extend the VAR framework to the functional domain, develop the method, and derive the theoretical results. For future work, one can consider adding exogenous variables to the VFAR model, extending the VARX framework in the functional domain, to develop the VFARX model. In application, one can jointly forecast the liquidity supply and demand of a basket of stocks, rather than just an individual stock that was presented in this paper, and include other exogenous variables (in VFARX) such as oil prices, or electricity prices, that may affect the liquidity of certain stocks. Most important, the VFAR model is general, has high interpretability, and can be used for other multiple functional time series modeling and forecasting.

Acknowledgments

We would like to thank the editor and two anonymous referees for their constructive comments to help improve the quality of this paper.

Disclosure statement

No potential conflict of interest was reported by the authors.

Funding

The research of Ying Chen is supported by the Academic Research Funding R-155-000-178-114 and IDS Funding R-155-000-185-64 at the National University of Singapore. Support from IRTG 1792 'High Dimensional Non Stationary Time Series', Humboldt-Universität zu Berlin, is gratefully acknowledged.

References

Aït-Sahalia, Y., Mykland, P. and Zhang, L., How often to sample a continuous-time process in the presence of market microstructure noise. *Rev. Financ. Stud.*, 2005, **18**, 351–416.

Almgren, R. and Chriss, N., Optimal execution of portfolio transactions. *J. Risk.*, 2000, **3**, 5–39.

Antoniadis, A. and Sapatinas, T., Wavelet methods for continuous-time prediction using Hilbert-valued autoregressive processes. *J. Multivar. Anal.*, 2003, **87**, 135–158.

Benston, G. and Hagerman, R., Determinants of bid-asked spreads in the over-the-counter market. *J. Financ. Econ.*, 1974, **1**, 353–364.

Besse, P., Cardot, H. and Stephenson, D., Autoregressive forecasting of some functional climatic variations. *Scand. J. Stat.*, 2000, **27**, 673–687.

Bosq, D., *Linear Processes in Function Spaces: Theory and Applications*, 2000 (Springer: New York).

Chaudhuri, K., Kim, M. and Shin, Y., Forecasting distributions of inflation rates: A functional Autoregressive Approach. *J. R. Stat. Soc.: Ser. A (Stat. Soc.)*, 2016, **179**, 65–102.

Chen, Y. and Li, B., An adaptive functional autoregressive forecast model to predict electricity price curves. *J. Bus. Econ. Stat.*, 2017, **35**(3), 371–388.

Chordia, T., Sarkar, A. and Subrahmanyam, A., An empirical analysis of stock and bond market liquidity. *Rev. Financial Stud.*, 2005, **18**(1), 85–129.

Cooper, K., Groth, J. and Avera, W., Liquidity, exchange listing, and common stock performance. *J. Econ. Bus.*, 1985, **37**, 19–33.

Fleming, M. and Remolona, E., Price formation and liquidity in the U.S. treasury market: The response to public information. *J. Financ.*, 1999, **54**, 1901–1915.

Foucault, T., Kadan, O. and Kandel, E., Limit order book as a market for liquidity. *Rev. Financ. Stud.*, 2005, **18**, 1171–1217.

Geman, S. and Hwang, C.R., Nonparametric maximum likelihood estimation by the method of sieves. *Ann. Stat.*, 1982, **10**, 401–414.

Gomber, P., Schweickert, U. and Theissen, E., Liquidity dynamics in an electronic open limit order book: An event study approach. *Eur. Financ. Manage.*, 2015, **21**, 52–78.

Grenander, U., *Abstract Inference*, 1981 (Wiley: New York).

Groß-Klußmann, A. and Hautsch, N., Predicting bid ask spreads using long-memory autoregressive conditional Poisson models. *J. Forecast.*, 2013, **32**, 724–742.

Guillas, S., Rates of convergence of autocorrelation estimates for autoregressive Hilbertian processes. *Stat. Probab. Lett.*, 2001, **55**, 281–291.

Härdle, W., Hautsch, N. and Mihoci, A., Modelling and forecasting liquidity supply using semiparametric factor dynamics. *J. Empir. Financ.*, 2012, **19**, 610–625.

Härdle, W., Hautsch, N. and Mihoci, A., Local adaptive multiplicative error models for high-frequency forecasts. *J. Appl. Economet.*, 2015, **30**, 529–550.

Härdle, W. K., Chen, S., Liang, C. and Schienle, M., Time-varying limit order book networks. IRTG 1792 Discussion Paper 2018-016, IRTG 1792, Humboldt Universität zu Berlin, Germany, 2018.

Harris, L., Liquidity, trading rules and electronic trading systems. Technical report, NYU Salomon Center Series in Finance and Economics, 1990.

Huberman, G. and Halka, D., Systematic liquidity. *J. Financ. Res.*, 2001, **24**, 161–178.

Hwang, C., Gaussian measure of large balls in a Hilbert space. *Proc. Am. Math. Soc.*, 1980, **78**, 107–110.

Johansen, S., Estimating and hypothesis testing of cointegration vectors in Gaussian vector autoregressive models. *Econometrica*, 1991, **59**, 1551–1580.

Mourid, T. and Bensmain, N., Sieves estimator of the operator of a functional autoregressive process. *Stat. Probab. Lett.*, 2006, **76**, 93–108.

Stoll, H., The pricing of security dealer services: An empirical study of NASDAQ stocks. *J. Financ.*, 1978, **33**, 1153–1172.

Zhang, L., Mykland, P. and Aït-Sahalia, Y., A tale of two time scales: Determining integrated volatility with noisy high-frequency data. *J. Am. Stat. Assoc.*, 2005, **100**, 1394–1411.

Appendix 1. Derivation of the B-spline coefficient relationship as shown in Section 3

$$X_t^{(a)}(\tau) = \sum_{h=1}^{\infty} p_h^a B_{h,m}(\tau)$$

$$+ \int_0^1 \left\{ \sum_{j=1}^{\infty} \sum_{i=1}^{\infty} c_j^{aa} d_{t-1,i}^a B_{j,m}(\tau - s) B_{i,m}(s) \right\} \, ds$$

$$+ \int_0^1 \left\{ \sum_{j=1}^{\infty} \sum_{i=1}^{\infty} c_j^{ab} d_{t-1,i}^b B_{j,m}(\tau - s) B_{i,m}(s) \right\} \, ds$$

$$+ \sum_{j=1}^{\infty} d_j^a(\varepsilon_t^{(a)}) B_{j,m}(\tau)$$

$$= \sum_{h=1}^{\infty} p_h^a B_{h,m}(\tau) + \sum_{j=1}^{\infty} d_j^a(\varepsilon_t^{(a)}) B_{j,m}(\tau)$$

$$+ \sum_{h=1}^{\infty} \sum_{i=1}^{\infty}$$

$$\times \left\{ \sum_{j=1}^{\infty} \left(\frac{w_{j+m} - w_{j+1}}{w_{j+m} - w_j} - \frac{w_{j+m+1} - w_{j+2}}{w_{j+m+1} - w_{j+1}} \right) c_j^{aa} - c_h^{aa} \right\}$$

$$\times \frac{w_{i+m} - w_i}{m} d_{t-1,i}^a B_{h,m}(\tau)$$

$$+ \sum_{h=1}^{\infty} \sum_{i=1}^{\infty}$$

$$\times \left\{ \sum_{j=1}^{\infty} \left(\frac{w_{j+m} - w_{j+1}}{w_{j+m} - w_j} - \frac{w_{j+m+1} - w_{j+2}}{w_{j+m+1} - w_{j+1}} \right) c_j^{ab} - c_h^{ab} \right\}$$

$$\times \frac{w_{i+m} - w_i}{m} d_{t-1,i}^b B_{h,m}(\tau),$$

$$X_t^{(b)}(\tau) = \sum_{h=1}^{\infty} p_h^b B_{h,m}(\tau)$$

$$+ \int_0^1 \left\{ \sum_{j=1}^{\infty} \sum_{i=1}^{\infty} c_j^{bb} d_{t-1,i}^b B_{j,m}(\tau - s) B_{i,m}(s) \right\} \, ds$$

$$+ \int_0^1 \left\{ \sum_{j=1}^{\infty} \sum_{i=1}^{\infty} c_j^{ba} d_{t-1,i}^a B_{j,m}(\tau - s) B_{i,m}(s) \right\} \, ds$$

$$+ \sum_{j=1}^{\infty} d_j^b(\varepsilon_t^{(b)}) B_{j,m}(\tau)$$

$$= \sum_{h=1}^{\infty} p_h^b B_{h,m}(\tau) + \sum_{j=1}^{\infty} d_j^b(\varepsilon_t^{(b)}) B_{j,m}(\tau)$$

$$+ \sum_{h=1}^{\infty} \sum_{i=1}^{\infty}$$

$$\times \left\{ \sum_{j=1}^{\infty} \left(\frac{w_{j+m} - w_{j+1}}{w_{j+m} - w_j} - \frac{w_{j+m+1} - w_{j+2}}{w_{j+m+1} - w_{j+1}} \right) c_j^{bb} - c_h^{bb} \right\}$$

$$\times \frac{w_{i+m} - w_i}{m} d_{t-1,i}^b B_{h,m}(\tau)$$

$$+ \sum_{h=1}^{\infty} \sum_{i=1}^{\infty}$$

$$\times \left\{ \sum_{j=1}^{\infty} \left(\frac{w_{j+m} - w_{j+1}}{w_{j+m} - w_j} - \frac{w_{j+m+1} - w_{j+2}}{w_{j+m+1} - w_{j+1}} \right) c_j^{ba} - c_h^{ba} \right\}$$

$$\times \frac{w_{i+m} - w_i}{m} d_{t-1,i}^a B_{h,m}(\tau). \tag{A1}$$

Rearranging the above equations gives the relationship of the B-spline coefficients in (3).

Next we show how the expansion was obtained in (A1). We only show for the first integral in (A1) as the expansion other integrals can be obtained similarly.

$$\int_0^1 \left\{ \sum_{j=1}^{\infty} \sum_{i=1}^{\infty} c_j^{aa} d_{t-1,i}^a B_{j,m}(\tau - s) B_{i,m}(s) \right\} \, ds$$

$$= \sum_{j=1}^{\infty} c_j^{aa} \int_0^1 B_{j,m}(\tau - s) \left\{ \sum_{i=1}^{\infty} d_{t-1,i}^a B_{i,m}(s) \right\} \, ds$$

$$= \sum_{j=1}^{\infty} c_j^{aa} \left\{ \frac{1}{m} \sum_{i=1}^{\infty} d_{t-1,i}^a (w_{i+m} - w_i) B_{j,m}(\tau - s) \right\} \Bigg|_{s=0}^{s=1}$$

$$+ \sum_{j=1}^{\infty} c_j^{aa} \int_0^1 \left[\frac{1}{m} \sum_{i=1}^{\infty} d_{t-1,i}^a (w_{i+m} - w_i) \right.$$

$$\left\{ \frac{m}{w_{j+m} - w_j} B_{j,m-1}(\tau - s) \right.$$

$$\left. \left. - \frac{m}{w_{j+m+1} - w_{j+1}} B_{j+1,m-1}(\tau - s) \right\} \right] ds$$

$$= - \sum_{j=1}^{\infty} \sum_{i=1}^{\infty} \frac{d_{t-1,i}^a (w_{i+m} - w_i)}{m} c_j^{aa} B_{j,m}(\tau)$$

$$+ \sum_{j=1}^{\infty} \sum_{i=1}^{\infty} \frac{d_{t-1,i}^a (w_{i+m} - w_i)}{m} c_j^{aa} \int_{\tau-1}^{\tau} \left\{ \frac{m}{w_{j+m} - w_j} B_{j,m-1}(z) \right.$$

$$\left. - \frac{m}{w_{j+m+1} - w_{j+1}} B_{j+1,m-1}(z) \right\} dz$$

$$= - \sum_{h=1}^{\infty} \sum_{i=1}^{\infty} \frac{d_{t-1,i}^a (w_{i+m} - w_i)}{m} c_h^{aa} B_{h,m}(\tau)$$

$$+ \sum_{h=1}^{\infty} \sum_{i=1}^{\infty} \sum_{j=1}^{\infty} \left(\frac{w_{j+m} - w_{j+1}}{w_{j+m} - w_j} - \frac{w_{j+m+1} - w_{j+2}}{w_{j+m+1} - w_{j+1}} \right)$$

$$\times c_j^{aa} \frac{w_{i+m} - w_i}{m} d_{t-1,i}^a B_{h,m}(\tau)$$

$$= \sum_{h=1}^{\infty} \sum_{i=1}^{\infty} \left[\sum_{j=1}^{\infty} \left\{ \frac{w_{j+m} - w_{j+1}}{w_{j+m} - w_j} - \frac{w_{j+m+1} - w_{j+2}}{w_{j+m+1} - w_{j+1}} \right\} c_j^{aa} - c_h^{aa} \right]$$

$$\times \frac{w_{i+m} - w_i}{m} d_{t-1,i}^a B_{h,m}(\tau).$$

The second equality made use of integration by parts, with $(d/ds) B_{j,m}(\tau - s) = -((m/(w_{j+m} - w_j)) B_{j,m-1}(\tau - s) - (m/(w_{j+m+1} - w_{j+1})) B_{j+1,m-1}(\tau - s))$ and $\int \sum_{i=1}^{\infty} d_{t-1,i}^a B_{l,m}(s) \, ds = (1/m) \sum_{i=1}^{\infty} d_{t-1,i}^a (w_{i+m} - w_i)$. In the third equality, we made the substitution of $z = \tau - s$. For the fourth equality, we made use of the formula: $\int_{-\infty}^{\tau} B_{j,m}(z) \, dz = ((w_{j+m+1} - w_{j+1})/(m+1)) \sum_{h=1}^{\infty} B_{h,m+1}(\tau)$, and truncating the sum up till the Jth term. We also swapped the notation j for the first summation with h in the fourth equality.

Appendix 2. Derivation of the ML estimator in (eqn6)

For $t = 1, \ldots, n$, we write (5) compactly as the following:

$$Y = BZ + U. \tag{A2}$$

By applying vec operator to (A2) yields

$$\text{vec}(Y) = \text{vec}(BZ) + \text{vec}(U)$$

$$= (Z^\top \otimes I_K) \text{vec}(B) + \text{vec}(U)$$

or equivalently,

$$\mathbf{y} = (Z^\top \otimes I_K) \boldsymbol{\beta} + \mathbf{u},$$

where $\otimes$ is the Kronecker product.

Assuming

$$\mathbf{u} = \text{vec}(U) = \begin{bmatrix} u_1 \\ \vdots \\ u_n \end{bmatrix} \sim \mathcal{N}(0, I_n \otimes \Sigma_u),$$

the probabilistic density of $\mathbf{u}$ is

$$f_{\mathbf{u}}(\mathbf{u}) = \frac{1}{(2\pi)^{Kn/2}} |I_n \otimes \Sigma_u|^{-1/2} \exp \left\{ -\frac{1}{2} \mathbf{u}^\top (I_n \otimes \Sigma_u^{-1}) \mathbf{u} \right\}.$$

In addition,

$$\mathbf{u} = \begin{bmatrix} I_K & & & 0 \\ -C & \ddots & & \\ & \ddots & \ddots & \\ 0 & & -C & I_K \end{bmatrix} (\mathbf{y} - \mathbf{v}) + \begin{bmatrix} -C \\ 0 \\ \vdots \\ 0 \end{bmatrix} y_0,$$

where $\mathbf{v} = (v, \ldots, v)^\top$ is a $(Kn \times 1)$ vector. Consequently, $\partial \mathbf{u}/\partial \mathbf{y}^\top$ is a lower triangular matrix with unit diagonal which has unit determinant. Therefore using $\mathbf{u} = \mathbf{y} - (Z^\top \otimes I_K) \boldsymbol{\beta}$, the transition density is as follows:

$$g(X_t^{(a)}, X_t^{(b)}, X_{t-1}^{(a)}, X_{t-1}^{(b)}, \rho^{aa}, \rho^{ab}, \rho^{ba}, \rho^{bb}) = f_{\mathbf{y}}(\mathbf{y}) = \left| \frac{\partial \mathbf{u}}{\partial \mathbf{y}^\top} \right| f_{\mathbf{u}}(\mathbf{u})$$

$$= \frac{1}{(2\pi)^{Kn/2}} |I_n \otimes \Sigma_u|^{-1/2}$$

$$\exp \left\{ -\frac{1}{2} \left(\mathbf{y} - (Z^\top \otimes I_K) \boldsymbol{\beta} \right)^\top (I_n \otimes \Sigma_u^{-1}) \left(\mathbf{y} - (Z^\top \otimes I_K) \boldsymbol{\beta} \right) \right\}.$$

The (approximated) log-likelihood function is

$$\ell\left(X_1^{(a)}, \ldots, X_n^{(a)}, X_1^{(b)}, \ldots, X_n^{(b)}; \rho^{aa}, \rho^{ab}, \rho^{ba}, \rho^{bb}\right) = \ell(\boldsymbol{\beta}, \Sigma_u)$$

$$= -\frac{Kn}{2} \log 2\pi - \frac{n}{2} \log |\Sigma_u| - \frac{1}{2} \left(\mathbf{y} - (Z^\top \otimes I_K) \boldsymbol{\beta} \right)^\top$$

$$\times (I_n \otimes \Sigma_u^{-1}) \left(\mathbf{y} - (Z^\top \otimes I_K) \boldsymbol{\beta} \right)$$

$$= -\frac{Kn}{2} \log 2\pi - \frac{n}{2} \log |\Sigma_u| - \frac{1}{2} \sum_{t=1}^{n} \left(y_t - v - C y_{t-1} \right)^\top$$

$$\times \Sigma_u^{-1} \left(y_t - v - C y_{t-1} \right)$$

$$= -\frac{Kn}{2} \log 2\pi - \frac{n}{2} \log |\Sigma_u| - \frac{1}{2} \sum_{t=1}^{n} \left(y_t - C y_{t-1} \right)^\top$$

$$\times \Sigma_u^{-1} \left(y_t - C y_{t-1} \right) + v^\top \Sigma_u^{-1} \sum_{t=1}^{n} \left(y_t - C y_{t-1} \right)$$

$$- \frac{n}{2} v^\top \Sigma_u^{-1} v$$

$$= -\frac{Kn}{2} \log 2\pi - \frac{n}{2} \log |\Sigma_u| - \frac{1}{2} \text{tr}\left((Y - BZ)^\top \Sigma_u^{-1} (Y - BZ) \right)$$

and the first order partial differentiations are as follows:

$$\frac{\partial \ell}{\partial \boldsymbol{\beta}} = (Z \otimes I_K)(I_n \otimes \Sigma_u^{-1}) \left(\mathbf{y} - (Z^\top \otimes I_K) \boldsymbol{\beta} \right)$$

$$= (Z \otimes \Sigma_u^{-1}) \mathbf{y} - (ZZ^\top \otimes \Sigma_u^{-1}) \boldsymbol{\beta}, \tag{A3}$$

$$\frac{\partial \ell}{\partial \Sigma_u} = -\frac{n}{2} \Sigma_u^{-1} + \frac{1}{2} \Sigma_u^{-1} (Y - BZ)(Y - BZ)^\top \Sigma_u^{-1}.$$

By equating the first order partial derivatives in (A3) to zero, we obtain the maximum likelihood estimators in (6).

Appendix 3. Proof of Theorem 3.1

The growth of J_n is determined by the following two conditions:

Con1: If there exists a sequence $\{\rho_{J_n}\}$ such that $\rho_{J_n} \in \Theta_{J_n} \forall n$ and $H(\rho_{0|\Theta_{J_n}}, \rho_{J_n}) \to H(\rho_{0|\Theta_{J_n}}, \rho_{0|\Theta_{J_n}})$, then $\|\rho_{J_n} - \rho_{0|\Theta_{J_n}}\|_{\mathscr{S}} \to 0$; meaning each $\|\rho_{J_n}^{xy} - \rho_{0|\Theta_{J_n}}^{xy}\|_{\mathscr{S}} \to 0$, for $xy = aa, ab, ba, bb$. Here $\rho_{0|\Theta_{J_n}}$ denotes the projection of the set of true operators ρ_0 on the sieve Θ_{J_n}.

Con2: There exists a sequence $\{\rho_{J_n}\}$ described in **Con1** such that $H(\rho_{0|\Theta_{J_n}}, \rho_{J_n}) \to H(\rho_{0|\Theta_{J_n}}, \rho_{0|\Theta_{J_n}})$.

Fix $\delta > 0$. Following Mourid and Bensmain (2006), we only need to show that

$$P(D_{J_n} \cap M_{J_n}^n \neq \emptyset) = 0, \quad (A4)$$

because if (A4) holds, then with probability 1

$$\inf_{\varphi \in M_{J_n}^n} H(\rho_{0|\Theta_{J_n}}, \rho) \geq H(\rho_{0|\Theta_{J_n}}, \rho_{J_n}) - \delta,$$

for all n sufficiently large. Since δ is arbitrary, and

$$H(\rho_{0|\Theta_{J_n}}, \rho_{J_n}) \to H(\rho_{0|\Theta_{J_n}}, \rho_{0|\Theta_{J_n}}),$$

by condition **Con2** we deduce

$$\liminf_{\rho \in M_{J_n}^n} \inf H(\rho_{0|\Theta_{J_n}}, \rho) \geq H(\rho_{0|\Theta_{J_n}}, \rho_{0|\Theta_{J_n}}) \quad \text{a.s.}$$

Combining with

$$H(\rho_{0|\Theta_{J_n}}, \rho) \leq H(\rho_{0|\Theta_{J_n}}, \rho_{0|\Theta_{J_n}}),$$

we have

$$\lim_{n \to +\infty} \sup_{\rho \in M_{J_n}^n} |H(\rho_{0|\Theta_{J_n}}, \rho) - H(\rho_{0|\Theta_{J_n}}, \rho_{0|\Theta_{J_n}})| = 0 \quad \text{a.s.} \quad (A5)$$

Fix $\varepsilon > 0$, and for each n choose $\psi_n \in M_{J_n}^n$ such that

$$\frac{d(\rho_{0|\Theta_{J_n}}, \psi_n)}{1 + d(\rho_{0|\Theta_{J_n}}, \psi_n)} > \sup_{\rho \in M_{J_n}^n} \frac{d(\rho_{0|\Theta_{J_n}}, \rho))}{1 + d(\rho_{0|\Theta_{J_n}}, \rho))} - \varepsilon.$$

Condition **Con1** combined with (A5) imply that

$$d(\rho_{0|\Theta_{J_n}}, \psi_n) \to 0 \quad \text{a.s.}$$

Hence,

$$\limsup_{\rho \in M_{J_n}^n} \sup \frac{d(\rho_{0|\Theta_{J_n}}, \rho))}{1 + d(\rho_{0|\Theta_{J_n}}, \rho))} \leq \varepsilon.$$

Since ε is arbitrary, we deduce that $M_{J_n}^n \to \rho_{0|\Theta_{J_n}}$, which is the desired result. Therefore, it suffices to prove (A4).

For now, n and J_n are fixed. Then

$$(D_{J_n} \cap M_{J_n}^n \neq \emptyset)$$

$$\subseteq \left\{ \sup_{\rho \in D_{J_n}} \ell(X_1^{(a)}, \ldots, X_n^{(a)}, X_1^{(b)}, \ldots, X_n^{(b)}; \rho) \right.$$

$$\geq \ell(X_1^{(a)}, \ldots, X_n^{(a)}, X_1^{(b)}, \ldots, X_n^{(b)}; \rho_{J_n}) \Big\}$$

$$\subseteq \bigcup_{k=1}^{l_{J_n}} \left\{ \sup_{\rho \in \Gamma_k} \prod_{i=1}^n g\left(X_i^{(a)}, X_i^{(b)}, X_{i-1}^{(a)}, X_{i-1}^{(b)}, \rho\right) \right.$$

$$\leq \prod_{i=1}^n g\left(X_i^{(a)}, X_i^{(b)}, X_{i-1}^{(a)}, X_{i-1}^{(b)}, \rho_{J_n}\right) \Big\}$$

$$\subseteq \bigcup_{k=1}^{l_{J_n}} \left\{ \prod_{i=1}^n g\left(X_i^{(a)}, X_i^{(b)}, X_{i-1}^{(a)}, X_{i-1}^{(b)}, \Gamma_k\right) \right.$$

$$\leq \prod_{i=1}^n g\left(X_i^{(a)}, X_i^{(b)}, X_{i-1}^{(a)}, X_{i-1}^{(b)}, \rho_{J_n}\right) \Big\}.$$

Next we bound the probability of this latter set and called it π.

$$\pi \leq \sum_{k=1}^{l_{J_n}} P\left[\prod_{i=1}^n g\left(X_i^{(a)}, X_i^{(b)}, X_{i-1}^{(a)}, X_{i-1}^{(b)}, \Gamma_k\right) \right.$$

$$\leq \prod_{i=1}^n g\left(X_i^{(a)}, X_i^{(b)}, X_{i-1}^{(a)}, X_{i-1}^{(b)}, \rho_{J_n}\right) \right]$$

$$= \sum_{k=1}^{l_{J_n}} P\left[\exp \sum_{i=1}^n \left\{ t_k \log \frac{g(X_i^{(a)}, X_i^{(b)}, X_{i-1}^{(a)}, X_{i-1}^{(b)}, \Gamma_k)}{g(X_i^{(a)}, X_i^{(b)}, X_{i-1}^{(a)}, X_{i-1}^{(b)}, \rho_{J_n})} \right\} \geq 1 \right]$$

$$\leq \sum_{k=1}^{l_{J_n}} \mathsf{E}_{\rho_{0|\Theta_{J_n}}} \left[\exp \left\{ t_k \log \frac{g(X_t^{(a)}, X_t^{(b)}, X_{t-1}^{(a)}, X_{t-1}^{(b)}, \Gamma_k)}{g(X_t^{(a)}, X_t^{(b)}, X_{t-1}^{(a)}, X_{t-1}^{(b)}, \rho_{J_n})} \right\} \right]^n$$

for any nonnegative arbitrary $t_1, \ldots, t_k$ and conditionally to $X_{i-1}^{(a)}$ and $X_{i-1}^{(b)}$, the laws of the real r.v. $g(X_i^{(a)}, X_i^{(b)}, X_{i-1}^{(a)}, X_{i-1}^{(b)}, \Gamma_k)$ and $g(X_i^{(a)}, X_i^{(b)}, X_{i-1}^{(a)}, X_{i-1}^{(b)}, \rho_{J_n})$ are images of g by the translations of the laws ε_i which are i.i.d. Hence, we get

$$\pi \leq l_{J_n}(\varphi_{J_n})^n.$$

Finally, result (A4) is deduced by condition (ii) of Theorem 3.1 and by the Borel–Cantelli lemma.

Appendix 4. Proof of consistency result in Theorem 3.2

Without loss of generality, we assume that p_j^a and p_j^b are all zeros. For non-zero cases, the same consistency results can be obtained. We check the condition **Con1**. We replace J_n by J in the remaining of this section for notational simplicity, and let all summation be from 1 to J. Using the definition of the entropy, we have

$$H(\rho_{0|\Theta_J}, \rho_{0|\Theta_J}) - H(\rho_{0|\Theta_J}, \rho_{\Theta_J})$$

$$= H(\kappa_{0|\Theta_J}, \kappa_{0|\Theta_J}) - H(\kappa_{0|\Theta_J}, \kappa_{\Theta_J})$$

$$= -\frac{1}{2} \log |\Sigma_u| + \frac{1}{2} \log |\Sigma_{u,J}| + \mathsf{E}\left(-\frac{1}{2} x^\top \Sigma_u^{-1} x + \frac{1}{2} x_J^\top \Sigma_{u,J}^{-1} x_J \right),$$

where

$$x = \begin{bmatrix} d_{t,1}^a - \sum_i \left(\sum_j q_j c_j^{aa} - c_1^{aa} \right) \frac{w_{i+m} - wi}{m} d_{t-1,i}^a \\ - \sum_i \left(\sum_j q_j c_j^{ab} - c_1^{ab} \right) \frac{w_{i+m} - wi}{m} d_{t-1,i}^b \\ \vdots \\ d_{t,J}^a - \sum_i \left(\sum_j q_j c_j^{aa} - c_J^{aa} \right) \frac{w_{i+m} - wi}{m} d_{t-1,i}^a \\ - \sum_i \left(\sum_j q_j c_j^{ab} - c_J^{ab} \right) \frac{w_{i+m} - wi}{m} d_{t-1,i}^b \\ d_{t,1}^b - \sum_i \left(\sum_j q_j c_j^{ba} - c_1^{ba} \right) \frac{w_{i+m} - wi}{m} d_{t-1,i}^a \\ - \sum_i \left(\sum_j q_j c_j^{bb} - c_1^{bb} \right) \frac{w_{i+m} - wi}{m} d_{t-1,i}^b \\ \vdots \\ d_{t,J}^b - \sum_i \left(\sum_j q_j c_j^{ba} - c_J^{ba} \right) \frac{w_{i+m} - wi}{m} d_{t-1,i}^a \\ - \sum_i \left(\sum_j q_j c_j^{bb} - c_J^{bb} \right) \frac{w_{i+m} - wi}{m} d_{t-1,i}^b \end{bmatrix},$$

$$
x_J = \begin{bmatrix}
d_{t,1}^a - \sum_i \left(\sum_j q_j c_{j,J}^{aa} - c_{1,J}^{aa} \right) \dfrac{w_{i+m} - w_i}{m} d_{t-1,i}^a \\[2mm]
\quad - \sum_i \left(\sum_j q_j c_{j,J}^{ab} - c_{1,J}^{ab} \right) \dfrac{w_{i+m} - w_i}{m} d_{t-1,i}^b \\[2mm]
\vdots \\[2mm]
d_{t,J}^a - \sum_i \left(\sum_j q_j c_{j,J}^{aa} - c_{J,J}^{aa} \right) \dfrac{w_{i+m} - w_i}{m} d_{t-1,i}^a \\[2mm]
\quad - \sum_i \left(\sum_j q_j c_{j,J}^{ab} - c_{J,J}^{ab} \right) \dfrac{w_{i+m} - w_i}{m} d_{t-1,i}^b \\[2mm]
d_{t,1}^b - \sum_i \left(\sum_j q_j c_{j,J}^{ba} - c_{1,J}^{ba} \right) \dfrac{w_{i+m} - w_i}{m} d_{t-1,i}^a \\[2mm]
\quad - \sum_i \left(\sum_j q_j c_{j,J}^{bb} - c_{1,J}^{bb} \right) \dfrac{w_{i+m} - w_i}{m} d_{t-1,i}^b \\[2mm]
\vdots \\[2mm]
d_{t,J}^b - \sum_i \left(\sum_j q_j c_{j,J}^{ba} - c_{J,J}^{ba} \right) \dfrac{w_{i+m} - w_i}{m} d_{t-1,i}^a \\[2mm]
\quad - \sum_i \left(\sum_j q_j c_{j,J}^{bb} - c_{J,J}^{bb} \right) \dfrac{w_{i+m} - w_i}{m} d_{t-1,i}^b
\end{bmatrix}.
$$

Here Σ_u, c_j^{aa}, c_j^{ab}, c_j^{ba}, and c_j^{bb} denote the covariance matrix and B-spline coefficients for the kernel $\kappa_{0|\Theta_J}$; and $\Sigma_{u,J}$, $c_{j,J}^{aa}$, $c_{j,J}^{ab}$, $c_{j,J}^{ba}$, and $c_{j,J}^{bb}$ denote the covariance matrix and B-spline coefficients for the kernel κ_J. κ_J is the set of kernel functions for ρ_J with $\rho_J \in \Theta_J$; and $\kappa_{0|\Theta_J}$ is the projection of the set of true kernel functions κ_0 on Θ_J. Assuming $\Sigma_u = \Sigma_{u,J}$, we have

$$
H(\rho_{0|\Theta_J}, \rho_{0|\Theta_J}) - H(\rho_{0|\Theta_J}, \rho_{\Theta_J})
$$
$$
= \mathsf{E}\left(-\frac{1}{2} x^\top \Sigma_u^{-1} x + \frac{1}{2} x_J^\top \Sigma_u^{-1} x_J \right)
$$
$$
= \frac{1}{2} \sum_{r,s} (\Sigma_u^{-1})_{r,s} \mathsf{E}\Big\{ (x_J)_r (x_J)_s - (x)_r (x)_s \Big\},
$$

where $(\Sigma_u^{-1})_{r,s}$ is the rth row, sth column of Σ_u^{-1}, $(x_J)_r$ is the rth element of x_J, and $(x)_r$ is the rth element of x.

Since the only difference between $(x_J)_r (x_J)_s$ and $(x)_r (x)_s$ are the different B-spline coefficients, we can group the individual terms of the expansion of $(x_J)_r (x_J)_s$ and the expansion $(x)_r (x)_s$ together. After canceling out the common terms not containing the B-spline coefficients, each of the grouped terms will contain a product of some common terms and the subtraction between the B-spline coefficients (of the same index) of the two kernels or the subtraction between the product of B-spline coefficients of one kernel and that of the other kernel (of the same combination of indices). Hence, if $H(\kappa_{0|\Theta_J}, \kappa_{\Theta_J}) \to H(\kappa_{0|\Theta_J}, \kappa_{0|\Theta_J})$ as $n, J \to \infty$, we have $c_{j,J}^{aa} \to c_j^{aa}$, $c_{j,J}^{ab} \to c_j^{ab}$, $c_{j,J}^{ba} \to c_j^{ba}$, $c_{j,J}^{bb} \to c_j^{bb}$ and consequently $\rho_J \to \rho_{0|\Theta_J}$.

For the condition **Con2** and (i) of Theorem 3.1, we follow similar arguments as in Mourid and Bensmain (2006). To verify Theorem 3.1 (ii), we define

$$
\varphi(t) = \mathsf{E}_{\kappa_{0|\Theta_J}} \left\{ \exp\left(t \log \frac{g(X_t^{(a)}, X_t^{(b)}, X_{t-1}^{(a)}, X_{t-1}^{(b)}, \Gamma_k)}{g(X_t^{(a)}, X_t^{(b)}, X_{t-1}^{(a)}, X_{t-1}^{(b)}, \kappa_J)} \right) \right\},
$$

where $g(X_t^{(a)}, X_t^{(b)}, X_{t-1}^{(a)}, X_{t-1}^{(b)}, \Gamma_k) = \sup_{\psi \in \Gamma_k} g(X_t^{(a)}, X_t^{(b)}, X_{t-1}^{(a)}, X_{t-1}^{(b)}, \psi)$. Furthermore, we have $\varphi(0) = 1$ and $\varphi' = \mathsf{E}_{\kappa_{0|\Theta_J}} \log(g(X_t^{(a)}, X_t^{(b)}, X_{t-1}^{(a)}, X_{t-1}^{(b)}, \Gamma_k) / g(X_t^{(a)}, X_t^{(b)}, X_{t-1}^{(a)}, X_{t-1}^{(b)}, \kappa_J))$.

For a fixed $\kappa \in \Gamma_k$, we have

$$
A = \mathsf{E}_{\kappa_{0|\Theta_J}} \log g(X_t^{(a)}, X_t^{(b)}, X_{t-1}^{(a)}, X_{t-1}^{(b)}, \Gamma_k)
$$
$$
\quad - \mathsf{E} \log g(X_t^{(a)}, X_t^{(b)}, X_{t-1}^{(a)}, X_{t-1}^{(b)}, \kappa)
$$
$$
= \mathsf{E}_{\kappa_{0|\Theta_J}} \sup_{\psi \in \Gamma_k} \Big\{ \log g(X_t^{(a)}, X_t^{(b)}, X_{t-1}^{(a)}, X_{t-1}^{(b)}, \psi)
$$
$$
\quad - \log g(X_t^{(a)}, X_t^{(b)}, X_{t-1}^{(a)}, X_{t-1}^{(b)}, \kappa) \Big\}
$$
$$
= \mathsf{E}_{\kappa_{0|\Theta_J}} \sup_{\psi \in \Gamma_k} \Big\{ -\frac{1}{2} \log |\Sigma_{u,\psi}| + \frac{1}{2} \log |\Sigma_{u,\kappa}|
$$
$$
\quad - \frac{1}{2} x_\psi^\top \Sigma_{u,\psi}^{-1} x_\psi + \frac{1}{2} x_\kappa^\top \Sigma_{u,\kappa}^{-1} x_\kappa \Big\},
$$

where x_ψ and x_κ have the same form as x_J, with J replaced by ψ and κ, respectively. $\Sigma_{u,\psi}$, $c_{j,\psi}^{aa}$, $c_{j,\psi}^{ab}$, $c_{j,\psi}^{ba}$, and $c_{j,\psi}^{bb}$ denote the covariance matrix and B-spline coefficients for the kernel ψ, while $\Sigma_{u,\kappa}$, $c_{j,\kappa}^{aa}$, $c_{j,\kappa}^{ab}$, $c_{j,\kappa}^{ba}$, and $c_{j,\kappa}^{bb}$ denote that for the kernel κ.

Assuming $\Sigma_{u,\psi} = \Sigma_{u,\kappa} = \Sigma_u$, we have

$$
A = \mathsf{E}_{\kappa_{0|\Theta_J}} \sup_{\psi \in \Gamma_k} \left\{ \frac{1}{2} \sum_{r,s} (\Sigma_u^{-1})_{r,s} \Big((x_\psi)_r (x_\psi)_s - (x_\kappa)_r (x_\kappa)_s \Big) \right\},
$$

where $(\Sigma_u^{-1})_{r,s}$ is the rth row, sth column of Σ_u^{-1}, $(x_\psi)_r$ is the rth element of x_ψ, and $(x_\kappa)_r$ is the rth element of x_κ.

We follow the similar conditions and arguments in Mourid and Bensmain (2006) and obtain $A \le C_1 / J^{\eta/2}$, where C_1 is a constant. In addition, for $\delta > 0$,

$$
\varphi'(0) = H(\kappa_{0|\Theta_J}, \kappa) - H(\kappa_{0|\Theta_J}, \kappa_J) + A \le C_2 J^{-\eta/2} - \delta.
$$

Using Taylor expansion and the results from Hwang (1980) such that $\varphi''(t) \le C_3 J^2$, we have $\varphi(1/J^2) \le 1 - \delta/C_4 J^2$, where C_2, C_3, and C_4 are constants. Since $\varphi_J = \sup_k \inf_{t \ge 0} \varphi(t)$, we can deduce that for sufficiently large J, we have

$$
l_J(\varphi_J)^n \le C J^{C J^{1+\eta}} \left(1 - \frac{\delta}{C J^2} \right)^n,
$$

which is summable if $J = \mathcal{O}(n^{1/3-\delta})$ for $\delta > 0$ (see Hwang 1980). Note that C is a constant. Finally, we can apply Theorem 3.1 to obtain the result that the ML estimator $\widehat{\kappa}$ obtained on Θ_{J_n} converges to the projected true set of kernel functions $\kappa_{0|\Theta_J}$. As $n, J_n \to \infty$, $\kappa_{0|\Theta_J} \to \kappa_0$ because each $\kappa_{xy,0|\Theta_J}$ in $\kappa_{0|\Theta_J}$ is just the B-spline truncation of the corresponding true kernel $\kappa_{xy,0}$ in κ_0 on Θ_{J_n}.

Forecasting market states

PIER FRANCESCO PROCACCI and TOMASO ASTE

(*Received 30 June 2018; accepted 6 May 2019; published online 9 July 2019*)

We propose a novel methodology to define, analyze and forecast market states. In our approach, market states are identified by a reference sparse precision matrix and a vector of expectation values. In our procedure, each multivariate observation is associated to a given market state accordingly to a minimization of a penalized Mahalanobis distance. The procedure is made computationally very efficient and can be used with a large number of assets. We demonstrate that this procedure is successful at clustering different states of the markets in an unsupervised manner. In particular, we describe an experiment with one hundred log-returns and two states in which the methodology automatically associates states prevalently to pre- and post-crisis periods with one state gathering periods with average positive returns and the other state periods with average negative returns, therefore discovering spontaneously the common classification of 'bull' and 'bear' markets. In another experiment, with again one hundred log-returns and two states, we demonstrate that this procedure can be efficiently used to forecast off-sample future market states with significant prediction accuracy. This methodology opens the way to a range of applications in risk management and trading strategies in the context where the correlation structure plays a central role.

1. Introduction

Markets do not always behave in the same way. In common terminology, there are periods of 'bull' market in which prices are more likely to rise and periods of 'bear' market in which prices are more likely to fall. These different 'states' of markets are commonly attributed in the literature to unobservable, or latent, regimes representing a set of macroeconomic, market and sentiment variables.

Many time series models presented in the literature tried to capture this phenomenon. Among the most popular methods, it is worth mentioning the TAR models (Tong 1978), trying to estimate 'structural breaks' in the time series process, and the Markov Switching models (Hamilton 1989), where the change in regimes are parametrized by means of an unobserved state variable typically modeled as Markov chain. However, the application of TAR models in finance is frequently criticized since it cannot be established with certainty when a structural break has occurred in economic time series and the prior knowledge of major economic events could lead to bias in inference (Campbell *et al.* 1997). Markov switching models, on the other hand, are highly affected by the curse of dimensionality. In particular, for slightly more complex dynamics than the original proposal (Hamilton 1989), we need to rely on variational inference techniques or MCMC methods (Tsay 2005, Kim and Nelson 1999). This implies that, in a multivariate context and particularly if we aim to extract information on the switching from the correlation structure, estimation becomes difficult to perform.

Other approaches focus on clustering of observations into groups: 'similar' data objects are discovered on the basis of some criteria for comparisons. Most works related to clustering of time series are classified into two categories: subsequence time series clustering and point clustering. Subsequence clustering involves the clustering of sliding windows of data points and usually aim to discover repeated patterns. Examples are Dynamic Time Warping (Liao 2005), Hierarchical methods (Nevill-Manning and Witten 1997) or pattern discovery (Ren *et al.* 2017). In point clustering methods, instead, each multivariate observation at each time instance *t* is assigned to a cluster. In most popular approaches, however, this is done based on a distance metric (Grabarnik and Särkkä 2001, Focardi and Fabozzi 2004, Zolhavarieh *et al.* 2014, Hendricks *et al.* 2016, Hallac *et al.* 2016).

In a multivariate context, different 'states' of markets are not only reflected in the gains and losses, but also in the relative dynamics of prices. Indeed, the correlation structure changes between bull and bear periods indicating that there are structural differences in these market states. Most common approaches in the industry assume—for convenience—a stationary correlation structure (Black and Litterman 1992, Duffie and Pan 1997). However, it is well established that correlations among stocks are not constant over time (Lin *et al.* 1994, Ang and Bekaert 2002, Musmeci *et al.* 2016) and increase substantially in periods of high market volatility, with, asymmetrically, larger increases for downward moves (see, for example, Ang and Chen 2002, Cizeau *et al.* 2010, Schmitt *et al.* 2013). Indeed, various approaches have been proposed in the literature to model and predict time-varying correlations. Examples are, for instance, the generalized autoregressive conditional heteroskedasticity (GARCH) models by Bollerslev (1990) or the Dynamic Conditional Correlation (DCC) model by Engle (2002). However, most of these models are not able to cope with more than a few assets due to the curse of dimensionality having numbers of parameters that increase super-linearly with the number of variables (Danielsson 2011). Other approaches have been focusing on the study of changes in a time-varying correlation matrix computed from a rolling window. This is, for instance, the case of estimators like the RiskMetrics (Longerstaey and Spencer 1996 or Lee and Stevenson 2003). However, since these approaches use only a small part of the data, these estimators have large variances and, in case of high dimensionality, may lead to inconclusive estimates (Laloux *et al.* 1999).

Hallac *et al.* (2017) introduced a clustering algorithm called TICC (Toeplitz Inverse Covariance Clustering), originally proposed for electric vehicles, where classification into states is constructed from a likelihood measure associate with a referential sparse precision matrix (inverse covariance matrix). Instead of considering each observation in isolation, however, in their approach they cluster short subsequences of observations so that the covariance matrix constructed on the subsequences provides a representation of the cross-time partial correlations. In this setting, then, by imposing a Toeplitz constraint to the precision matrix of each regime, the cross-time partial correlations are constrained to be constant and, hence, covariance-stationarity is enforced. This method has a number of appealing features from a financial perspective, although the structure of data considered by the authors is significantly different from noisy data in finance.

In this paper, we build on Hallac *et al.* (2017) and propose a similar Covariance-based Clustering. However, we consider single observations and do not enforce Toeplitz structure on the precision matrix. We, therefore, call this methodology ICC—Inverse Covariance Clustering. Analogous to Hallac *et al.* (2017), we also enforce temporal coherence by penalizing frequent switches between market states and favoring temporal consistency. Another difference is that we do not directly maximize the likelihood, but rather we assign states to clusters accordingly to their Mahalanobis distance (De Maesschalck *et al.* 2000). We experiment with this methodology in the context of financial time series and provide a detailed analysis of the role played by sparsity and temporal consistency, while assessing the significance of the clusters. Finally, we

show that the cluster classification can be used for one step ahead off-sample prediction.

Our approach simplifies and clarifies the definition of 'market state' by identifying each state with a sparse precision matrix and a vector of expectation values which are associated to a set of multivariate observations clustered together accordingly with a given procedure. In the following, the precision matrix of market state 'k' is denoted with J_k and it represents the structure of partial correlations between the system's variables. In the multivariate normal case, two nodes are conditionally independent if and only if the corresponding element of J_k is equal to zero. A sparse precision matrix provides an easily interpretable and intuitive structure of the market state with all the most relevant dependencies directly interconnected in a sparse network. Furthermore, sparsity reduces the number of parameters from order n^2 (with n the number of variables) to order n preventing overfitting (Lauritzen 1996) and filtering out noisy correlations (Barfuss *et al.* 2016, Musmeci *et al.* 2017).

The *segmentation procedure* starts by setting the number of clusters K (in the present paper we limit to $K = 2$) and assigns multivariate observations to clusters randomly. From these K sets of data we compute the sample means μ_k and the precision matrices J_k and we then iteratively re-assign points to the cluster with smallest

$$\mathcal{M}_{t,k} = d_{t,k}^2 + \gamma \mathbb{1}\{\mathcal{K}_{t-1} \neq k\}, \qquad (1)$$

where $X_t = [x_{t,1}, x_{t,2}, \ldots, x_{t,n}]$ is the n-stocks multivariate observation at time $t (= 1, \ldots, T)$; μ_k is the vector of the means for cluster k; J_k is the (sparse) precision matrix for cluster k; $d_{t,k}^2 = (X_t - \mu_k)^T J_k (X_t - \mu_k)$ is the square Mahalanobis distance of observation X_t in cluster k with respect to the cluster centroid μ_k; γ is a parameter penalizing state switching; $\mathcal{K}_{t-1}$ is the cluster assignment of the observation at time $t - 1$. We considered as well clustering with respect to maximum likelihood and minimum Euclidean distance, however, we report only about the procedure with Mahalanobis distance which is the one providing the best results. Specifically, Euclidean distance is very efficient in distinguishing positive and negative returns but does not distinguish well between pre- and post-crisis periods. The maximum likelihood instead identifies very well the crisis period but then it is much less clean in classifying the 'bull' and 'bear' market states. Let us note that the Mahalanobis distance clustering used is producing high likelihood although not maximal.

The clustering assignment procedure is made computationally efficient by using the Viterbi algorithm (Viterbi 1967, Bishop 2006) that transforms an otherwise $O(K^T)$ procedure into $O(KT)$ (Appendix 1). Further, the sparse precision matrix J_k is computed efficiently from the observations in each cluster by means of the TMFG-LoGo network filtering approach (Massara *et al.* 2015, Barfuss *et al.* 2016). TMFG-LoGo approach has proven to be more efficient and better performing, particularly when only a few data are available (Barfuss *et al.* 2016, Aste and Di Matteo 2017), with respect to other techniques such as GLASSO (Friedman *et al.* 2008). Implementation has been performed with an in-house built-for-purpose python package. This is the first time this methodology is introduced and applied to financial data and market states analytics.

In this paper, we report results for two experiments performed over a dataset of daily closing prices of $n = 2490$ US stocks entering among the constituents of the Russel 1000 index (*RIY index*) traded between 02/01/1995 and 31/12/2015. For each asset $i = 1, \ldots, n$, we calculated the corresponding daily log-returns $r_i(t) = \log(P_i(t)) - \log(P_i(t-1))$, where $P_i(t)$ is the closing price of stock i at time t.

2. Clustering

As mentioned in the introduction, our primary goal is to efficiently cluster noisy, multivariate time series into meaningful regimes, while controlling for temporal consistency. In this first experiment, we considered the entire dataset between 02/01/1995 and 31/12/2015 and estimated two referential market states. In order to explore the role of each building block of our algorithm and to compare it to a traditional baseline method, we investigate five models:

(a) ICC Model—sparse precision matrix and temporal consistency
(b) ICC Model—full precision matrix and temporal consistency
(c) ICC Model—sparse precision matrix
(d) ICC Model—full precision matrix
(e) Gaussian Mixture Model—full covariance

Model (a) is the present proposed ICC methodology. Model (b) considers full precision matrices J_k instead of sparse ones. Model (c) relaxes temporal consistency allowing for $\gamma = 0$ in equation 1. Model (d) has $\gamma = 0$ full precision matrices. Finally, Model (e) is a conventional Gaussian Mixture Model (Bishop 2006) that has been chosen as a baseline method given the similarities with the ICC approach. We analyzed and compared the resulting clusters both in terms of market

properties to which the two clusters are associated and in terms of temporal consistency. First, we focused on a subset of 100 stocks chosen at random among those that have been continuously traded throughout the observed period. Random choice of the basket is to avoid selection bias. We then consider random resamplings to assess the robustness when different stocks are considered.

We optimized the temporal consistency parameter by grid-searching as described in Appendix 1 and used $\gamma = 16$ for ICC Sparse (a) and $\gamma = 14.7$ for ICC Full (b) in both the experiments presented in this paper. The two referential precision matrices, J_1 and J_2, obtained with this experiment had 344 non-zero entries (dependency network edges) of which 142 were common to both states showing a good level of differentiation, but also significant overlaps between the two market states. The number of points assigned to each cluster was respectively 3295 for cluster 1 and 1704 for cluster 2. Figure 1 reports with colored background the points' assignment for the two clusters. We can observe there is a good spatial consistency. For instance, the average number of consecutive days in cluster 1 is 25.3 days. We also note that cluster 1 (blue background) tend to be associated with periods of rising market prices whereas cluster 2 (orange background) appears more present during crisis and market downturns. We indeed discovered that—automatically—the methodology assigns '*bull*' market periods (positive mean returns) to cluster 1 and '*bear*' market periods (negative mean returns) to cluster 2. We can for instance observe in figure 1(a) that 52 consecutive observations during the 2001–2002 *.com* bubble crisis and 211 consecutive observations during the 2007–2008 global financial crisis have been assigned to the *bear* cluster 2. From figure 1(b) we observe that the *bull* cluster 1 has, indeed, average positive returns for all stocks whereas the *bear* cluster 2 has average negative returns. Furthermore, also the standard deviations are different between the two cluster assignments.

To compare the two clusters on a risk-adjusted basis, we computed the Sharpe ratio (Sharpe 1966, 1994) for each stock

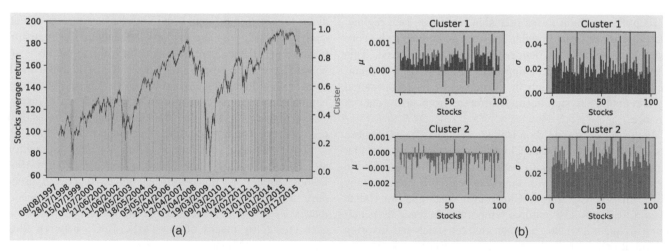

(a)   (b)

Figure 1. Clustering segmentation for experiment 1 over the whole dataset. Panel (a) reports the cumulative average return at each time t across the 100 stocks; in this picture, the blue background corresponds to time instances assigned to Cluster 1 and the orange background correspond instead to time instances assigned to Cluster 2. Panel (b) reports mean and standard deviation of each of the 100 stocks respectively computed using the returns assigned to each of the 2 clusters. We observe that Cluster 1 exhibits positive mean returns ('*bull*' state) and lower levels of volatility for all the considered stocks, while for cluster 2 all the stocks present negative mean returns ('*bear*' state) and higher levels of volatility. (a) Time series segmentation results and (b) mean (*left*) and standard deviation (*right*) of each stock for each temporal cluster.

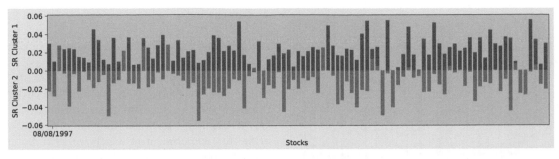

Figure 2. Estimated Sharpe Ratio (SR) for each of the 100 stocks in the sample. The blue bars report the SR computed from log-returns in Cluster 1, whereas the red bars report the SR computed from log-returns in Cluster 2.

Table 1. Positive/negative Sharpe ratio for ('bull','bear') states.

	Median	5th percentile	95th percentile
GMM	(69,64)	(48,53)	(75,81)
ICC Full, $\gamma = 0$	(77,78)	(67,71)	(92,98)
ICC Sparse, $\gamma = 0$	(85,87)	(69,75)	(96,95)
ICC Full, $\gamma = 14.7$	(73,74)	(68,65)	(78,80)
ICC Sparse, $\gamma = 16$	(75,81)	(65,69)	(86,90)

Note: Median, 5th and 95th percentiles obtained from 100 random resamples of the stocks composing the dataset.

Table 2. Temporal consistency metrics.

	Median	5th percentile	95th percentile
	Number of switches		
GMM	785	540	874
ICC Full, $\gamma = 0$	1203	992	2176
ICC Sparse, $\gamma = 0$	1157	727	1421
ICC Full, $\gamma = 14.7$	204	54	306
ICC Sparse, $\gamma = 16$	208	120	298
	Segment length		
GMM	5.07	2.4	11.8
ICC Full, $\gamma = 0$	3.3	1.68	4.38
ICC Sparse, $\gamma = 0$	3.5	2.8	6.65
ICC Full, $\gamma = 14.7$	22.64	14.6	38.26
ICC Sparse, $\gamma = 16$	23.6	18	55.27

Note: Number of switchings and segment lengths over 100 resamplings.

in each cluster. We found for the *bull* cluster an average annualized Sharpe ratio equal to 1.2, with 5th and 95th 5th and 95th percentiles respectively equal to 0.84 and 1.78, while the *bear* cluster had average −0.96, with −1.03 and −0.24 as 5th and 95th 5th and 95th percentiles. It is therefore clear that the two clusters have very different risk–return profiles. Figure 2 reports the Sharpe ratios in the two clusters for the 100 stocks. In order to verify robustness and generality of the results, we computed the same quantities for 100 other randomly chosen baskets of 100 stocks. For all resampled baskets of stocks we found a consistent clusterization in *bull* and *bear* regimes with Sharpe ratios for at least 75% of stocks larger than zero for the bull state and significantly smaller than zero for the bear state. Across the 100 resamplings, the two clusters had average number of elements respectively equal to 3451 and 1293.

Sparsity and Temporal Consistency. In order to assess the role of sparsity and temporal consistency, we performed the same analysis on the 'alternative' ICC Models (b)–(d) and the GMM (e).

Table 1 summarizes the number of stocks having positive/negative Sharpe ratio in both clusters over 100 resamplings. In the table, each couple refers to the number of stocks having positive SR in *bull* (left) and negative SR in *bear* (right) states. We found that, in the absence of temporal consistency constraints, both the ICC models (c, d) meaningfully classify clusters with and without sparsity. However, when temporal consistency is considered, ICC Full (b) is significantly affected by the constraint while ICC Sparse (a) provides robust results. GMM delivered the worst clusters in terms of risk/return significance.

Focusing on temporal consistency, table 2 reports the number of switches and the segment length resulting from the cluster assignments of the five models. When no temporal

consistency is enforced (c,d), ICC provides the less temporal consistent results with small differences related to sparsity. This also explains the good results obtained by the models in terms of risk/return significance. When constrained to be temporal consistent, ICC Full (b) shows large variability in temporal consistency across samples with some having only a few switches over the whole period and others having several hundreds. ICC Sparse (a) is instead more consistent with a few hundred switches over the whole period which are less than 1/3 of the switches in GMM (e).

3. Role of sparsity

In previous works (Barfuss *et al.* 2016), the TMFG-LoGo approach has proven to perform better than other filtering approaches including GLasso and Ridge providing the additional advantages of efficiency and fixed sparsity level with no need to calibrate hyperparameters (Massara *et al.* 2015). In this section, we motivate the choice of TMFG-LoGo filtering procedure in terms of statistical significance by comparing the performances of the TMFG-LoGo to the cross-validated Ridge l_2 penalized inverse covariance (Ridge) on our dataset. We considered the widely used Ridge penalization as robust estimate of the empirical inverse covariance matrix and compared it to TMFG-LoGo and show that, when applied to our

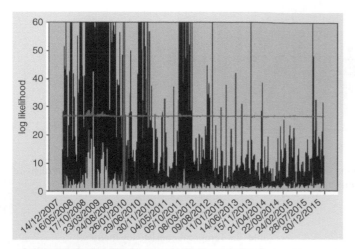

Figure 3. Train and test log likelihood observation-wise using TMFG (red line) and Ridge (black line) precision matrices. The green vertical line divides train and test set. Ridge peaks reach values outside the range up to 320.

Table 3. TMFG and Ridge log likelihood metrics—means, 5th and 95th percentiles—computed in train (top panel) and test (bottom panel) set.

	Average	5th percentile	95th percentile
Train set			
$\mathcal{L}_{\text{Ridge}}$	41.70	2.19	188.85
$\mathcal{L}_{\text{TMFG}}$	26.71	26.53	27.22
Test set			
$\mathcal{L}_{\text{Ridge}}$	8.08	1.39	27.64
$\mathcal{L}_{\text{TMFG}}$	26.55	26.44	26.73

Note: TMFG and Ridge precision matrices are estimated using $q = 500$ observations.

dataset, TMFG-LoGo produces more stable likelihood results than Ridge. We used 40% of the data (from 31/12/2007 to 31/12/2015) as test set, and we considered as train sets the q observations preceding the test set (until 30/12/2007). The penalization parameter of Ridge was defined by cross validating within the train set. To compare TMFG-LoGo and the cross-validated Ridge we computed the log-likelihoods $\mathcal{L}_{s,k} = 1/2(\log |\mathbf{J}_k| - d_{s,k}^2 - p\log(2\pi))$ using the two covariance estimates and compared them. Figure 3 shows the likelihood observation-wise computed in train and in test using the TMFG-LoGo and Ridge precision matrices estimated over $q = 500$ observations. The TMFG-LoGo likelihoods are much more stable over time suggesting that the procedure was successful in filtering out noise. Table 3 reports details on mean, 5th and 95th 5th and 95th percentiles of the likelihoods computed in the train and test set. As previously mentioned, TMFG-LoGo likelihoods are much more stable with 5th and 95th 5th and 95th varying a few percent only for TMFG-LoGo and instead varying of more than one order of magnitude in Ridge. We found similar results for TMFG-LoGo and Ridge when different values of q are considered. Note that Ridge log likelihoods have large differences between train and test. This is a typical indication of overfitting. Conversely, TMFG presents small differences indicating that the LoGo procedure acts as a topological penalize.

4. Forecasting

In the second experiment we used our methodology to forecast future states of the market form previous observations.

To this end, we used the first 65% of the data (from 02/01/1995 to 05/02/2009) as train set from which we extracted the two referential precision matrices and means $(\mathbf{J}_1, \boldsymbol{\mu}_1)$ and $(\mathbf{J}_2, \boldsymbol{\mu}_2)$ (note they are different form the ones of the first experiment in which we used the entire dataset instead). We then forecasted the probability that, given an observation at time t, the observation at a following time $t + h$ would belong to state k. This is achieved by performing a logistic regression using the log likelihood ratio of the two clusters (Neyman and Pearson 1933) from a rolling window of length Δ:

$$\mathcal{R}_t = \sum_{s=t-\Delta+1}^{t} \mathcal{L}_{s,1} - \mathcal{L}_{s,2}, \qquad (2)$$

where $\mathcal{L}_{s,k} = 1/2(\log |\mathbf{J}_k| - d_{s,k}^2 - p\log(2\pi))$ is the log-likelihood of observation $\mathbf{X}_s$ when associated with cluster $k = 1$ or 2. In our experiment, we considered $\Delta = 24$ days, since this is the average length of segments obtained from ICC (a) in the first experiment. Figure 4 provides a visual representation of the likelihood ratio computed for each cluster and of its evolution as compared to market movements. The green vertical line divides the train set form the test set. The logistic regression of market states $\mathcal{K}_t$ against the log likelihood ratio $\mathcal{R}_t$ can be written as

$$P(\mathcal{K}_{t+h} = 1, 2 \mid \mathcal{R}_t = x) = \frac{1}{1 + e^{-(\beta_0 + \beta_1 x)}}, \qquad (3)$$

where the parameters β_0 and β_1 are estimated through maximum likelihood (Bishop 2006). We estimated all parameters $(\mathbf{J}_1, \mathbf{J}_2, \boldsymbol{\mu}_1, \boldsymbol{\mu}_2, \gamma, \beta_0$ and $\beta_1)$ in the train set and estimated a threshold or cut-off point of 0.54 by cross-validation in the train set. We then used these parameters to predict, in the test set, the next day state given the log-likelihood ratio $\mathcal{R}_t = x$. Specifically, we predict $\widehat{\mathcal{K}}_{t+1} = 1$ if $P(\mathcal{K}_{t+1} = 1 \mid \mathcal{R}_t = x) > 0.54$ and $\widehat{\mathcal{K}}_{t+1} = 2$ otherwise. For instance, for the day 30-Mar-2010 (test set) we predicted a *bull* state with probability $P(\mathcal{K}_{30-Sep} = 1 \mid \mathcal{R}_{29-Mar}) = 0.77$, where $\mathcal{R}_{29-Mar}$ was computed using the observations from 06-Mar to 29-Mar-2010 ($\Delta = 24$ days, all in the test set) and the parameters $\boldsymbol{\mu}_k, \mathbf{J}_k, \gamma$, β_0 and β_1 were the ones calibrated on the train set with data until 31/04/2009.

To assess the goodness of our approach we compared test set predictions with the classification performed over the whole period in the first experiment (see figure 1). We used three metrics (Hastie *et al.* 2008) to assess the performance of our classification method: the True Positive Rate *TPR* (number of elements correctly assigned to cluster 1 divided by total number of elements in cluster 1), the True Negative Rate *TNR* (number of elements correctly assigned to cluster 2 divided by total number of elements in cluster 2) and Accuracy *ACC* (number of correct predictions in cluster 1 or 2 divided by total number of elements). In order to test for the robustness of our method, we randomly resampled the 100 stocks and performed the classification experiment considering the new dataset. We repeated this process 100 times and stored

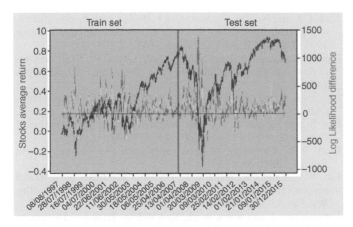

Figure 4. Log likelihood ratio and mean returns across train and test sets. The log likelihood ratio of the two states $\mathcal{R}_t$ was computed using the $\Delta = 28\,days$. The green vertical bar indicates the end of the train set and the beginning of the test set. We estimated J_1 and J_2 in train and held it fixed for the computation of $\mathcal{R}_t$ also in the test set. The black horizontal line identifies $\mathcal{R}_t = 0$ level, i.e. the level above which the *bull* state is more likely. Coherently with previous findings, we can identify persistent market states with a more frequent bull market and regions of bear market.

Table 4. Out-of-sample performance metrics using the ICC log likelihood ratio as independent variable.

	Median	5th percentile	95th percentile
TPR	0.68	0.51	0.93
TNR	0.52	0.39	0.78
ACC	0.54	0.47	0.69

Note: Median, 5th and 95th percentiles obtained from 100 random resamples of the stocks composing the dataset.

the three performance metrics *TPR*, *TNR* and *ACC*. Table 4 presents a summary of the results obtained. A good level of *ACC* is obtained across resamplings with only the 5th percentile falling slightly below 50%. As we can see, *TPR* is higher than 50% at the 5th percentile while *TNR* presents a good median result, but a low 5th percentile showing that it can be difficult to correctly forecast. This indicates that there is a tendency to over-assign time-instances to cluster 1 (*bull* state) and conversely missing predictions for the less frequent *bear* state. Nonetheless, we verified (by using the hypergeometric distribution as reported in Aste and Di Matteo (2017)) that these *TNR* are statistically significant at 0.01 level indicating that there is, indeed, significant prediction power also for the bear state. Let us stress that the present forecasting exercise is not optimized and there are several ways these performances can be improved. However, this is beyond the purpose of the present paper where we privileged simplicity over performances.

To compare the previous results with a baseline method, we estimated the logistic regression in equation 3 using the fraction of stocks that at time $t-1$ were presenting positive returns as independent variable. Aim being to compare our ICC log-likelihood to a much simplified version of the information about the correlation structure. Same estimation scheme is used and a threshold of 0.61 is obtained by cross

Table 5. Out-of-sample performance metrics using the fraction of positive stocks as independent variable.

	Median	5th percentile	95th percentile
TPR	0.71	0.67	1
TNR	0.24	0.0	0.77
ACC	0.47	0.38	0.62

Note: Median, 5th and 95th percentiles obtained from 100 random resamples of the stocks composing the dataset.

validation. Results are reported in table 5. While this simplified information still provides a median accuracy close to 50%, the model has overall inferior performances with respect to the ICC log likelihood ratio case reported in table 4.

5. Conclusions

In this paper, we presented a novel methodology to define, identify, classify and forecast market states. In addition to accuracy, intuitiveness and forecasting power, our procedure is numerically very efficient and able to process high dimensional datasets. We reported two experiments to illustrate that the method is efficient and reliable in identifying and predicting accurate and interpretable structures in multivariate, non-stationary financial datasets. These two examples use two clusters and 100 variables, however, we verified that analogous results hold for larger or smaller numbers of variables and similarly interesting classifications emerge also when three or more clusters are used. The choice of two clusters has been only motivated by simplicity. The fact that they turned out to be respectively populated mostly with average positive and negative returns associated with pre- and post-crisis periods was unexpected by us and opens potentials for completely novel ways to use multivariate analytics for the forecasting of stock market returns. This also greatly simplified the interpretation of these states as 'bull' and 'bear' markets. Of course, in reality, there are more than two market states and common definition of bull and bear markets are often blurry. In this work we did not attempt to optimize results favoring, instead, simplicity and interpretability and, therefore, there is a large open domain of exploration to refine the methodology. We also adopted several methodological choices that can be modified in future works. For instance, the segmentation with the Mahalanobis distance turned out to be a powerful tool in the reported experiments, however, there is a broad range of possible metrics for clustering and experiments with Euclidean distance or Likelihood also produce interesting results. Further, the choice of TMFG network over other possible information filtering networks or other sparsification methodologies can be investigated. Temporal consistency could had also being performed differently by using a hidden Markov model approach (see note in Appendix 1). The choice of logistic regression to forecast market state is just one simple possibility among many regression options that might make better use of the information content of our regimes' structures. All these and other methodological choices have been motivated by simplicity and intuitiveness. Since one of the main achievements of our methodology is computational efficiency allowing one to apply the methodology to high dimensional datasets, further work will include new sources of information (e.g. news, economic indicators, sentiment).

Disclosure statement

No potential conflict of interest was reported by the authors.

References

Ang, A. and Bekaert, G., International asset allocation with time-varying correlations. *Rev. Financial Stud.*, 2002, **15**, 1137–1187.

Ang, A. and Chen, J., Asymmetric correlations of equity portfolios. *J. Financ. Econ.*, 2002, **63**, 443–494.

Aste, T. and Di Matteo, T., Causality network retrieval from short time series. ArXiv preprint arXiv:1706.01954, 2017.

Barfuss, W., Massara, G.P., di Matteo, T. and Aste, T., Parsimonious modeling with information filtering networks. *Phys. Rev. E*, 2016, **94**, 062306.

Bishop, C.M., *Pattern Recognition and Machine Learning*, 2006 (Springer-Verlag: New York).

Black, F. and Litterman, R., Global portfolio optimization. *Financ. Anal. J.*, 1992, **48**, 28–43.

Bollerslev, T., Modelling the coherence in short-run nominal exchange rates: A multivariate generalized ARCH model. *Rev. Econ. Stat.*, 1990, **4**, 498–505.

Campbell, J.Y., Lo, A.W. and MacKinlay, A.C., *The Econometrics of Financial Markets*, 1997 (Princeton University Press: Princeton, NJ).

Cizeau, P., Potters, M. and Bouchaud, J.P., Correlation structure of extreme stock returns. *Quant. Finance*, 2010, **1**, 217–222.

Danielsson, J., *Financial Risk Forecasting: The Theory and Practice of Forecasting Market Risk with Implementation in R and Matlab*, 2011 (Wiley-Blackwell: Hoboken).

De Maesschalck, R., Jouan-Rimbaud, D. and Massart, D.L., The Mahalanobis distance. *Chemometr. Intell. Lab. Syst.*, 2000, **50**, 1–18.

Duffie, D. and Pan, J., An overview of value at risk. *J. Derivatives*, 1997, **4**, 7–49.

Engle, R., Dynamic conditional correlation. *J. Bus. Econ. Stat.*, 2002, **20**, 339–350.

Focardi, S.M. and Fabozzi, F.J., A methodology for index tracking based on time-series clustering. *Quant. Finance*, 2004, **4**, 417–425.

Friedman, J., Hastie, T. and Tibshirani, R., Sparse inverse covariance estimation with the graphical lasso. *Biostatistics*, 2008, **9**, 432–441.

Grabarnik, P. and Särkkä, A., Interacting neighbour point processes: Some models for clustering. *J. Stat. Comput. Simul.*, 2001, **68**, 103–125.

Hallac, D., Nystrup, P. and Boyd, S., Greedy Gaussian segmentation of multivariate time series. ArXiv e-prints, 2016.

Hallac, D., Vare, S., Boyd, S.P. and Leskovec, J., Toeplitz inverse covariance-based clustering of multivariate time series data. CoRR, abs/1706.03161, 2017.

Hamilton, J.D., A new approach to the economic analysis of non-stationary time series and the business cycle. *Econometrica*, 1989, **57**, 357–384.

Hastie, T., Tibshirani, R. and Friedman, J., *The Elements of Statistical Learning*, 2008 (Springer: New York).

Hendricks, D., Gebbie, T. and Wilcox, D., Detecting intraday financial market states using temporal clustering. *Quant. Finance*, 2016, **16**, 1657–1678.

Kim, C.J. and Nelson, C., *State-Space Models with Regime Switching: Classical and Gibbs-Sampling Approaches with Applications*, 1999 (The MIT Press: Cambridge, MA).

Laloux, L., Cizeau, P., Bouchaud, J.P. and Potters, M., Noise dressing of financial correlation matrices. *Phys. Rev. Lett.*, 1999, **83**, 1467–1470.

Lauritzen, S.L., *Graphical Models*, 1996 (Oxford University Press: Oxford).

Lee, S. and Stevenson, S., Time weighted portfolio optimisation. *J. Prop. Investment Finance*, 2003, **21**, 233–249.

Liao, W.T., Clustering of time series data – a survey. *Pattern Recogn.*, 2005, **38**, 1857–1874.

Lin, W.L., Engle, R. and Ito, T., Do bulls and bears move across borders? International transmission of stock returns and volatility. *Rev. Financ. Stud.*, 1994, **7**, 507–38.

Longerstaey, J. and Spencer, M., RiskMetrics Technical Document, J.P. Morgan/Reuters, 1996.

Massara, G.P., di Matteo, T. and Aste, T., Network filtering for big data: Triangulated maximally filtered graph. CoRR, abs/1505.02445, 2015.

Musmeci, N., Aste, T. and Di Matteo, T., What does past correlation structure tell us about the future? An answer from network filtering. ArXiv e-prints, 2016.

Musmeci, N., Nicosia, V., Aste, T., Di Matteo, T. and Latora, V., The multiplex dependency structure of financial markets. *Complexity*, 2017, **2017**, 13.

Nevill-Manning, C.G. and Witten, I.H., Identifying hierarchical structure in sequences: A linear-time algorithm. *J. Artif. Intell. Res.*, 1997, **7**, 67–82.

Neyman, J. and Pearson, E.S., IX. On the problem of the most efficient tests of statistical hypotheses. *Philos. Trans. R. Soc. London A: Math. Phys. Eng. Sci.*, 1933, **231**, 289–337.

Ren, L., Wei, Y., Cui, J. and Du, Y., A sliding window-based multi-stage clustering and probabilistic forecasting approach for large multivariate time series data. *J. Stat. Comput. Simul.*, 2017, **87**, 2494–2508.

Schmitt, T.A., Chetalova, D., Schäfer, R. and Guhr, T., Non-stationarity in financial time series: Generic features and tail behavior. *EPL (Europhys. Lett.)*, 2013, **103**, 58003.

Sharpe, W.F., Mutual fund performance. *J. Bus.*, 1966, **39**, 119–138.

Sharpe, W.F., The Sharpe ratio. *J. Portf. Manag.*, 1994, **21**, 49–58.

Tong, H., On a threshold model. In *Pattern Recognition and Signal Processing*, edited by C. H. Chen, 1978 (Sijthoff and Noordhoff: Amsterdam).

Tsay, R., *Analysis of Financial Time Series*, 2nd ed., 2005 (Wiley: Hoboken, NJ).

Viterbi, A., Error bounds for convolutional codes and an asymptotically optimum decoding algorithm. *IEEE Trans. Inf. Theory*, 1967, **13**, 260–269.

Zolhavarieh, S., Aghabozorgi, S. and Wah Teh, Y., A review of subsequent time series clustering. *Sci. World J.*, 2014, **2014**, 312521.

Appendix. The Viterbi algorithm

Figure 1 provides a visualization of the problem of assigning points to clusters. Based on the parameters estimates (μ_k and J_k via TMFG-LoGo), we compute the Mahalanobis distance of every multivariate observation obtaining, for each cluster k and for each observation t, a value $d_{t,k}^2 = (X_t - \mu_k)^T J_k (X_t - \mu_k)$.

We need to consider the best *sequence* of latent states which is not the set of best individual states. In particular, if we introduce a cost parameter γ that penalizes cluster switching, the problem complexity becomes combinatorial, since we need to account for the whole sequence or *path* of assignations. In particular, given K potential cluster assignment of T points (multivariate observations), the number of potential paths grows exponentially with the length of the chain to K^T possible assignments of points to clusters. Based on a dynamic programming approach, the Viterbi algorithm

(Viterbi 1967) provides an efficient solution with complexity $O(KT)$ (*i.e. linear*) to this problem, searching the space of the paths and finding the most efficient path. The Viterbi algorithm in the convenient formulation by Hallac *et al.* (2017) is sketched in Algorithm 1.

Algorithm 1 Viterbi algorithm

Input

$d_{t,k}^2 =$ square Mahalanobis distance of observation t if assigned to state k

$\gamma =$ time consistency parameter

Initialize

    PreviousCost = array of K zeros

    CurrentCost = array of K zeros

    PreviousPath = array of K elements

    CurrentPath = array of K elements

for each observation $t = 1, ..., T$ **do**

    for each state $k = 1, ..., K$ **do**

        MinVal = index of minimum value of Previous-Cost

        if PreviousCost [*MinVal*] $+ \gamma >$ Previous Cost [k] **then**

            CurrentCost [k] $=$ Previous Cost [k] $+ d_{t,k}^2$

            CurrentPath [k] $=$ Previous Path [k]. append [k]

        else

            CurrentCost[k] $=$ PreviousCost[*MinVal*] $+ \gamma + d_{t,k}^2$

            CurrentPath[k] $=$ PreviousPath[*MinVal*].append[k]

        PreviousCost=CurrentCost

        PreviousPath=CurrentPath

FinalMinVal=index of minimum value of CurrCost

FinalPath=CurrPath[FinalMinVal]

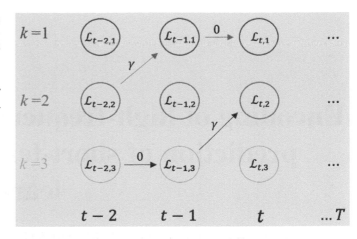

Figure A.1. Example of two among the K^T possible paths considering $K = 3$ clusters and T observations. $\mathcal{L}_{t,j}$ represents the log likelihood of the multivariate observation at time t if assigned to cluster j. If an observation is assigned to same cluster as the previous one, no penalty is applied, otherwise a *cost* weighted by the parameter γ is added.

A more general formulation can be implemented by describing the paths as Markov chains and introducing a transition probability between the states. However, under the Markov chain formalism the expression in equation (2) for the likelihood ratio is no longer consistent because it implies iid multivariate observations.

Encoding of high-frequency order information and prediction of short-term stock price by deep learning

DAIGO TASHIRO, HIROYASU MATSUSHIMA ⓘ, KIYOSHI IZUMI and HIROKI SAKAJI

(Received 2 July 2018; accepted 6 May 2019; published online 9 July 2019)

Predicting the price trends of stocks based on deep learning and high-frequency data has been studied intensively in recent years. Especially, the limit order book which describes supply-demand balance of a market is used as the feature of a neural network; however these methods do not utilize the properties of market orders. On the other hand, the order-encoding method of our prior work can take advantage of these properties. In this paper, we apply some types of convolutional neural network architectures to order-based features to predict the direction of mid-price trends. The results show that smoothing filters which we propose to employ rather than embedding features of orders improve accuracy. Furthermore, inspection of the embedding layer and investment simulation are conducted to demonstrate the practicality and effectiveness of our model.

1. Introduction

Is it possible to predict the rapidly fluctuating prices of financial products? In response to this question, many theoretical and empirical studies have been conducted by practitioners and researchers in various fields. In recent years, following the proposal of the Efficient Market Hypothesis and the publication of empirical research refuting it, information technology (especially machine learning and deep learning) has been increasingly applied for financial and economic analyses. These techniques offer the ability to recognize patterns and uncover the knowledge and rules hidden within the data. They have achieved promising results in market forecasting.

While many studies of market forecasts have been conducted, the behavior of the market is changing dramatically. Along with computerization, which has sped up trading on the market, strategies to conduct automated transactions, such as algorithmic trading and high-frequency trading (HFT), have been put to practical use. The order data and transaction data from the market can be observed at a very high sampling frequency, and the volume of data has become enormous. It is expected that this data, called 'high-frequency data', can be leveraged for various purposes.

Research has been conducted to explore the application of deep learning to high-frequency trading data. In particular, many studies using order book data have been reported (Tsantekidis *et al.* 2017, Dixon 2018).

For example, the trend in the mid-price was predicted using a neural network that takes the order prices and quantities of 'asks' (i.e. sell orders) and 'bids' (i.e. buy orders) as reported in the order book information as the inputs. It exhibited better prediction accuracy than machine learning.

Market orders, which represent trader's strong intentions and promises to issue prompt payment, greatly influence the market and there is a strong correlation between the market orders and the market return. In addition, limit orders and cancelation orders may also affect prices and must be considered (Eisler *et al.* 2012, Cont *et al.* 2014). However, it is challenging to deal with order book information using existing methods because it is difficult to determine whether a decrease in the best ask or best bid in the order book is due to a successful order or a cancelation of an order. Hence, a neural network can be used to differentiate successful orders by inputting the order series itself into a model.

In this paper, we propose methods to predict short-term price trends using deep learning based on the high-frequency order series which includes all order types.

First, we propose the order-encoding method that can be used to convert order book information of varying quality into input variables for the neural network. Then, we propose an extension of a convolutional neural network (CNN) called an average convolutional neural network (A-CNN) that can be used to acquire a learned model that extracts features to predict price given order book information. Furthermore, we propose an A-CNN+ that is improved to overcome the problems associated with the A-CNN. The proposed approach may ultimately be used to improve the operational performance of algorithmic trading.

The remainder of this paper is organized as follows; Section 2 describes the relevant prior work in this field. In Section 3, we present the proposed method. In Section 4, we describe the experimental validation of the proposed technique on historical price-trend data and compare the results with those obtained by other approaches. In Section 5, we present the results of a simulation of stock price prediction including the simulated improvements in revenue that can be attained using different parameters in the proposed approach. Finally, conclusions are presented in Section 6.

2. Related works

In this section, we describe previous researches involving applications of machine learning to high-frequency trading data. Kercheval predicted the fluctuation in the mid-price by using a support vector machine (SVM) (Hearst *et al.* 1998) based on features such as the bid price and the bid-ask spread (Kercheval and Zhang 2015). Similarly, Fletcher predicted the exchange rate between the Euro and the US dollar using an SVM based on the limit order books (Fletcher and Taylor 2015).

Tsantekidis pointed out that irrational human behavior cannot be captured in designed features and mathematical models, which limits the accuracy of the approach (Tsantekidis *et al.* 2017). Thus, in recent years, market forecasting has been performed without feature extraction using neural networks based on the raw book orders as inputs. Tsantekidis used a neural network to predict trends in the mid-price (Tsantekidis *et al.* 2017). Tsantekidis predicted the mid-price from the ask/bid prices and the quantity of orders accumulated on the order books using long short-term memory (LSTM) (Hochreiter and Schmidhuber 1997); this approach exhibited better performance than SVM. A single learned model was acquired by LSTM using the order book data of five normalized stocks collected over 10 days. However, the shape and fluidity of the order book can vary depending on the stocks. Furthermore, with regard to the prices in the market, it is considered difficult to normalize the data from the order books because it has power-law characteristics and multiple peaks. Therefore, learned models must be created to every stock and a large amount of data is needed for the learning process.

Further, more serious problems are involved in the classification of the market orders. When market orders are used as explanatory variables, it is possible to dynamically trace the strength and balance of the ask and bid at each point in time. However, when the best ask or best bid on the market order decreases, it is impossible to determine whether it is due to the completion of a market order or an order cancelation. With the

emergence of HFT in recent years, cancel orders are becoming frequent, which will make this issue even more difficult to address.

Other studies have used neural networks to predict market prices using current prices, quantities, and order books as the inputs (Dixon *et al.* 2017, Sirignano 2019). Dixon focused on market orders and proposed an extended method to generate features based on the ratio of buy and sell orders from a past order series and add the features to the input vector (Dixon 2018).

However, no studies have successfully predicted market prices by directly inputting a time series of all order types into a CNN as we propose herein.

3. Proposed method

The method proposed in this study is presented as follows: First, we describe the process used to encode market orders. Then, we describe the initial version of the A-CNN. Lastly, we describe the modification of the A-CNN to address its flaws, giving rise to the A-CNN+.

3.1. Order-encoding method

The features of an order are represented as different variables; price, quantity, and time of the order are represented as numerical values (quantitative variables) and buy and sell orders are represented as categorical information (qualitative variables).

In this section, we describe the method used to encode orders before inputting them into the neural network. The order-encoding is done in two stages:

(i) Categorization: convert all qualitative variables to categorical variables belonging to orders.
(ii) Conversion: convert all variables into a single qualitative variable.

The first step is executed as follows for each variable:

order type: The order type (buy, sell, order, limit, and cancel) is a categorical qualitative variable and is used without modification.

price: When qualitative variables are input to a neural network, normalization is generally required. However, the price distribution of the orders is asymmetrical (i.e. a power-law distribution) and multimodal, so it is difficult to calculate standard deviation of it. In addition, preprocessing is difficult because the orders associated with different stock code have different distributions. Therefore, in this paper, we consider the relative price, which is defined as the difference between the price and the mid-price, rather than the absolute price. Figure 1(top) shows the frequency distribution of the relative prices of the orders and the mid-prices at the time of ordering. Figure 1 (bottom) shows the frequency

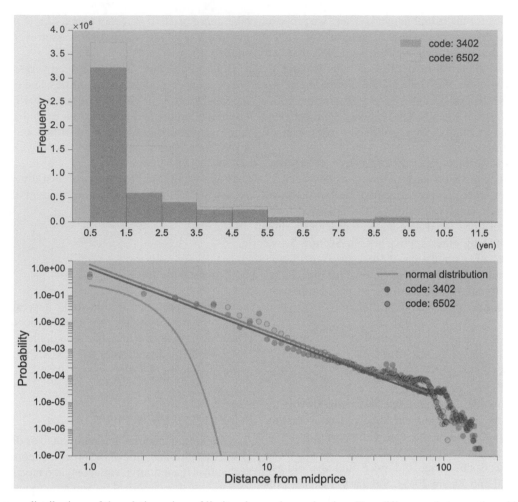

Figure 1. Frequency distributions of the relative prices of limit orders and cancel orders. Top: differences between the mid-price and order price when the orders are placed. Bottom: frequency distributions on a log-log graph: the black curve shows a normal distribution.

distributions of normalized order quantity plotted on a log-log graph. As shown in figure 1 (bottom), although the frequency distributions for stock codes 3402 and 6502 differ, both distributions decrease at prices farther away from the mid-price. Furthermore, it is confirmed that these frequency distributions are similar to power-law distributions, for which averages and standard deviations cannot be identified. Since it is difficult to standardize different price ranges for various stock codes, it is categorized rather than numerical information and used. Also, with relative price, the limit order far from the mid-price is considered to have less impact on price. For these reasons, it is suggested that categorization of order information is superior to normalization.

time difference: When analyzing high-frequency data, it is difficult to classify what kinds of orders have been made. However, assuming that the order type varies with the participants in the order market, it is hypothesized that the accuracy of the market prediction can be improved by associating the information about the participant placing an order with the other order information. To do this, the time-difference relative the previous order is used to classify orders that occur at millisecond intervals as orders made by mechanical traders. Thus, approximate classification information about which transactions are conducted by a particular trader can be included.

Here, by using equation 1, the embedding order, x_t, can calculated at time t.

$$x_t = w_{embed} x_i^{onehot}. \tag{1}$$

The product of the order type (represented by the onehot vector) and the embedding matrix, w, is calculated to derived the embedding vector, x_t, of the order.

The second step in the encoding process is conducted as follows: In order to unify multiple categorical variables and express them as a single variable, the order to be input to the neural network is first normalized. Figure 2 provides a concrete schematic of the order-encoding method. The direct product of plurality of categories represented by matrices is calculated. It can be seen that prices far from mid-price

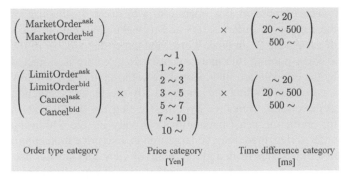

Figure 2. Order-encoding used in this study.

(which have less influence) are categorized together. The time-difference categories are set with the expectation that it is possible to further differentiate automated orders as high-frequency automated orders (if the time difference is less 20 ms) and relatively low-frequency orders (if the time difference is between 20 and 500 ms).

Although even at the same price, limit orders and cancel orders hold different meanings, this feature-representation method of encoding orders to be input to a neural network helps to achieve the objective of dealing with both market orders and limit orders. In addition, this method can make the relationship between the first layer of the neural network and the order information unique, and facilitate the evaluation of the convolution layer.

3.2. Prediction model using average order embedding

Convolutional neural networks (CNN) have been successful for tasks, such as document classification, not only image recognition but also in natural language processing (Kim 2014, Johnson and Zhang 2015). In this research, we used CNN for the order time series because CNN has invariance with respect to position.

CNN performs maximum pooling in the sequence direction post convolution. Even if the limit orders or cancel orders concentrate behind the series, recognizing the market order and learning features and patterns of price trends is possible using

CNN. Hence, we used a model that uses CNN to convolve local order sequences and extract patterns.

Sequence S unified by constant n by padding using the embedding vector x_t of the order x_t is represented as $x_{1:n} = [x_1, x_2, \ldots, x_n]$. The local matrix $x_{i:i+h}$ was convolved, and a new feature c_i was obtained by applying an activation function. When this convolution was performed on $(x_{1:h}, x_{2:h+1}, \ldots, x_{n-h+1:n})$ with a stride width of 1, a new feature vector $c = [c_1, c_2, \ldots, c_{n-h+1}]^T \in \mathbb{R}^{n-h+1}$ was obtained. By performing maximum pooling on the c, a feature amount $\hat{c} = \max(c)$ was obtained from one filter. This process was performed for some convolution filters. Features $\hat{c} = [\hat{c}_1, \hat{c}_2, \ldots, \hat{c}_{k_{conv}}]^T$ obtained via convolution using k_{conv} filters and maximum pooling was input to the entire fully connected layer. Using the SoftMax function, we converted the output class obtained from the fully connected layer.

Several sizes of convolution filters were prepared to change the length of the sequence to extract the pattern based on its size. For example, if the filter was large size, the global relationship of orders was captured, whereas if the filter was small size, the local relationship was captured.

3.3. Average convolutional neural network: A-CNN

In the time series data for financial markets, even if a certain price trend is observed, few clear patterns exist in the microstructure, such as order units. In a time series of orders, it is assumed that the order interaction for a local range captured by the convolution filter is small. To reduce these effects by averaging a certain number of orders, we propose using average-CNN (A-CNN) as a prediction model, which uses averaging of order embedding.

Figure 3 shows an overview of A-CNN. A-CNN uses a two-dimensional (2D) embedding matrix (i.e. order embedding) as input. By using proposed order-encoding method, various plural order information in one stock code is calculated as w_{embed}, which is represented as the matrix of embedding size (column) and the number of orders (row) in figure 3. Average pooling was applied to the embedded matrix, $x_{1:n}$, with a window width of $1 \times l_{pool}$ pool. Padding was performed with a padding size of l_{pad} with respect to

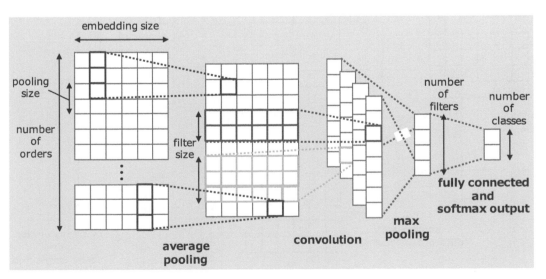

Figure 3. Structure of A-CNN.

the order time series direction prior to pooling. The feature matrix post pooling is represented as $x_{\mathrm{pool}} \in \mathbb{R}^{e \times \lfloor l_{\mathrm{pad}} + n/l_{\mathrm{pool}} \rfloor}$ with the floor function as $\lfloor x \rfloor$. Next, feed forward propagation and learning were conducted similar to CNN.

The effect of averaging also aids in capturing the market order interactions. CNN cannot extract market order features when the interval for the market order is larger than the size of the convolution filter. By adding the averages, extending the length of the order series captured by the filter to $l_{\mathrm{pool}} \times h$ is possible. Based on the above described method, capturing the interactions between the orders of execution with a low occurrence frequency is possible. However, when some market orders are present in the pooling window l_{pool} it is a disadvantage that they are averaged.

Consider an example, wherein using the order-encoding method, order book information was assigned according to each categorized item in figure 2, '1' was assigned to the applicable category, '0' was otherwise assigned, and the 0/1 embedding matrix was input into the neural network. Because the embedding matrix is represented as 0/1, when max pooling is used in the pooling layer, many variables of the matrix through the pooling layer may be 1. Hence, we considered max pooling to be inappropriate, and we used average pooling instead.

3.4. A-CNN+

Next, we propose the A-CNN+ model, which is shown in figure 4, as an extension of the A-CNN described in the previous subsection. Multiple averaging matrices are created by performing average pooling on the order embedding matrix using different window widths. A convolution filter is then prepared for each averaging matrix and convolution and maximum pooling are applied. These vectors are input to the entire fully connected layer as in a CNN.

The purpose of this operation is to diversify the size of the context of orders series and to make convolution filters of various sizes. In other words, the larger the window of the average pooling, the more extensively a feature is extracted by the convolution filter. Conversely, the smaller the window for average pooling, the more locally the feature extraction is performed. Here, we hypothesize that the useful pattern for predicting price fluctuations can vary in size within the order series; there may be large trends, like price momentum in a time series from a global point of view, and smaller patterns, such as microeconomic interactions from a local point of view. By using pooling windows and convolution filter windows of various widths, the A-CNN+ can correspond to patterns of various lengths. Based on this way, the model can synergistically capture a larger variety of relationships between orders.

4. Experiment

4.1. Data set

In this experiment, dataset comprised 20 stocks of FLEX-FULL historical data, which include data from the Tokyo Stock Exchange over 245 business days between 1 July 2013 to 30 June 2014. Two classes (Up, Down) and three classes (Up, Down, Neutral) classification problem were set for each issue for which the mid-price was the target of prediction.

This dataset was selected in consideration of the practice of algorithmic trading. The order sequence (event-driven) to be input to the price-prediction model to decide the price trend (the output) is aligned with the order timing (time-driven) via a transaction algorithm. More specifically, as shown figure 5, a delimiter is set every 30 seconds to delimit one encoded ordered sequence and several such order sequences

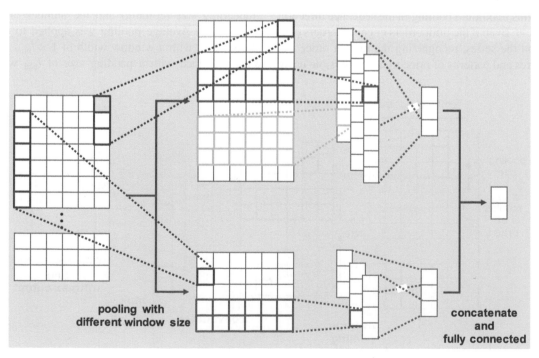

Figure 4. Structure of the A-CNN+.

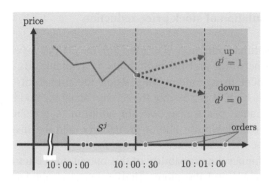

Figure 5. Sampling of a series, $\mathcal{S}^j$, and labeling in two-class classification.

are acquired. It should be noted that although the divided order sequence, $\mathcal{S}^j$, has a variable length, it can be handled effectively on the prediction model side.

As shown figure 5, the output class (the price trend, d^j) corresponding to $\mathcal{S}^j$ was for the time period beginning 30 seconds after the last time point in the input interval. In this experiment, the following classification problems are considered.

- two-class classification to predict up/down price
- three-class classification to predict up/neutral/down price

4.2. Results

The data from each issue over the course of one year is divided in a ratio of 7:1.5:1.5 as learning data, verification data, and evaluation data, respectively. Using the data from each of the 20 stock codes, learning was conducted using the learning data and a parameter search was carried out (Appendix). The model with the best performance on the verification data was selected for use with the evaluation data. The F1 scores for each class in the evaluation data were obtained and the average of the F1 scores was used as the evaluation metric.

Figure 6 shows the experimental results including the F1 scores obtained in the two-class mid-price-prediction experiment on the evaluation data. Logistic regression, nonlinear SVM, multi-layer perceptron (MLP), and a CNN were also applied for comparison. Here, the A-CNN and A-CNN+ provided higher scores than the other baseline methods, indicating that the proposed method outperformed the baseline methods for all issues. In some cases, the A-CNN outperformed A-CNN+ but in other cases, the A-CNN+ was better (figure 7).

4.3. Analysis

In this section, we analyze the convolutional layer. There is a vector representing each order with a norm corresponding to

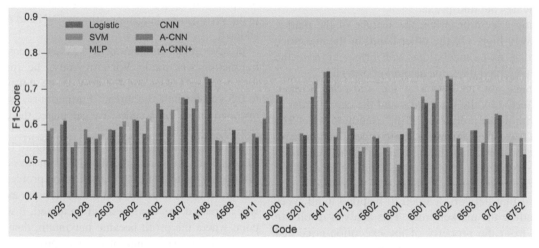

Figure 6. F1 scores of the mid-price prediction for each stock code using two-class classification; the vertical axis represents the F1 score and the horizontal axis denotes each stock code.

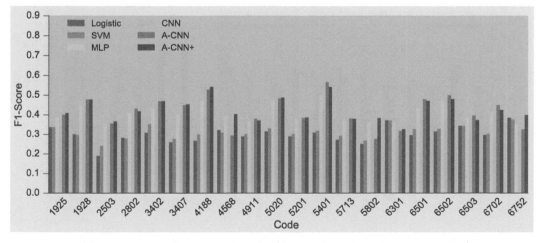

Figure 7. F1 scores of the mid-price prediction for each stock code using three-class classification.

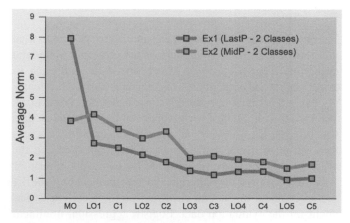

Figure 8. Norm averages of the embedding vectors in the A-CNN model.

the strength of firing of the neural network. Figure 8 shows the average of norms for the two-class classification problem in case of which forecasting targets are execution-price and mid-price. In figure 8, the average of the norms of the embedding vectors from the market sales orders (*MO*), limit orders (*LO*), and cancelation orders (*C*) in each price range are calculated for all the stock codes. The numbers (e.g. *LO*1 and *C*2) represent price categories: 1, 2, 3, 4, and 5 indicate the price categories ~ 1, $1 \sim 2$, $2 \sim 3$, $3 \sim 5$, and $5 \sim 7$, respectively, as shown figure 2. *LastP* indicates the execution-price and *MidP* indicates the mid-price.

In forecasting execution price, the weight of the market order is relatively high. On the other hand, in the mid-price prediction, orders and cancelations with prices close to the mid-price are weighted the same as market orders.

This is because the prediction of the mid-price is more likely to be affected by the limit order and the cancel order in comparison with to the prediction of the execution price. The mid-price fluctuate by entering a limit order and a cancel order near the best ask and the best bid, but the execution-price change only as a result of entering a market order. Since the mid-price also fluctuates depending on the market order, it is considered that network learned to respond to all types of orders including the market order. This analysis result can be convinced from the property of the execution price and the mid-price, it shows that the proposed method works as intended.

5. Simulation of stock price reduction

The Softmax function was used for the output layer of the neural network, and the probability is available. By making investment using output only when the probability by the model is high, it is possible to increase accuracy and improve performance per transaction. In addition, a threshold was set for the maximum output probability, and the investment behavior was determined.

The higher the probability of this output, the better features are captured and the more reliable output is obtained. As a reason for the above, figure 9 is shown. In figure 9, the bar graph indicates the precision (vertical axis on the left), and the line graph indicates the ratio of the number of samples whose output probability exceeds the threshold value (vertical axis on the right). The threshold values were set to 0.50, 0.55, and 0.60. The chance rate (i.e. vertical axis on the right) indicates the proportion to the total number of samples in the evaluation data. The precision is when a threshold is set for the output of each evaluation data. The precision was calculated using the number of samples whose output exceeded each threshold value. As the threshold value was set higher, the evaluation value increased, and the number of times to output a probability exceeding the high threshold decreased.

When conducting investment simulations, we compared a two-class classification problem with a three-class classification problem using profit. The model with the highest F1 value in the verification data among the A-CNN and A-CNN+ was adopted.

In investment simulation, it was set to cost each time a transaction was made. For simplicity, the spread was uniformly set to 1 yen, and the cost of one transaction was set to 0.5 yen for half the thread. Furthermore, assuming that it operated on all stock codes, we calculated the profit obtained from this portfolio.

The corresponding result is shown in figure 10. Profits were calculated as we varied the thresholds in investment simulations. As a feature of each classification problem, we showed that profit became positive at a certain point as the threshold was increased. As the threshold increased, it went through a point where the profit became maximum, then decayed, and approached 0. The range of positive profit means that profit exceeds the cost of half-spread in one transaction. Although

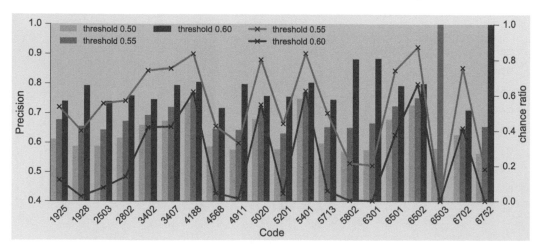

Figure 9. Ratio of the precision and prediction opportunities when the threshold was set to output (two-class classification).

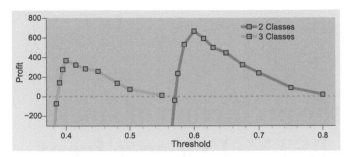

Figure 10. Changes in profit as a function of testing different thresholds. Total profit for all brands with a set cost.

using large threshold the accuracy of the prediction could be increased, the sum of profits declined because the number of transactions become decrease.

From these results, we showed that the proposed order-encoding method and averaging of the embedding matrix are practical. In addition, this result show that the two-class classification can generate larger profit than the three-class classification and can increase the positive profit in many thresholds. This results suggest that the two-class classification was easier to learn than the three-class classification.

6. Conclusion

In this research, in order to predict the short-term trend of stock price, we proposed an order-encoding method and improved CNN models (A-CNN, A-CNN+) which are suitable for capturing features of the orders. Through experiments using large-scale high-frequency trading data, the experimental results showed that the proposed method is superior to other benchmark methods. Furthermore, it was confirmed that the convolutional layer performed as intended. Especially in prediction of mid-price, we confirmed that an improved CNN by the proposed method can learn to capture features of the order book.

The experimental results suggest that the learned model responds strongly to the ordering process in all tasks. In the prediction of mid-price, we found that the limit orders and cancel orders close to the mid-price are important as same as the market orders. Finally, investment simulations were conducted to demonstrate a practical application to buying and selling according to the model predictions by the proposed method. Positive results were achieved through investment simulations, and the practicality of the model is suggested. Furthermore, the performance was improved by setting a threshold for the probability of output, and results show that the two-class classification model outperforms the three-class classification model.

In future works, the incorporation of more detailed order book information will be explored. In this paper, we focused on information on the type and price of orders sampled in fixed time interval. By introducing more fluid information, it is potentially that prediction accuracy is improved. In addition, it is necessary to develop the method to utilize it.

Disclosure statement

No potential conflict of interest was reported by the authors.

ORCID

Hiroyasu Matsushima ⓘ http://orcid.org/0000-0001-7301-1956

References

Cont, R., Kukanov, A. and Stoikov, S., Price impact of order book events. *J. Financ. Econ.*, 2014, **12**, 47–48.

Dixon, M., Polson, N. and Sokolov, V., Deep learning for spatio-temporal modeling: Dynamic traffic flows and high frequency trading. *Appl. Stoch. Models. Bus. Ind.*, 2017, 1–20.

Dixon, M., Sequence classification of the limit order book using recurrent neural networks. *J. Comput. Sci.*, 2018, **24**, 277–286.

Eisler, Z., Bouchaud, J.P. and Kockelkoren, J., The price impact of order book events: Market orders, limit orders and cancellations. *Quant. Finance*, 2012, **12**, 1395–1419.

Fletcher, T. and Taylor, J.S., Multiple kernel learning with fisher kernels for high frequency currency prediction. *Comput. Econ.*, 2015, **15**, 1315–1329.

Hearst, M., Dumais, S., Osuna, E., Platt, J. and Scholkopf, B., Support vector machines. *IEEE Intell. Syst. Appl.*, 1998, **13**, 18–28.

Hochreiter, S. and Schmidhuber, J., Long short-term memory. *Neural. Comput.*, 1997, **9**, 1735–1780.

Johnson, R. and Zhang, T., Effective use of word order for text categorization with convolutional neural networks. Proceedings of the 2015 Conference of the North American Chapter of the Association for Computational Linguistics: Human Language Technologies, pp. 103–112, 2015.

Kercheval, A. and Zhang, Y., Modeling high-frequency limit order book dynamics with support vector machines. *Quant. Finance*, 2015, **15**, 1315–1329.

Kim, Y., Convolutional neural networks for sentence classification. *Empirical Methods Nat. Lang. Process.*, 2014, 1746–1751.

Sirignano, J.A., Deep learning for limit order books. *Quant. Finance*, 2019, **19**, 549–570.

Tsantekidis, A., Passalis, N., Tefas, A., Kanniainen, J., Gabbouj, M. and Iosifidis, A., Using deep learning to detect price change indications in financial markets. Proceedings of the 25th European Signal Processing Conference, pp. 2511–2515, 2017.

Appendix

Parameters

Here, search parameters related to each method used in this paper are described. Parameters were searched using grid search.

Table A1. A-CNN: ReLU was used for the activation function.

Parameter	Range
dimensions of the embedding layer	[3, 5, 10]
Size and num. of filter (size:num.)	[3:20, 5:20, 7:20, 3:5, 5:5, 7:5, 10:5]
Pooling size	[5, 10, 15]

Table A2. A-CNN+: Size of filter is fixed as 20. ReLU was used for the activation function.

Parameter	Range
dimensions of the embedding layer	[3, 5, 10]
Number of filter	[3, 5, 7, 3, 5, 7, 10]
Size of average pooling	[5, 10, 5, 10, 15]

Attention mechanism in the prediction of stock price movement by using LSTM: Evidence from the Hong Kong stock market

SHUN CHEN ⓘ and LEI GE ⓘ

(Received 7 June 2018; accepted 6 May 2019; published online 9 July 2019)

State-of-the-art methods using attention mechanism in Recurrent Neural Networks have shown exceptional performance targeting sequential predictions and classifications. We explore the attention mechanism in Long–Short-Term Memory (LSTM) network based stock price movement prediction. Our proposed model significantly enhances the LSTM prediction performance in the Hong Kong stock market. The attention LSTM (AttLSTM) model is compared with the LSTM model in Hong Kong stock movement prediction. Further parameter tuning results also demonstrate the effectiveness of the attention mechanism in LSTM-based prediction method.

1. Introduction

Predicting stock price movement is one of the most challenging tasks in the financial world (Booth *et al.* 2014, Al-Hmouz *et al.* 2015, Barak and Modarres 2015, Jiang *et al.* 2018, Rodrigues and Lleo 2018), since the stock market is essentially dynamic, complicated, nonlinear, chaotic and nonparametric in nature (Abu-Mostafa and Atiya 1996). Accurate prediction in stock price movement is very important for trading strategy development (Kim and Han 2000). Many researchers from different areas have obtained various results in predicting stock markets.

It is of interest to study stock price movements using the data from stock markets, especially the Hong Kong stock market. Hong Kong is the largest source of foreign direct investment for the Chinese mainland. The Hong Kong stock market is one of the largest stock markets in the world. It has the advantage that Hong Kong is the bridge between the western world and eastern worlds. The exchange rules in the Hong Kong stock market make it be a very mature market. It has about one hundred years' history and has around 2000 listed companies from all over the world (Wiki 2018).

Recently, a large number of deep learning techniques are used to study the mechanism of the stock market and have put forward many new results. LSTM-based method for China stock returns prediction was proposed in Chen *et al.* (2015).

They used pre-process techniques to transfer the Chinese stocks into sequences which were used to be the inputs of the LSTM. Their methods were compared with the random prediction method. Daily stock price prediction was proposed for Sri Lankan stock market by using RNN in Samarawickrama and Fernando (2017). In this paper, the authors used the GRU network which is a special RNN to do prediction in the specified stock market. CNN-LSTM neural network for quantitative strategy analysis in stock markets was researched in Liu *et al.* (2017). Their researches combined the convolutional neural network and long short-term memory neural network to study quantitative stock selection strategy. However, to the best of our knowledge, attention mechanism has not been used in LSTM-based stock movement prediction, which is one of the main contributions of this paper.

Attention mechanism is currently acknowledged as an effective method in sequential learning applications, image recognition, etc (LeCun *et al.* 2015). After the researches proposed by Bahdanau *et al.* (2015) and Vaswani *et al.* (2017), the attention mechanism has attracted plenty of interest in deep learning. In Chorowski *et al.* (2015), the attention-based models for speech recognition were given. Their results show a competitive improvement compared with transitional models which did not use attention mechanism. In Yang *et al.* (2016), attention mechanism was used in document classification. The authors proposed hierarchical attention networks which contained two levels of attention mechanisms to construct the document representations. In Zhang *et al.* (2018), an hierarchical attention network was applied in multi-modal social image popularity prediction. The user-guided attention mechanisms were introduced in this paper to hierarchically attend both visual and textual modalities.

Those works motivate our research on the attention mechanism in LSTM-based stock movement prediction. We use the Hong Kong stock data as input variables, which can be directly obtained from software.

The remainder of this paper is organized as follows. In Section 2, RNN, LSTM, and attention mechanism are proposed. In Section 3, attention LSTM is proposed and some data preparations are given. In Section 4, experiments are given to show the effectiveness of the attention mechanism in LSTM-based prediction. In Section 5, conclusions are drawn.

2. Research methodology

2.1. Theory of recurrent neural network

The key feature in a Recurrent Neural Network (RNN) is that the network has at least one feed-back connection. This means that the activations can form a loop. This fundamental feature makes RNN have the advantage in temporal process and sequences learning tasks, such as, sequence recognition and temporal prediction. One common type of the recurrent neural network architectures is that a standard Multi-Layer Perceptron (MLP) with loops inside. Those loops make the recurrent neural network have the power of memorizing previous state. One simple recurrent neural network can be found in the figure 1.

The recurrent neural network can be described as a dynamical system in state space model. The detail formula is given in the following equations:

$$s_t = f_s(W_i x_t + W_s s_{t-1}),$$
$$y_t = f_o(W_o s_t), \tag{1}$$

where x_t is the neural network inputs, y_t is the neural network outputs, W_i is the connection weight matrix between inputs

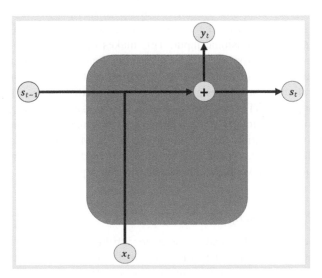

Figure 1. Recurrent neural network.

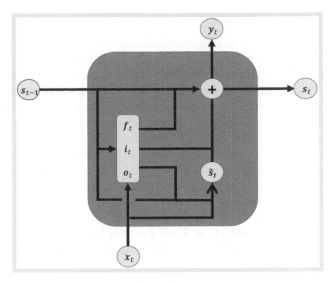

Figure 2. Long–short-term memory network.

and hidden layer, W_s is the connection weight matrix between delayed hidden layer and current hidden layer, W_o is the connection weight matrix between hidden layer and outputs, f_s is the hidden unit activation function, and f_o is the output unit activation function.

From (1), the memory of the recurrent neural network is represented by the time-delayed state s_{t-1}. This shows the memory mechanism in the recurrent neural network.

2.2. Theory of long–short-term memory RNN

An RNN composed of long–short-term memory blocks is often called an LSTM network. This LSTM architecture contains a set of recurrently connected subnets, which are call memory blocks. In each memory block, there exist memory cell which stores the state, input gate which controls what to learn, forget gate which controls what to forget, and output gate which controls the amount of contents to modify. The main difference between LSTM and traditional RNN is that the LSTM blocks can use the introduced gates to decide whether to keep the existed memory while the traditional RNN blocks overwrite its content at each time step. One simple long–short-term memory network can be found in the figure 2.

The detail formula can be given in the following equations:

$$\begin{aligned} i_t &= \sigma_g(W_i s_{t-1} + U_i x_t + b_i), \\ o_t &= \sigma_g(W_o s_{t-1} + U_o x_t + b_o), \\ f_t &= \sigma_g(W_f s_{t-1} + U_f x_t + b_f), \\ \tilde{s}_t &= \phi(W(o_t \odot s_{t-1}) + U x_t + b), \\ s_t &= f_t \odot s_{t-1} + i_t \odot \tilde{s}_t, \\ y_t &= o_t \odot \sigma_y(s_t), \end{aligned} \tag{2}$$

where three gates at time step t are represented by i_t (input gate), o_t (output gate), and f_t (forget gate). The s_t and s_{t-1} are the current and prior states, x_t is the current input, y_t is the output, W, U are the weights, b is the bias, σ_g, ϕ, σ_y are activation functions, and $\odot$ denotes the element-wise multiplication.

2.3. Theory of attention

In neuroscience and computational neuroscience, the attention mechanism has been widely studied (Desimone and Duncan 1995, Itti *et al.* 1998). This common mechanism comes from the fact that many animals focus on only specific parts of their visual view to give adequate responses. So many neural computation researches conclude that one only need the most pertinent piece of the information to make further neural process, rather than using all the information. This mechanism has also been widely used in recent deep learning researches, such as, image recolonization, speech recognition and language translation.

To illustrate the attention mechanism, the work (Bahdanau *et al.* 2015) consider an RNN Encoder-Decoder in Cho *et al.* (2014) and Sutskever *et al.* (2014): an encoder reads the input sequence of vectors $x = (x_1, \ldots, x_{T_x})$ into a vector c. This approach is often explained in an RNN structure in the following form:

$$s_t = f(x_t, s_{t-1}, c_t)$$

and

$$c = q(s_1, \ldots, s_{T_x}),$$

where s_t is the hidden state, c is the output vector of the RNN which is generated by the hidden states. In attention model, the context vector c_t is strongly related to the sequence of annotations $(h_1, \ldots, h_{T_x})$ to which an encoder maps the input sentence. The information about the whole input sequence with a strong focus on the parts surrounding the t-th word of the input sequence is contained in the annotation h_t. Details can be found in the following explanations. figure 3 shows the attention mechanism in neural network.

A weighted sum of those annotations h_t forms the context vector c_t:

$$c_t = \sum_{j=1}^{T_x} \alpha_{tj} h_j,$$

where the weight α_{tj} of each annotation h_j is given by

$$\alpha_{tj} = \frac{\exp(e_{tj})}{\sum_{k=1}^{T_x} \exp(e_{tk})}$$

in which

$$e_{tj} = a(s_{t-1}, h_j).$$

The function $a(s_{t-1}, h_j)$ is an alignment model which is used to describe the matching ability between the inputs around position j and the outputs at position t. The score is calculated by using the RNN hidden state s_{t-1} and the j-th annotation h_j of the input sentence.

The attention mechanism in neural network equips a neural network which has the ability to focus on a subset of its inputs: it always selects important inputs. In figure 3, the attention mechanism aims to select the important inputs in the input sequences $\{x_1, x_2, \ldots, x_{T_x}\}$ by using the weight α_{tj}.

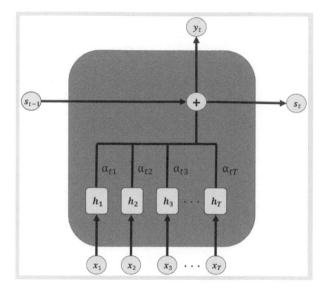

Figure 3. Attention mechanism.

3. Research design

3.1. Attention LSTM

Long–short-term memory network has been proven to be an effective deep learning model in sequential tasks. Two layered LSTM network is used in this paper with dropout followed on each layer. In attention LSTM model, we use the attention layer before the LSTM layer, see figure 4. The LSTM layer takes the output of the attention layer as the input with the activation function assumed to be *tanh*. The dropout is applied in the LSTM layer. At the end of the two LSTM layers, we add a dense layer to obtain two-valued outputs which are the prediction classes (increasing movement and decreasing movement). Finally, BatchNormalization layer is applied after the dense layer. The output of the BatchNormalization layer is passed into a softmax classification layer.

For comparison purpose, we also give the LSTM network without attention in figure 5.

In this paper, we use a double LSTM network. As one may know, even training a simple LSTM model can take plenty of time and system resources. In this paper, we use lots of features as the input of the LSTM network which is a high dimensional input. This makes the training procedure of the proposed model take more time. So we use the double LSTM model for the illustration on the effectiveness of attention mechanism in LSTM-based prediction. In addition, one LSTM network can certainly be used. However, it should be pointed out that a deeper LSTM structure may show better prediction results than a single LSTM network. Considering time, resources limitation and prediction accuracy requirement, we use double LSTM in this paper.

3.2. Data description

The research data and the predictor attributes selected in this study are described in this section. Predicting direction of daily close price movement for stocks in Hong Kong market is the main research objective in this paper.

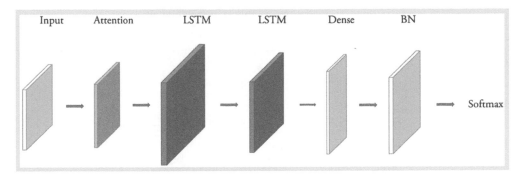

Figure 4. Attention long–short-term memory network architecture.

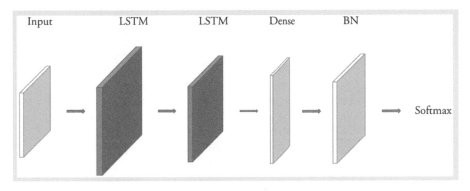

Figure 5. Long–short-term memory network architecture.

3.3. Feature selection

Several main technical indicators and their corresponding formulas are discussed in table 1, which are designed to be the inputs of the AttLSTM and LSTM models. Some features are selected based on the program in Fang (2018).

The prediction movement of the stock is calculated based on the stock close price p_t of each trading day. The formula is

$$p_{chg}(t) = \begin{cases} 1, & p_{t+1} - p_t > 0 \\ 0, & p_{t+1} - p_t \leq 0 \end{cases} \qquad (3)$$

This way, the prediction output of each model is converted to be '1' or '0', where '1' indicates the increase movement and '0' indicates decreasing or equal movement. In practice, predicting stock price movement direction and predicting the precise price are both important. In this paper, although we do not predict the precise price, the obtained prediction results on the stock price movement still can help to make trading decisions to long/short stocks or adjust positions. Especially, we have built a simple 'Long-Only' strategy to show the profitability by using the prediction results of proposed models.

The detailed technical indicators are discussed as follows.

ROCP Rate of Change Percentage is the percentage change between the price today and the price of last day. A positive/negative ROCP means an upward/downward momentum.

MA Moving Average is the average value of sequential data in a specified time period.

EMA Exponential Moving Average is similar to Moving Average, except the average calculation is not based on equal weight. Larger weight is given to the latest data and less weight to the early data. This type of MA reacts faster to recent price change than a simple MA.

MACD Moving Average Convergence/Divergence is an indicator mainly to reveal the change in the momentum of stock price trend. A momentum oscillator is constructed by subtracting the longer EMA from the shorter EMA. The MACD fluctuates above and below the zero line as the MA converges, crosses and diverges.

RSI Relative Strength Index is an indicator measures the relative strength between the momentum of positive change in price and the momentum of negative change during a specified time period. RSI has a range from 0 to 100 and is considered to reveal overbought or oversold of a stock.

VROCP Volume Rate of Change Percentage measures a volume trend of a stock. A positive VROCP means the market support the price to continue moving in the current trend while a negative VROCP means a lack support on the moving in the current trend, and the current price trend maybe disappear or reverse.

Boll Bollinger Bands include three indicators which are middle band, upper band and lower band. Middle band could be calculated by moving average. Upper/lower band is obtained by middle band plus/minus K times an N-period standard deviation. These three bands are supposed to reveal high or low stock price.

Table 1. Used technical indicators with formula.

Technical indicator	Full name	Formula
ROCP	Rate of Change Percentage (using close price)	$\mathrm{ROCP}(i) = \dfrac{S_{i,\mathrm{close}} - S_{i-1,\mathrm{close}}}{S_{i-1,\mathrm{close}}}$
OROCP	Rate of Change Percentage (using open price)	$\mathrm{OROCP}(i) = \dfrac{S_{i,\mathrm{open}} - S_{i-1,\mathrm{open}}}{S_{i-1,\mathrm{open}}}$
HROCP	Rate of Change Percentage (using high price)	$\mathrm{HROCP}(i) = \dfrac{S_{i,\mathrm{high}} - S_{i-1,\mathrm{high}}}{S_{i-1,\mathrm{high}}}$
LROCP	Rate of Change Percentage (using low price)	$\mathrm{LROCP}(i) = \dfrac{S_{i,\mathrm{low}} - S_{i-1,\mathrm{low}}}{S_{i-1,\mathrm{low}}}$
MA	Moving Average	$\mathrm{MA}(N) = \dfrac{1}{N}\Sigma_{i=1}^{N} S_{i,\mathrm{close}}$
MACP	Moving Average Change Percentage	$\mathrm{MACP}(N) = \dfrac{\mathrm{MA}(N) - S_{\mathrm{close}}}{S_{\mathrm{close}}}$
MACD	Moving Average Convergence/Divergence	$\mathrm{DIF}(i) = \mathrm{EMA}(N_{\mathrm{fast}}) - \mathrm{EMA}(N_{\mathrm{slow}})$ $\mathrm{DEA}(i) = \alpha * \mathrm{DEA}(i-1) + (1-\alpha) * \mathrm{DIF}(i)$ $\mathrm{MACD}(i) = 2 * (\mathrm{DIF}(i) - \mathrm{DEA}(i))$
DIFROCP	Rate of Change Percentage (using DIF)	$\mathrm{DIFROCP}(i) = \dfrac{\mathrm{DIF}(i) - \mathrm{DIF}(i-1)}{\mathrm{DIF}(i-1)}$
DEAROCP	Rate of Change Percentage (using DEA)	$\mathrm{DEAROCP}(i) = \dfrac{\mathrm{DEA}(i) - \mathrm{DEA}(i-1)}{\mathrm{DEA}(i-1)}$
MACDROCP	Rate of Change Percentage (using MACD)	$\mathrm{MACDROCP}(i) = \dfrac{\mathrm{MACD}(i) - \mathrm{MACD}(i-1)}{\mathrm{MACD}(i-1)}$
RSI	Relative Strength Index	$\mathrm{RSI}(N) = 100 - \dfrac{100}{(1 + \mathrm{EMA}(N)_{up}/\mathrm{EMA}(N)_{\mathrm{down}})}$
RSIROCP	Rate of Change Percentage (using RSI)	$\mathrm{RSIROCP}(N)_i = \dfrac{\mathrm{RSI}(N)_i - \mathrm{RSI}(N)_{i-1}}{\mathrm{RSI}(N)_{i-1}}$
VROCP	Volume Rate of Change	$\mathrm{VROCP}(i) = \arctan((V_i - V_{i-1})/V_{i-1})$
BOLL	Bollinger Bands	$\mathrm{BOLL}(N,K)_{\mathrm{middle}} = \mathrm{MA}(N),$ $\sigma = \mathrm{Std}(\{S_{i,\mathrm{close}}, S_{i-1,\mathrm{close}}, \ldots, S_{i-N+1,\mathrm{close}}\})$ $\mathrm{BOLL}(N,K)_{\mathrm{upper}} = \mathrm{MA}(N) + K * \sigma,$ $\mathrm{BOLL}(N,K)_{\mathrm{lower}} = \mathrm{MA}(N) - K * \sigma$
VMAROCP	Volume Moving Average Rate of Change Percentage	ROCP based on volume MA See MA and ROCP
VMACP	Volume Moving Average Change Percentage	MACP based on volume MA See MACP
PRICE VOLUME	ROCP × VROCP	$\mathrm{PRICE-}_{\mathrm{VOLUME}} = \mathrm{ROCP} \times \mathrm{VROCP}$

VMA Volume Moving Average is similar to VROCP, except VMA is based on volume moving average and VROCP is based on daily volume. VMA measures a volume trend of a stock with a positive/negative value revealing that the market support/do not support the price to continue moving in current trend.

4. Evaluation

We carry out some comparative experiments on stocks in Hong Kong market by using AttLSTM and LSTM to evaluate the performance of the attention mechanism. The time span of the transaction data of these stocks is within the range from 1 January 2005 to 31 December 2017. Same training set

and testing set of each stock data are chosen for comparison between AttLSTM and LSTM-based stock price movement prediction.

4.1. Experiment setup

The Hong Kong stock data are downloaded by using TongDaXin software. We choose the stock codes between 00809.HK and 00899.HK to evaluate the performance of the proposed AttLSTM model. The testing set of the chosen stocks contains the nearest 700 trading days. The rest data in history is chosen to be the training set. For each training set, we hold out 30% of its data for validation in the training process and the remaining 70% are used to train models. The details can be found in figure 6. For easy comparison, we set up the parameters tobe the same in AttLSTM and

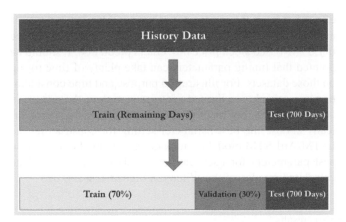

Figure 6. Train, validation, and test data.

Table 2. System environment.

CPU	Intel(R) Core(TM) i7-7700K
RAM	32G
GPU	NVIDIA TITAN X (Pascal) & NVIDIA TITAN Xp
System	Windows 10
Python Version	Python 3.5.4
Keras Version	Keras 2.0.9
CUDA Version	CUDA V9.0.176
Tensorflow Version	Tensorflow 1.7.0

LSTM. Batch size is set to be 512. Learning rate is set to be 0.001. Dropout rate is set to be 0.2. The input step for the stock sequence is set to be 10. The epoch number is set to be 1000. We use early stopping to avoid the over-fitting. The setting of early stopping is based on the non-increasing in validation accuracy. The code running environment is shown in table 2. We use 'AttLSTM Win' to count the number of winning datasets. If the 'AttLSTM Architecture' shows higher or equal prediction accuracy compared with 'LSTM Architecture' in one dataset, the 'AttLSTM Win' number increases one, otherwise the number remains the same.

4.2. Results

The experimental results are listed in table 3. The basic features of each trading day only contain the following values: close price, open price, high price, low price, volume. The other technique indicators are calculated by using Python package TA-Lib (Fortier 2018). From table 3, the AttLSTM shows prediction accuracy improvement in 56 stocks out of 72 stocks. Wilcoxon signed rank test is used to compare the median rank of the AttLSTM model and LSTM model. The null hypothesis and alternative hypothesis is given by the following formula:

$$H_0 : \text{Median}_{\text{AttLSTM}} = \text{Median}_{\text{LSTM}}.$$

$$H_a : \text{Median}_{\text{AttLSTM}} \neq \text{Median}_{\text{LSTM}}.$$

The calculated p-value of the Wilcoxon Signed Test is less than $6.0E-6$ which provides the evidence that the AttLSTM maintains or improves the overall stock movement prediction accuracy. In addition, we also conduct the McNemar's test

Table 3. Comparison results.

NAME	LSTM	AttLSTM	NAME	LSTM	AttLSTM
00809.HK	0.6171	**0.6243**	00810.HK	0.5000	**0.5914**
00811.HK	0.5300	**0.5343**	00812.HK	0.6329	**0.6529**
00813.HK	**0.5300**	**0.5300**	00814.HK	0.5829	**0.5900**
00815.HK	0.5071	**0.5329**	00816.HK	0.4757	**0.5886**
00817.HK	**0.5043**	0.4971	00818.HK	0.6014	**0.6114**
00819.HK	**0.5157**	0.4957	00821.HK	0.6314	**0.6486**
00822.HK	**0.6614**	0.6586	00825.HK	0.4943	**0.5757**
00826.HK	0.5086	**0.5229**	00827.HK	0.4943	**0.5871**
00829.HK	0.5571	**0.6571**	00830.HK	0.6414	**0.6714**
00831.HK	0.5943	**0.6329**	00832.HK	**0.5771**	0.5729
00833.HK	**0.5829**	**0.5829**	00834.HK	0.5914	**0.6071**
00836.HK	**0.5186**	0.4814	00837.HK	0.5543	**0.5686**
00838.HK	0.5929	**0.5971**	00840.HK	0.6300	**0.6343**
00841.HK	0.6471	**0.6586**	00842.HK	0.5629	**0.6071**
00844.HK	0.5929	**0.6043**	00845.HK	0.6157	**0.6314**
00848.HK	0.6371	**0.6557**	00850.HK	0.6329	**0.6357**
00851.HK	**0.6243**	0.6243	00852.HK	0.6329	**0.6471**
00853.HK	**0.5500**	0.5371	00855.HK	0.5443	**0.5500**
00856.HK	**0.5614**	**0.5614**	00857.HK	0.5500	**0.5600**
00858.HK	0.6614	**0.6943**	00859.HK	0.6057	**0.6357**
00860.HK	0.6200	**0.6329**	00861.HK	0.5014	**0.5243**
00862.HK	0.6557	**0.6786**	00865.HK	0.8143	**0.8371**
00866.HK	**0.6257**	0.6157	00867.HK	**0.5257**	0.5100
00868.HK	**0.5271**	0.5186	00871.HK	**0.6029**	0.5886
00872.HK	**0.6486**	**0.6486**	00874.HK	0.5314	**0.5314**
00875.HK	0.5500	**0.5614**	00876.HK	0.6214	**0.6314**
00877.HK	0.5386	**0.5429**	00878.HK	0.5186	**0.5514**
00880.HK	**0.5529**	**0.5529**	00881.HK	**0.5529**	0.5429
00882.HK	0.5229	**0.5329**	00883.HK	0.5329	**0.5457**
00884.HK	**0.5314**	0.5300	00885.HK	0.6614	**0.6986**
00886.HK	**0.6157**	0.5971	00887.HK	0.6329	**0.6514**
00888.HK	**0.6800**	0.6786	00889.HK	0.6371	**0.6386**
00891.HK	0.6400	**0.6571**	00893.HK	0.5143	**0.6214**
00894.HK	**0.6386**	**0.6386**	00895.HK	0.5286	**0.5314**
00896.HK	0.6071	**0.6214**	00897.HK	**0.6357**	0.6286
00898.HK	**0.6557**	**0.6557**	00899.HK	0.6400	**0.6443**
AttLSTM Win	56	Total Num	72	AttLSTM Win	77.78%

Note: The bold values are those greater prediction accuracies between AttLSTM model and LSTM model in the corresponding stock.

Table 4. Contingency table.

	LSTM Correct	LSTM Incorrect
AttLSTM Correct	25938	4295
AttLSTM Incorrect	3537	16630

analysis. The calculated p-value of the McNemar's test is less than $1.0E-17$. This also shows the power of attention mechanism in LSTM-based stock movement prediction. The contingency table for all the datasets is given by table 4.

4.3. Results after parameter tuning

The deep learning models' (AttLSTM and LSTM) parameters used for tuning are input size, batch size and learning rate. To effective train the AttLSTM and LSTM model, we test two levels of input size, three levels of batch size and two levels of learning rate. These parameters and their levels are summarized in table 5. We use the parameter setting which

Table 5. AttLSTM(LSTM) parameters and corresponding test levels.

Parameters	Levels
Input Size	[10, 20]
Batch Size	[512, 256, 128]
Learning Rate	[0.001, 0.1]

has the highest prediction accuracy on validation dataset to do the test. For illustration purpose, we use the stock with the stock code between 00500.HK and 00537.HK to show the

effectiveness of the attention mechanism. The detailed results are shown in table 6, which also show the attention advantage in LSTM-based stock price movement prediction. It should be pointed that tuning parameters can take plenty of time to run on those datasets. For illustration purpose and time consideration, we only choose limited parameters to show the results. In addition, the tuning method used in this paper will automatically choose the best parameter setting for constructing the LSTM/AttLSTM model in stock movement prediction. Those best parameters for each dataset are shown in table 7. The calculated p-value of the Wilcoxon Signed Test is 0.025.

Table 6. Comparison results.

NAME	LSTM	AttLSTM	NAME	LSTM	AttLSTM
00500.HK	0.5857	**0.6057**	00503.HK	0.5300	**0.5700**
00505.HK	0.6271	**0.6343**	00506.HK	0.5214	**0.5414**
00508.HK	**0.6729**	**0.6729**	00509.HK	0.6514	**0.6557**
00510.HK	0.5971	**0.6757**	00511.HK	0.5029	**0.5114**
00512.HK	0.6014	**0.6186**	00513.HK	0.6300	**0.6314**
00515.HK	0.6086	**0.6114**	00517.HK	**0.5500**	0.5443
00518.HK	0.6314	**0.6529**	00519.HK	**0.6457**	0.6343
00521.HK	**0.6300**	0.6171	00522.HK	**0.5186**	0.4786
00524.HK	**0.6786**	0.6671	00525.HK	0.4986	**0.5357**
00526.HK	0.6614	**0.6643**	00527.HK	0.7329	**0.7357**
00528.HK	**0.6371**	**0.6371**	00529.HK	0.6100	**0.6286**
00530.HK	0.5429	**0.5471**	00531.HK	0.6543	**0.6743**
00532.HK	**0.6814**	0.6771	00533.HK	**0.5857**	**0.5857**
00535.HK	0.6171	**0.6300**	00536.HK	0.6357	**0.6386**
AttLSTM Win	22	Total Num	28	AttLSTM Win	78.57%

Note: The bold values are those greater prediction accuracies between AttLSTM model and LSTM model in the corresponding stock.

Table 7. Best parameter comparison.

NAME	AttLSTM			LSTM		
	Input size	Batch size	Learning rate	Input size	Batch size	Learning rate
00500.HK	20	128	0.001	10	128	0.100
00503.HK	10	256	0.100	20	512	0.001
00505.HK	10	256	0.100	20	512	0.100
00506.HK	10	256	0.001	10	512	0.100
00508.HK	10	512	0.001	10	512	0.001
00509.HK	10	512	0.001	10	256	0.100
00510.HK	20	128	0.001	20	512	0.001
00511.HK	20	256	0.100	10	512	0.100
00512.HK	20	256	0.001	10	256	0.100
00513.HK	10	512	0.001	10	128	0.001
00515.HK	10	128	0.100	10	128	0.100
00517.HK	20	128	0.100	10	256	0.100
00518.HK	10	128	0.100	20	512	0.100
00519.HK	10	512	0.001	20	256	0.001
00521.HK	20	128	0.100	10	128	0.100
00522.HK	10	256	0.100	10	128	0.100
00524.HK	10	256	0.001	10	512	0.100
00525.HK	10	256	0.001	10	128	0.100
00526.HK	10	512	0.001	10	512	0.001
00527.HK	10	512	0.001	10	256	0.100
00528.HK	10	256	0.001	10	256	0.001
00529.HK	20	128	0.001	10	512	0.100
00530.HK	10	512	0.001	20	512	0.001
00531.HK	20	256	0.100	20	256	0.100
00532.HK	20	512	0.001	20	256	0.100
00533.HK	20	512	0.001	20	512	0.001
00535.HK	20	256	0.001	10	256	0.001
00536.HK	20	256	0.001	10	128	0.100

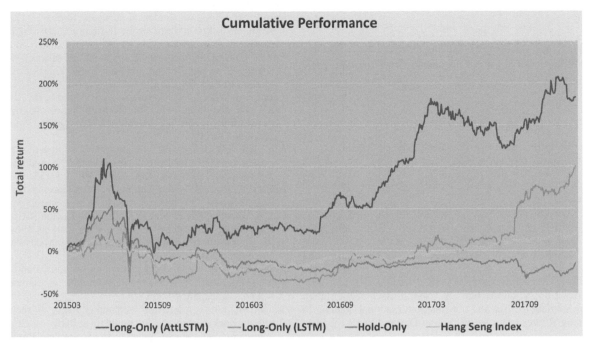

Figure 7. Cumulative performance.

4.4. Trading strategy

A simple 'Long-Only' strategy is constructed. We aim to show that a profitable strategy can be build based on the prediction results by the proposed model. We take 700 days as the investment trading days which is the prediction days in the experiments. The observed stocks are those listed in the table 6. We use the prediction results of the proposed model to make a selection on those stocks. For each day t, all wealth will be equally invested on those stocks which are predicted to have positive movements. If all observed stocks are predicted to have negative movements, no investment would be made on those stocks. The trading price of each stock is the close price of that day. The Hang Seng Index is used as a benchmark. Another benchmark 'Hold-Only' strategy is that we invest equal wealth on those stocks at the first day and hold them until the last day. The total return after d days' trading is

$$\text{total return} = \prod_{t=1}^{d}(1 + \text{return}_t) - 1.$$

The performance of the proposed strategy is shown in figure 7.

The trading performance in figure 7 shows that the simple 'Long-Only' strategy is better than the benchmark strategy and the Hang Seng Index. During the 700-day period, the stocks in table 6 contribute 19 600 observations. The base percentage of positive and negative movement days over all 700 days for all the stocks are 37.12% and 62.88%. The calculated positive movement recalls for AttLSTM model and LSTM model are 11.41% and 12.16%. The calculated positive movement precisions for AttLSTM model and LSTM model are 43.92% and 40.86% which are greater than the base percentage 37.12%. The calculated negative movement recalls for AttLSTM model and LSTM model are 91.40%

and 89.61%. The calculated negative movement precisions for AttLSTM model and LSTM model are 63.60% and 63.34% which are greater than the base percentage 62.88%. It shows that attention-based LSTM model has better prediction performance in stock movement than the LSTM model. In addition, figure 7 also shows the power of attention mechanism in the simple 'Long-Only' strategy.

5. Conclusion

In this paper, the attention mechanism has been explored in LSTM-based stock price movement prediction. The Hong Kong market stocks are chosen to verify the effectiveness of the attention mechanism. The performance of proposed models has been evaluated on more than one hundred Hong Kong stocks. In addition, the parameter tuning results also show the improvement of the attention mechanism in LSTM based prediction. What's more, a simple 'Long-Only' strategy is proposed to verify the profitability of the attention mechanism in LSTM-based stock price movement prediction.

Acknowledgments

We gratefully acknowledge the support of NVIDIA Corporation with the donation of the Titan X Pascal GPU used for this research.

Disclosure statement

No potential conflict of interest was reported by the authors.

Funding

This work is supported by Huazhong University of Science and Technology Double First-Class Funds for Humanities and Social Sciences.

ORCID

Shun Chen ⓘ http://orcid.org/0000-0002-8318-7960
Lei Ge ⓘ http://orcid.org/0000-0001-8715-0797

References

Abu-Mostafa, Y.S. and Atiya, A.F., Introduction to financial forecasting. *Appl. Intell.*, 1996, **6**, 205–213.

Al-Hmouz, R., Pedrycz, W. and Balamash, A., Description and prediction of time series: A general framework of granular computing. *Expert Syst. Appl.*, 2015, **42**, 4830–4839.

Bahdanau, D., Cho, K. and Bengio, Y., Neural machine translation by jointly learning to align and translate. International Conference on Learning Representations 2015, San Diego, CA, 1–15, May, 2015.

Barak, S. and Modarres, M., Developing an approach to evaluate stocks by forecasting effective features with data mining methods. *Expert Syst. Appl.*, 2015, **42**, 1325–1339.

Booth, A., Gerding, E. and McGroarty, F., Automated trading with performance weighted random forests and seasonality. *Expert Syst. Appl.*, 2014, **41**, 3651–3661.

Chen, K., Zhou, Y. and Dai, F., A LSTM-based method for stock returns prediction: A case study of China stock market. Proceedings of the 2015 IEEE International Conference on Big Data, Santa Clara, CA, 2823–2824, October, 2015.

Cho, K., Merrienboer, B.V., Gulcehre, C., Bahdanau, D., Bougares, F., Schwenk, H. and Bengio, Y., Learning phrase representations using RNN Encoder–Decoder for statistical machine translation. Proceedings of the 2014 Conference on Empirical Methods in Natural Language Processing, Doha, Qatar, 1724–1734, October, 2014.

Chorowski, J.K., Bahdanau, D., Serdyuk, D., Cho, K. and Bengio, Y., Attention-based models for speech recognition. 28th Annual Conference on Neural Information Processing Systems, Montreal, Canada, 577–585, December, 2015.

Desimone, R. and Duncan, J., Neural mechanisms of selective visual attention. *Annu. Rev. Neurosci.*, 1995, **18**, 193–222.

Fang, X., DeepTrade_keras on GitHub, 2018. Available online at: https://github.com/happynoom/DeepTrade_keras (accessed 10 March 2018).

Fortier, M., TA-Lib: Technical analysis library – Home, 2007. Available online at: https://www.ta-lib.org/ (accessed 20 February 2018).

Itti, L., Koch, C. and Niebur, E., A model of saliency-based visual attention for rapid scene analysis. *IEEE Trans. Pattern. Anal. Mach. Intell.*, 1998, **20**, 1254–1259.

Jiang, Z.Q., Wang, G.J., Canabarro, A., Podobnik, B., Xie, C., Stanley, H.E. and Zhou, W.X., Short term prediction of extreme returns based on the recurrence interval analysis. *Quant. Finance*, 2018, **18**, 353–370.

Kim, K.J. and Han, I., Genetic algorithms approach to feature discretization in artificial neural networks for the prediction of stock price index. *Expert Syst. Appl.*, 2000, **19**, 125–132.

LeCun, Y., Bengio, Y. and Hinton, G., Deep learning. *Nature*, 2015, **521**, 436–444.

Liu, S., Zhang, C. and Ma, J., CNN-LSTM neural network model for quantitative strategy analysis in stock markets. Proceedings of the Neural Information Processing, Kuching, Malaysia, 198–206, November, 2017.

Rodrigues, A.A. and Lleo, S., Combining standard and behavioral portfolio theories: A practical and intuitive approach. *Quant. Finance*, 2018, **18**, 707–717.

Samarawickrama, A.J.P. and Fernando, T.G.I., A recurrent neural network approach in predicting daily stock prices an application to the Sri Lankan stock market. Proceedings of the 2017 IEEE International Conference on Industrial and Information Systems, Peradeniya, Sri Lanka, 1–6, December, 2017.

Sutskever, I., Vinyals, O. and Le, Q.V., Sequence to sequence learning with neural networks. Proceedings of the 27th International Conference on Neural Information Processing Systems, Montreal, Canada, 3104–3112, December, 2014.

Vaswani, A., Shazeer, N., Parmar, N., Uszkoreit, J., Jones, L., Gomez, A.N., Kaiser, L. and Polosukhin, I., Attention is all you need. Proceedings of the 30th International Conference on Neural Information Processing Systems, Long Beach, CA, 6000–6010, December, 2017.

Wiki, Hong Kong stock exchange. Available online at: https://en.wikipedia.org/wiki/Hong_Kong_Stock_Exchange (accessed 10 April 2018).

Yang, Z., Yang, D., Dyer, C., He, X., Smola, A. and Hovy, E., Hierarchical attention networks for document classification. Proceedings of the 2016 Conference of the North American Chapter of the Association for Computational Linguistics: Human Language Technologies, San Diego, CA, 1480–1489, June, 2016.

Zhang, W., Wang, W., Wang, J. and Zha, H., User-guided hierarchical attention network for multi-modal social image popularity prediction. Proceedings of the 2018 World Wide Web Conference, Lyon, France, 1277–1286, April, 2018.

Learning multi-market microstructure from order book data

GEONHWAN JU ⓘ, KYOUNG-KUK KIM ⓘ and DONG-YOUNG LIM ⓘ

(*Received 28 June 2018; accepted 6 May 2019; published online 10 July 2019*)

In this paper, we investigate market behaviors at high-frequency using neural networks trained with order book data. Experiments are done intensively with 110 asset pairs covering 97% of spot-futures pairs in the Korea Exchange. An efficient training scheme that improves the performance and training stability is suggested, and using the proposed scheme, the lead–lag relationship between spot and futures markets are measured by comparing the performance gains of each market data set for predicting the other. In addition, the gradients of the trained model are analyzed to understand some important market features that neural networks learn through training, revealing characteristics of the market microstructure. Our results show that highly complex neural network models can successfully learn market features such as order imbalance, spread-volatility correlation, and mean reversion.

1. Introduction

The wide adoption and large market share of high-frequency trading and algorithmic trading is no news in current financial markets. This practice, also called quantitative trading in the financial markets, has been brought about by three major components: first, the availability of huge and detailed trading data from financial markets, second, advances in computing power and storage capability, and third, significant developments in trading algorithms. Based on the SEC's concept release on equity market structure, high-frequency trading is responsible for 50% or higher of trading volumes in the US equity markets. Such a substantial proportion of high-frequency trading brings the demand for revisiting some stylized facts derived from low-frequency data, and analyzing the nature of the market structure from the viewpoint of high-frequency dynamics. The main content of this paper is to accomplish this task using neural networks which are trained to predict short-term price movements with order book data, particularly because neural networks are known to perform well for large and complex datasets.

A great deal of effort to predict stock prices has already been devoted to by academic researchers and practitioners. There are many works which employ both support vector machines (SVM) or artificial neural networks (ANN) to develop a prediction system. We refer the reader to recent survey papers rather than enumerating all related studies. Sapankevych and Sankar (2009) provided a good survey of the SVM approach in financial market prediction and many applications for time series data. Li and Ma (2010) surveyed the application of ANNs in forecasting asset prices. After entering the high-frequency world, the form of data has changed from daily time series data to huge and high-dimensional TAQ historical data. Thus, ANN armed with a deep neural network that can accommodate 'big data' has become more preferable in predicting future price movements. Except for Kercheval and Zhang (2015) who use SVMs, neural network models, mainly recurrent neural network (RNN), are employed to learn future price movements from limit order books, as in Dixon (2017), Sirignano (2018) and Sirignano and Cont (2018).

In this paper, we suggest an efficient network architecture and training schemes to improve the performance and training stability, which ensures the capability of the network to learn various market features from raw data. The performance of two popular neural network architectures, multi-layer perceptron (MLP) and RNN, are compared and the results indicate that MLP outperforms RNN in terms of predictive power across a wide range of assets if various input features are preprocessed and fed into the network. After verifying the training stability and performance of the network, we measure the lead–lag relationship between the futures market and the spot market of the underlying at a high-frequency level, and identify market features that drive the price dynamics.

To investigate the lead–lag relationship between futures and spot markets with a tick-level data set, we define and compute a performance gain, a measure of how informative each market data set is to forecast price movements of the other market. When futures market data are used as additional input data for predicting the next spot price movements, there is a substantial increase in performance compared to the model solely trained with the spot market data. On the other hand, it turns out that stock market data is superfluous for looking ahead at futures prices. This shows the existence of information asymmetry between the futures and spot markets. This finding is consistent with the majority of results in the literature. See Kawaller *et al.* (1987), Stoll and Whaley (1990), Abhyankar (1999), Min and Najand (1999), Judge and Reancharoen (2014) and references therein. Furthermore, we find that such lead–lag relationships are observed regardless of trading activity level.

A gradient-based analysis method is proposed to interpret the market features that the network learned from market data. Many previous works focused on modeling the market dynamics with selected features such as bid/ask imbalance or order flows to analyze micro-movements (Cao *et al.* 2009, Cont *et al.* 2013, Gould and Bonart 2016, Yang and Zhu 2016). However, in terms of predictive power, recent approaches with machine learning techniques show better performance as in Kercheval and Zhang (2015), Dixon (2017), and Sirignano and Cont (2018). Machine learning models can handle high-dimensional features such as the full state of a limit order book. But one caveat is that little analysis has been done to interpret the market trained behaviors of predictive models. From the gradient of each input feature set, it is verified that models successfully learn peculiar market behaviors such as order imbalance, spread-volatility correlation, and mean reversion.

The rest of the paper is organized as follows. Section 2 describes the market data and experimental environments and introduces basic network architectures. An efficient network architecture and training scheme is proposed in Section 3. Finally, Section 4 reports the results of analyses on the lead–lag relationship and market microstructure.

2. Preliminaries

Let us first describe our dataset from the Korean stock/futures markets, and how input features are preprocessed from raw data in detail. Next, the basic architectures of MLP and RNN are introduced. Experimental environments including hyperparameters, frameworks, and hardware are also reported at the end of this section.

2.1. Data and market features

This study uses the entire intra-day limit orders and transactions data from the Korea Exchange, covering one month from 15 November to 13 December 2017. These records were

obtained during continuous normal trading hours, from 9:00 a.m. to 3:30 p.m. for 19 business days during the period. The dataset consists of 110 stocks and their nearby-maturity futures, representing about 97% of total pairs (110 out of 113) listed in the Korea Exchange. More specifically, the dataset includes

- tickers of the assets traded;
- submission, cancelation, and amendment of the limit orders and their time stamps;
- transaction time, price, quantity, and type (buy or sell).

From these records, we construct a basic limit order book (LOB) feature set:

$$\{\mathsf{p}_t^{a,i}, \mathsf{p}_t^{b,i}, \mathsf{v}_t^{a,i}, \mathsf{v}_t^{b,i}\}_{i=1}^{10}$$

where $\mathsf{p}_t^{a,i}$ is the ask price of the ith level at time t, and $\mathsf{v}_t^{a,i}$ represents the volume of the corresponding ask level of limit order book. Prices and volumes of bid orders are $\mathsf{p}_t^{b,i}$ and $\mathsf{v}_t^{b,i}$, respectively. For smaller i, the price is closer to the mid-price. Features include ticks with 0 volume to maintain the tick difference between levels consistent. By convention, the best bid/ask price is considered as the first level, i.e. $i = 1$.

Labels are calculated based on whether the target price will increase, stay or decrease over a small time interval Δt. The target price is the best bid/ask price in the futures/stock markets, and Δt is defined as a fixed time interval: $\{0.2\,\mathrm{s}, 0.5\,\mathrm{s}, 1\,\mathrm{s}, 2\,\mathrm{s}, 3\,\mathrm{s}, 4\,\mathrm{s}, 5\,\mathrm{s}\}$ where the time unit s is second.

In addition to the basic LOB features, we describe additional input features to improve the performance of the proposed model. This work is motivated by the path-dependency of price processes. Although most mathematical models for high-frequency trading assume that the price evolution follows a Markov process for analytical tractability, indeed, many empirical studies find evidence on the non-Markovian nature of price changes. See Cartea *et al.* (2015) and Sirignano and Cont (2018). Contrary to RNNs which is capable of analyzing sequential data by the network architecture, the activations in MLPs flow only from the input layer to the output layer. Thus, we need to manually supply historical information as inputs for MLPs to reach satisfactory results when the labels heavily rely on historical data. We use three different path dependent features: moving average prices, order flows, and arrival rates. By conducting comprehensive experiments, we find that the inclusion of such path dependent features is critical in improving the performance of MLPs.

We use seven different time windows $\{5\,\mathrm{s}, 10\,\mathrm{s}, 60\,\mathrm{s}, 120\,\mathrm{s}, 180, 240\,\mathrm{s}, 300\,\mathrm{s}\}$ for each time-sensitive feature, meaning that we calculate the values of each input feature by looking at the data between $t - u$ and t where $u = 5\,\mathrm{s}, 10\,\mathrm{s}$, etc. and t is the current time. The first time-sensitive quantity, moving average price is one of the most popular and simplest technical indicators to identify trends, and it is calculated by averaging the volume weighted average prices (VWAP). More specifically, there are two types of VWAP:

$$\frac{\mathsf{p}_t^{a,1}\mathsf{v}_t^{a,1} + \mathsf{p}_t^{b,1}\mathsf{v}_t^{b,1}}{\mathsf{v}_t^{a,1} + \mathsf{v}_t^{b,1}}, \quad \frac{\mathsf{p}_t^{a,1}\mathsf{v}_t^{b,1} + \mathsf{p}_t^{b,1}\mathsf{v}_t^{a,1}}{\mathsf{v}_t^{a,1} + \mathsf{v}_t^{b,1}}$$

where the latter of the two values is referred to as *smart price* in Kearns and Nevmyvaka (2013). The second time-sensitive feature is the order flow which is defined as the net difference of limit order volume changes at each price level during a fixed time window. Order flows with varying time windows at each of the price levels show how market participants' overall demand and supply change over time. Lastly, we introduce the arrival rate of all limit orders over a fixed window, to capture the two well-known intra-day trading patterns. When we plot transaction volumes with respect to the time of the day, it is typically U-shaped because trading is relatively more active at the beginning and at the end of the day. Notably, one can observe that transactions driven by market orders cluster together, which is the so-called volume clustering. These phenomena are well demonstrated in Cartea *et al.* (2015). Arrival rates enable models to determine whether the current market state is active or calm.

2.2. Network architecture and experimental design

Multi-layer Perceptron. An MLP is a basic form of feedforward neural networks, composed of one input layer, hidden layers, and one output layer. Let $X = (x_1 x_2 \cdots x_m)$ be an input vector and output Y where m is the number of input features. For price movements, there are three possible outcomes, *down*, *stay* and *up*, and the probability for each direction is calculated by applying a softmax function to the three output variables, which are called logits.

Consider a two-layer feed forward network with k nodes per layer as shown in figure 1. The input value for each node is computed by a weighted sum of the values for the previous nodes plus a bias term: in matrix form,

$$H^{(1)} = (h_1^{(1)} h_2^{(1)} \cdots h_k^{(1)}) = f(XW^{(1)} + b^{(1)}),$$

where $W^{(1)} = (w_{ij}^{(1)})_{\{1 \le i \le m, 1 \le j \le k\}}$ is the weight matrix, $b^{(1)} = (b_1^{(1)} b_2^{(1)} \cdots b_k^{(1)})$ is the bias vector and f is the activation function. Similarly, we can compute $H^{(2)} = f(H^{(1)}W^{(2)} + b^{(2)})$. Then, the output layer generates three output logits $\widehat{y}_i$, which are sent to a softmax function to obtain probabilities for each direction. We denote the final output $\widehat{Y} = \text{softmax}((\widehat{y}_1 \widehat{y}_2 \widehat{y}_3)) = \text{softmax}(H^{(2)}W^{(3)} + b^{(3)})$.

The goal of training the MLP model is to properly adjust the network parameters $\Theta = (W^{(1)}, W^{(2)}, W^{(3)}, b^{(1)}, b^{(2)}, b^{(3)})$

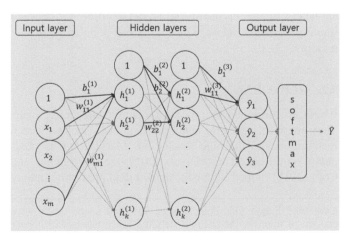

Figure 1. Architecture of an MLP.

Table 1. Configuration of an MLP model.

Number of hidden layers	2
Number of nodes per hidden layer	1000
Loss function	Negative log likelihood (NLL)
Activation function	ReLU
Normalization	Batch normalization
Optimizer	Stochastic gradient descent (SGD)

Notes: We searched the optimal architecture without overfitting or underfitting through experiments. The search range is [1,10] for the number of hidden layers, and [100,2000] for the number of hidden nodes per layer.

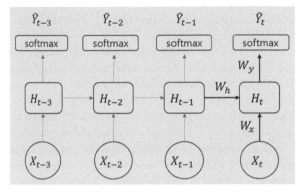

Figure 2. Architecture of a simple RNN model.

so that some suitable loss function $L(Y, \widehat{Y})$ is minimized. The most common approaches to minimize the loss function are stochastic gradient descent algorithms.

REMARK 1 When two or more hidden layers are used, we call it a deep neural network. As the number of hidden layers grows, the model becomes more capable of learning a very complex function. However, we might encounter tricky problems such as overfitting or vanishing gradient which extremely slows down the training. Several techniques have been proposed to alleviate these problems in many aspects. Glorot and Bengio (2010) found that a significant improvement can be achieved by replacing the sigmoid function, $\sigma(x) = 1/(1 + e^{-x})$, with ReLU (Rectified Linear Unit) function, $\text{ReLU}(x) = \max(x, 0)$, as an activation function. Ioffe and Szegedy (2015) suggested 'batch normalization' whose function is two-fold. First, it normalizes scales and second, it shifts the output just before the activation function of each hidden layer, allowing each layer to learn more independently by reducing covariate shift. Table 1 summarizes the network architecture of our model.

Recurrent Neural Network. RNNs are designed to learn temporal behaviors of sequential data. Typical applications include natural language processing and image captioning. Figure 2 shows a simple RNN structure with k nodes per basic cell. Assume that an input at the time t denoted by X_t is a vector in $\mathbb{R}^m$ and an output at the time t denoted by $\widehat{Y}_t$ is a vector in $\mathbb{R}^3$ as in the previous example. The key property of RNNs is to use a sequence of inputs and outputs for training and prediction.

In the RNN, the recurrent nodes in the basic cell at time t are connected from the input as well as the hidden state from the previous time step $t - 1$:

$$H_t = f(X_t, H_{t-1}) = f(X_t W_x + H_{t-1} W_h + b)$$

where the weight variable W_x is a $m \times k$ matrix, the weight variable W_h is a $k \times k$ matrix, and the bias variable b is a vector in $\mathbb{R}^k$. Here, k is the number of nodes per each basic cell as in our MLP example. The final output $\widehat{Y}_t$ is obtained by applying softmax. That is, $\widehat{Y}_t = \text{softmax}((\widehat{y_1}\widehat{y_2}\widehat{y_3})) = \text{softmax}(H_t W_y + b_y)$ where the weight variable W_y is a $k \times 3$ matrix and $b_y \in \mathbb{R}^3$. Note that the weight parameters W_x, W_h and W_y are shared by all of the recurrent loops. Training RNNs is also done by regular backpropagation, so-called backpropagation through time. In this paper, we replicate the RNN architecture suggested in Dixon (2017), with 10 time steps and one hidden layer with 20 nodes.

Experimental Settings. All MLP models are trained for 160 epochs, with the learning rate of 0.005 for initial 130 epochs,† and 0.002 for remaining 30 epochs. For RNN models, the learning rate of 0.01, 0.005, 0.002 are used with the epoch schedule of 80, 130, 160. For both types of networks, we use the batch size of 3,000, ℓ_2 regularization parameter of 0.01, and the stochastic gradient descent (SGD) optimizer with momentum of 0.9.

The whole dataset is split into two, 15 days of the training set and four days of the test set, and all of the experiments are done with seven-fold cross-validation by changing training and test sets.‡ To address the label imbalance issue, the loss contribution of each label is set to be proportional to the inverse of the ratio of the label. To be specific, these label ratios are the ratios of the number of *down, stay,* or *up* labels to the number of samples. We use PyTorch 0.3, and all models are trained on a DGX-1 server with Dual Xeon E5-2698 and eight Tesla V100 GPUs.

Each training took 10 min on average using a single GPU, resulting in the total computation time of 130 h for all 110 assets with seven-fold cross-validation. The performance of the model is measured by the area under the receiver operating characteristic (ROC) curve or simply the area under the curve (AUC). Since AUC is a measure for binary classification, one-versus-all AUC scores of three directions (*down, stay, up*) are averaged to get the final score.

3. Experiments for the network design

Several experiments are done to determine the architecture and the training scheme in order to improve performance and stability. First, we introduce the multi-task training scheme that effectively prevents overfitting while providing predictions for multiple time windows at the same time, with little additional computational cost. We also compare two architectures, MLP and RNN. Although RNN is a common approach

for learning sequential features, we show that MLP is simple and effective in terms of prediction power when various preprocessed features are fed together.

3.1. Multi-task training

One of the most common problems with training from the imbalanced dataset is *overfitting*, the loss of generalization power due to fitting training data too closely. Overfitting easily occurs when the label imbalance is severe while the model capacity is high. Figure 3 shows the typical training curve of an overfitted model. While training loss continuously decreases toward 0, test loss starts to increase after a certain point. Such occurrence of overfitting can be measured by comparing the maximum AUC score and the AUC score in the last epoch during the training, which is drawn as the red box in the right panel of figure 3.

The simplest remedy for overfitting is to stop training before the score starts to get worse. This strategy is called early stopping. This can be easy and effective, but if a model starts to overfit before fully learning the general features, it fails to achieve the maximum performance. This is why many regularization techniques like dropout or weight-decay (ℓ_2 regularization) are applied for neural networks. We suggest a simple method that can be applied to market prediction models, which we find reduces overfitting significantly.

One popular method to improve the performance and training stability of a neural network is to train feature-sharing tasks together. For example, since all image tasks share similar basic visual features like edges or color blobs, the overall performance of object detection/classification increases when the network is trained with additional images from multi-class dataset, instead of just a single class. For the market prediction model, the easiest way to get feature-sharing tasks is to generate labels for different time delays. With seven different time delays (0.2, 0.5, 1, 2, 3, 4, 5) in seconds,§ a total of 14 labels from the best bid/ask price movements were trained simultaneously for the output of 42 logits (*down, stay, up* logits for each label). As shown in figure 4, this multi-task training effectively prevents overfitting and improves the performance (2.3% on average) with little additional computational cost. Another advantage of this method is that trained models produce predictions for multiple time windows at the same time, without having to train multiple models separately for different labels. Figure 5 is the histogram of the difference between training loss and test loss, which is another popular overfitting measure.

3.2. MLP vs. RNN

RNNs are designed to process sequential data effectively. They are widely used for many practical tasks such as speech recognition and machine translation. Market data is obviously sequential. Thus, Dixon (2017) and Sirignano and Cont (2018) trained RNNs for market data prediction mainly

---

† Since the number of data varies with asset, longer training epochs are required for assets with less market activity. We find that 160 epochs are enough to guarantee the convergence for all assets.

‡ From the cross-validation results, we found that using training data whose dates are after the test set gives no performance gain on predicting the micro-movements. This is mainly due to the highly localized characteristics of the short-term price dynamics.

---

§ We tried longer time delays up to 60 s, and seven labels were enough to improve the training stability. Since labels with longer time delay are less correlated with short-term price movements, using more labels with longer time delays results in underfitting.

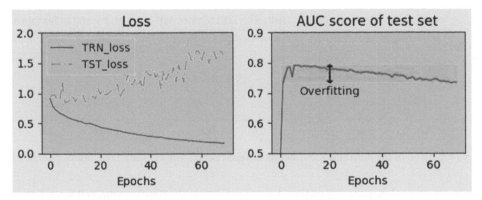

Figure 3. Training curves from the overfitted model: (left) training loss (TRN_loss) and test loss (TST_loss) are compared (right) AUC scores of the test set. All results are based on single task training (with label of 0.5 s) and the LOB data of futures prices of a single asset.

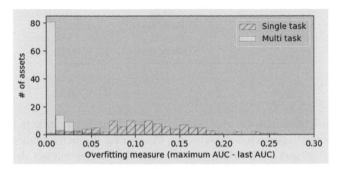

Figure 4. Overfitting measures from single task training and multi-task training. Histograms are based on overfitting measures of all the futures prices of 110 assets.

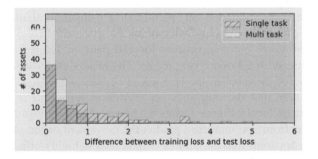

Figure 5. Difference between training and test loss for single task training and multi-task training.

with LOB states, expecting the networks to learn time-sensitive features of the market without any preprocessing.

Alternatively, one can preprocess selected time-sensitive features and feed them directly into an MLP model without recurrent loops. These two approaches are compared with three experimental settings: (1) MLP with LOB features, (2) RNN with LOB features, and (3) MLP with the full feature set. Here, we mean moving averages, arrival rates, and order flows in addition to LOB features by the full feature set. For RNN, two order flow features are fed together as in Dixon (2017). The first experiment only uses the current LOB status to predict price movements, while RNN predicts with 10 previous LOB states. By having the current LOB state only, we can study the existence of non-Markovian market dynamics. Somewhat surprisingly, the score difference between these two experiments is minor as shown in the left

two panels of in figure 6 although the higher score of RNN is ascribable to the trained time-sensitive features of RNN. On the other hand, when the MLP model is trained with the pre-processed feature set, the performance gain is significant and the variance is also reduced. See the right panel in figure 6.

Although we do not report in details, we find that batch normalization and adjusting loss weights for imbalanced labels stabilize the training process regardless of the price levels of assets considered or label ratios. For the rest of the paper, all results are obtained from the best-working setting, i.e. the MLP model with batch normalization layers trained with the multi-task scheme and the full feature set.

4. Market analysis using neural network models

This section provides an analysis of multi-market microstructure based on the trained neural network model. Section 4.1 examines the information inefficiency between the futures market and the spot market to investigate their lead–lag relationship. Next, Section 4.2 discusses how market features are interrelated to the micro-movements of market prices, by analyzing the gradients with respect to each feature set.

4.1. Multi-market information inefficiency

There is a rich literature on the lead–lag relationship between the futures and spot markets. Although reported findings are diverse in methodologies, countries, data frequency/period, the majority of them report that there is a tendency for the futures market to lead the spot market. To name a few, Kawaller *et al.* (1987) showed that S&P futures prices significantly affect subsequent S&P 500 index movements based on a vector auto-regression model. Stoll and Whaley (1990) gave a similar finding that S&P 500 and major market index futures tend to lead the stock market by about 5 min on average. Then, a variety of quantitative methods have been used to clarify the relationship between derivative markets and their underlying asset markets. We refer the reader to Judge and Reancharoen (2014) for an overview of the literature until 2014. More recently, Huth and Abergel (2014) studied a lead–lag relationship measured by a cross-correlation function using tick-by-tick data. They showed that the lead–lag

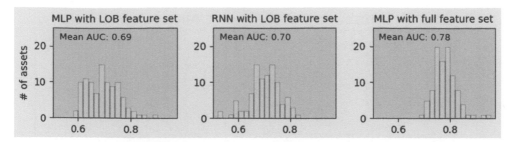

Figure 6. Comparison of the performances from three experimental settings for all the futures prices of 110 assets.

relationship is closely related to the level of liquidity, observing that more liquid assets tend to lead less liquid assets. Zhou and Wu (2016) used four different econometric models to see a high-frequency relationship between the futures market and the spot market. In Wang *et al.* (2017), a thermal optimal path method is employed to identify the long-term and the short-term relationship between the two markets in China.

Our analysis is distinguished from the literature in three ways. Firstly, on the contrary to popular econometric models such as vector auto-regression or other linear models that focus on the linear interdependence among multivariate time series, our method is able to capture non-linear relationships between futures and spot price dynamics as well as their LOB states. Secondly, the neural network model reflects short-term information inefficiency, which may dissipate in a very short time. Numerous papers investigated the existence of the lead–lag relationship in a variety of time scales, however, they usually focus on relatively low-frequency data so that it may be inadequate to extend those findings to the short-run causal relationship in a high-frequency setting. Lastly, our analysis covers almost every pair of futures contracts and their underlying assets in the Korea Exchange based on our massive and complete data set, whereas results in the literature are often based on stock index futures and underlying spot indices. This advantage enables us to look into any relationship between information asymmetry (the futures and spot markets) and liquidity asymmetry (various assets with different market activity levels).

In an ideal situation, the relationship between the price of a futures contract F_t and the price of the underlying asset S_t at the time t is given by

$$F_t = S_t e^{(r-d)(T-t)} \qquad (1)$$

where r is the risk-free interest rate, d is the dividend yield of the underlying asset and T is the maturity of the futures contract under the assumption that r and d are known and constant. In perfectly efficient markets, the violation of the relation (1) should disappear instantaneously. However, if there is information inefficiency between the two markets, the lead–lag relationship could arise. Indeed, many empirical studies reported that futures prices move first, and then pull stock prices to remove arbitrage.

To investigate such market behaviors, we consider four experimental settings $\mathscr{A}$, $\mathscr{B}$, $\mathscr{C}$, and $\mathscr{D}$ of which details are shown in table 2. For example, the network of Experiment $\mathscr{A}$ predicts the direction of spot prices using the full feature set from the spot market only. On the other hand, the network

Table 2. Four experimental settings to obtain performance gains.

Experiment	Input data	Prediction
$\mathscr{A}$	Spot	Spot
$\mathscr{B}$	Futures, spot	Spot
$\mathscr{C}$	Futures	Futures
$\mathscr{D}$	Futures, spot	Futures

of Experiment $\mathscr{B}$ uses all the features from both markets to predict spot price movements. Comparing the performances of $\mathscr{A}$ and $\mathscr{B}$ would reveal whether the futures market data is informative to forecast spot price movements, and we consider this as the performance gain from the futures market. Similarly, the performance gain from the spot market data for predicting futures price movements is estimated by comparing Experiment $\mathscr{C}$ and Experiment $\mathscr{D}$. For each asset and each cross-validation set, performance gains are calculated and averaged over cross-validations.

We carry out experiments for 110 pairs of futures contracts and their underlying assets. The results are visualized only for the label of the best ask price after 0.5 s. However, we note that the outcomes are consistent across all of the fourteen labels. Figure 7 plots the histograms of performance gains from one market to predict the movement of the other. It is apparent that the futures market data is highly effective to improve the predictability of spot price movements. Performance gains are positive for most assets as shown in the shaded bars in the figure. On the other hand, the performance gains from the spot market, that is, when the spot market data is an additional input, are distributed around zero. This implies that the spot market data is not significantly helpful for predicting futures market price movements. Such information asymmetry between the two markets illustrates the unidirectional flow of information from the futures market to the spot market across a wide range of asset pairs.

We also explore the behavior of information gain with respect to the degree of market activity, defined by the average LOB changes per day. Figure 8 depicts that information asymmetry between the two markets can be observed, irrespective of the degree of market activity.

Many papers argue that the causal relationship between futures prices and spot prices is attributed to high liquidity as well as low transaction cost and less restrictive regulations in the futures market. Along this line of arguments, we examine whether the predictive performance is influenced by liquidity asymmetry. To proxy liquidity asymmetry, we measure the

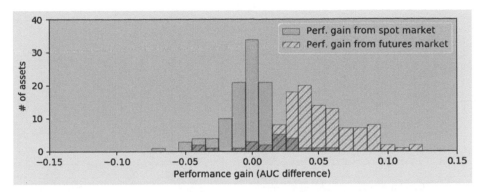

Figure 7. Illustration of performance gains from multi-market data.

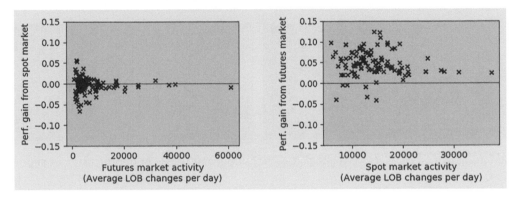

Figure 8. Performance gain with respect to market activity.

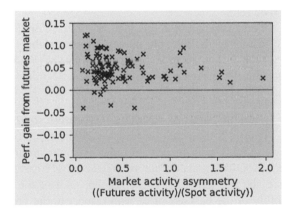

Figure 9. Performance gain with respect to the relative difference in market activity.

relative difference of market activities defined by

$$\frac{\text{average number of LOB changes in the futures market per day}}{\text{average number of LOB changes in the spot market per day}}.$$

As the value of market activity asymmetry is away from one, there is a large imbalance of liquidity between the two markets. Figure 9 indicates that there is no significant correlation between these quantities.

Lastly, we analyze the performance gains for different labels in order to check the persistence of the performance gain from the futures market in predicting spot price movements. As shown in figure 10, it is observed that the gain from multi-market data gradually decreases as the model predicts price movements for a longer time scale. This observation indicates that the contribution of the information from the futures market depreciates as the label time increases. Nevertheless, we emphasize that models trained with multi-market data still outperform models trained on a single market, on average even when the model predicts the spot price movements after 5 s.

4.2. Micro-movement analysis using gradients

4.2.1. Introduction. Previous studies on the relationship between high-frequency market features and short-term movements can be grouped into two categories: the first is the model-focused approach that concentrates on modeling the dynamics of micro-movements with selected input features, and the second is the prediction-focused approach which uses machine learning techniques to improve the predictive performance on price movements. Although the latter results in stronger predictive power, the downside is that it provides little information or intuition about the price dynamics. This is because it is highly non-trivial to interpret trained parameters due to the model complexity and the high dimensionality of input features. In this section, we visualize the effects of market features on price dynamics at a micro level by utilizing gradient information.

Gradient Visualization. Since the early 2010s, neural networks, especially convolutional neural networks, have become widely used for many image-related tasks such as object classification and detection. But, even the quite simple networks in practice contain more than hundreds of parameters, and this makes identifying the basis of network outputs

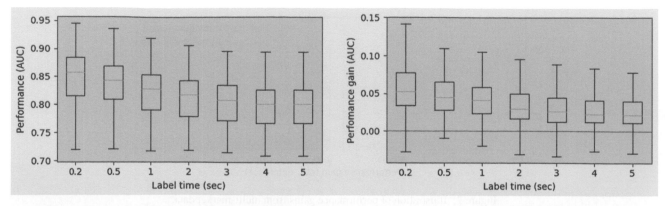

Figure 10. Performance and performance gain in predicting the spot price movements at each label time.

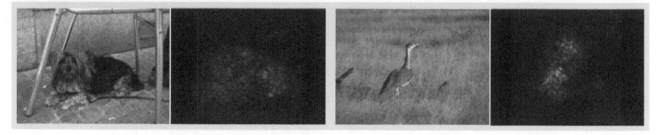

Figure 11. Gradient visualization of CNN. The first and third are images from the test set of ILSVRC-2013, and the others are images in Simonyan *et al.* (2014).

not straightforward. Many techniques have been proposed to visualize and interpret the outputs of trained networks. Among them, Simonyan *et al.* (2014) suggested a visualization technique based on the gradient of a specific label of interest with respect to input pixels. The idea behind this is simple. If there is a meaningful image area, which is basically a group of pixels, the prediction probability will be much more sensitive to the changes of pixels in that area than in other areas.

Figure 11 shows the original input images and gradient magnitudes of each pixel for *dog* and *bird* label, respectively. Left two images show that the gradient magnitudes of *dog* label are large in the region where the dog presents, and the gradient map of *bird* label on the right highlights the location of the bird.

A similar idea can be applied to analyze the influence of input features to the output of a network. For a neural network model G and an input vector $X = (x_1 x_2 \cdots x_m)$, an output $\widehat{Y} = G(X)$ and gradient $G_{x_i} = \partial G(X)/\partial x_i$ are calculated via feedforward and backpropagation. A positive G_{x_1} means that $\widehat{Y}$ increases as x_1 increases. If G_{x_2} is negative in addition, this implies that the change of the output $\Delta \widehat{Y}$ is positively correlated to the difference of two input changes, $\Delta x_1 - \Delta x_2$. We extend this simple relationship to multiple inputs to analyze gradient plots.

In our model, unlike images that objects can appear anywhere, the same type of information is fed to the exact same location. This means that gradients can be averaged over the whole dataset to observe the overall influence of each feature set on price movements. We visualize the average gradients of outputs only for the time window of 0.5 s, but the patterns are similar for other time windows as well. There are three output logits for each side of the market, so we have six plots from *down*, *stay*, and *up* logits of the best ask and bid price.

For the rest of this section, we present an analysis for four feature sets: LOB volume, LOB price, moving average price, and arrival rate.

All the results reported in this section are based on the prediction results of the best bid and ask prices in the futures markets with 110 assets utilizing the input data of the futures market. This corresponds to Experiment $\mathscr{C}$ in Section 4.1.

4.2.2. Gradient analysis of market features. *LOB Volumes.* Figure 12 shows the average gradients $G_{V^{a,i}}$, $G_{V^{b,i}}$ of six logit outputs with respect to order volumes around the mid-price. All the gradients are averaged over 110 assets. For instance, the top left panel is the gradient plot of the down probability of the best ask price with respect to the volumes at 10 price levels. The most prominent feature in the figure is the peak at the best ask with a positive sign and negative values at bid prices. See the dashed box in the top left panel. This visualizes a well-known correlation between the bid/ask order imbalance and price movement, as many existing studies indicate. For an illustration, assume the volume at the best ask grows and the volume at the best bid shrinks. This order imbalance increases the down probability of the best ask price and decreases the up probability of the best ask price, pushing the price levels downward. Similarly, for the up or down probability of the best bid price, we see that peaks are formed at the best bid and that bid/ask imbalance has similar effects on the target logit output.

Another interesting observation is that the effects of volumes on the bid (or ask) side on the down/up probabilities of the best bid (or ask) are not consistent across bid (or ask) price levels. See, for instance, the solid box in the bottom right panel. This might look counter-intuitive at first glance because the increases in bid orders beyond the best bid seem

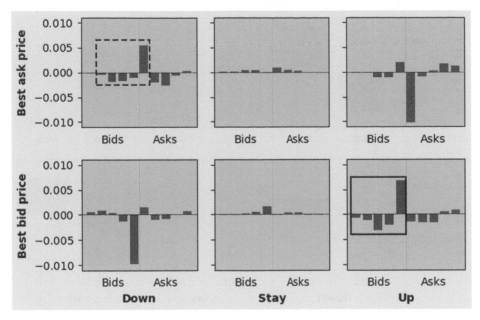

Figure 12. Gradients of down (left), stay (middle), up (right) probabilities of the best bid/ask prices with respect to the order volumes at 10 price levels. The dashed box in the top left panel highlights the effect of the bid/ask order imbalance on the price movement. The solid box in the bottom right panel highlights the effect of bid order imbalance on the price movement. All gradient plots are averaged over 110 assets.

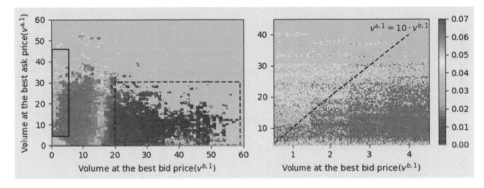

Figure 13. $G_{v^{b,1}}$ of up probability of the best ask price at different levels of $v_t^{b,1}$ and $v_t^{a,1}$, from Samsung Electronics futures. The plot in the right shows the area in the solid box. Notes: Since the levels of input features and gradients vary with assets, we choose a single asset for the visualization. To avoid overlapping points, each point with coordinate (x, y) is randomly moved to (x', y'), where $x' \sim \text{Unif}(x - 0.5, x + 0.5)$ and $y' \sim \text{Unif}(y - 0.5, y + 0.5)$.

to induce the downward price movement. However, one can argue that this phenomenon actually indicates another order imbalance feature, which may be called 'bid imbalance' or 'ask imbalance' depending on the type of the order. Suppose, for a fixed total volume of orders on the bid side, bid orders become biased toward the best bid. In other words, the orders beyond the best bid decrease while the volume at the best bid increases. Then, the gradient plot in the solid box of figure 12 implies that it leads to an increase in the probability of the best bid to go upward. One may think of this as the indication of the natural relationship between the market participants' average willingness-to-buy and the market price. To the best of the authors' knowledge, this kind of order imbalance has not been reported in the literature.

Although the overall influence of each input feature can be observed from the average gradients, a more closer look at individual assets' gradients reveals non-linear behaviors of the trained neural network. Figure 13 shows the gradient $G_{v^{b,1}}$, the sensitivity of the up probability of the best price for the Samsung Electronics futures with respect to the volume at the

best bid. Recall that the positivity of this gradient implies the upward price movement according to the volume increase at the best bid. Differently from figure 12, however, we visualize gradient values at varying levels of the volumes at the best bid/ask, delivering a sort of global behaviors at different levels of the inputs.

The gradient value peaks when the volume at the best bid is between 0 and 15 and decreases significantly when $v^{b,1}$ is larger than 20 as in the dashed box. This indicates the market characteristic that the influence of an additional bid order pushing the price upward diminishes as the existing order volume increases, and converges to zero if the volume becomes large enough. The gradient also decreases when the bid–ask imbalance exceeds a certain level as in the right panel of figure 13. The plot shows that the magnitude decreases when the bid–ask imbalance exceeds 10 (the area above the dashed line). In other words, the influence of the bid volume change diminishes as the imbalance becomes so severe that the market will remain imbalanced despite a few additional bid orders.

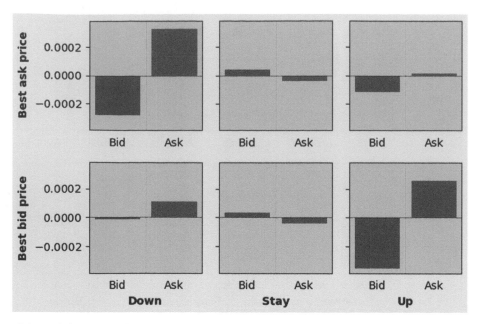

Figure 14. Gradients of down (left), stay (middle), up (right) probabilities of the best bid/ask prices with respect to bid/ask price levels. All gradient plots are averaged over 110 assets.

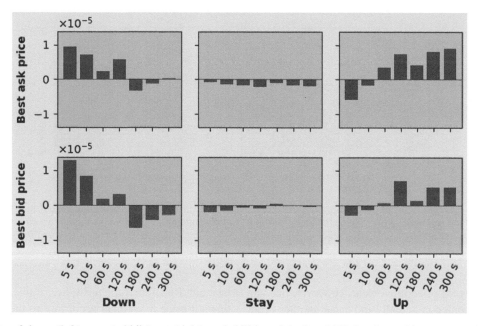

Figure 15. Gradients of down (left), stay (middle), up (right) probabilities of the best bid/ask prices with respect to the moving averages with varying lengths of time windows. All gradient plots are averaged over 110 assets.

LOB Prices. Next, we study the gradient plots of the target logit outputs with respect to the LOB price levels. Recall that we build up the LOB feature set including ticks with 0 volume. Hence, bid or ask prices levels are deterministic from the best bid/ask prices. Therefore, the gradients with respect to LOB prices boil down to the gradients with respect to the overall bid/ask price levels. This is nothing but the effect of change of variable. See figure 14 where each gradient plot has two values with respect to the bid price level and to the ask price level.

It is notable that the signs of gradients in the left and right columns are positive with respect to the ask price and negative with respect to the bid price while the values in the top left and bottom right corners are relatively greater. It turns out to be illuminating if we consider those gradients in terms of bid–ask spread and mid-price level rather than bid/ask price levels. Here, the bid–ask spread is $s_t = p_t^{a,1} - p_t^{b,1}$ and the mid-price is $m_t = (p_t^{a,1} + p_t^{b,1})/2$. With $\widehat{Y} = G(X)$, the partial derivatives G_{s_t} and G_{m_t} are calculated as $G_{p_t^{a,1}} - G_{p_t^{b,1}}$ and $2(G_{p_t^{a,1}} + G_{p_t^{b,1}})$, respectively.

In our experiments, the average G_{m_t} over all asset pairs is positive for *down* events and negative for *up* events. This implies that when the mid-price level increases, the best bid/ask prices at the next time stamp (0.5 s later in this set of experiments) have larger probabilities to go down and smaller probabilities to go up. This *mean reversion* behavior has long been observed in financial markets, and it is re-confirmed in our tick-level data.

Let us turn our attention to the gradient G_{s_t}. It is easily seen that G_{s_t} values are positive in the left and right columns whereas they are negative in the middle column from figure 14. This means, first, that the widening bid–ask spread affects the down/up probabilities of the best bid and ask prices positively, and reduces the probabilities of staying at the current price levels. In other words, there is a higher probability of price changes at the next time stamp, which can be interpreted as a positive correlation between tick-level price volatility and bid–ask spread. Bollerslev and Melvin (1994) quantified this relationship with a GARCH model, and Wyart et al. (2008) modeled the profitability of market makers, showing that adverse selection risk makes the bid–ask spread wider when the market is volatile. Zumbach (2004) also reported a strong empirical evidence for stocks included in FTSE 100. Secondly, the magnitudes of G_{s_t} are greater in the top left and bottom right panels, where the target probabilities are the probabilities of the spread narrowing events. One

plausible explanation for this is that, when the bid–ask spread widens, market participants are likely to place limit orders to fill up the order book.

Moving Average. The gradient plots for the moving average prices with varying time windows are shown in figure 15. For *down* logits, the gradient tends to decrease in the length of the time window, and increases for *up* logits regardless of whether it is for the best bid or the best ask. This observation implies that when the shorter-term moving averages increase, the best bid and ask prices have larger probabilities of going down and smaller probabilities of going up. On the contrary, when the longer-term moving averages increase, the best bid and ask prices have smaller probabilities of going down and larger probabilities of going up. In both cases, the best bid and ask prices tend to move together in a probabilistic sense. This discrepancy between short-term and long-term moving averages indicates the existence of the price reversion to the long-term moving average.

Arrival Rate. As shown in figure 16, the greater arrival rate increases the probability of price changes regardless of the

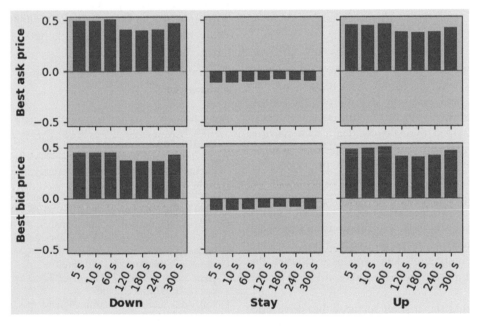

Figure 16. Gradients of down (left), stay (middle), up (right) probabilities of the best bid/ask prices with respect to the arrival rates of all limit orders in varying lengths of time windows. All gradient plots are averaged over 110 assets.

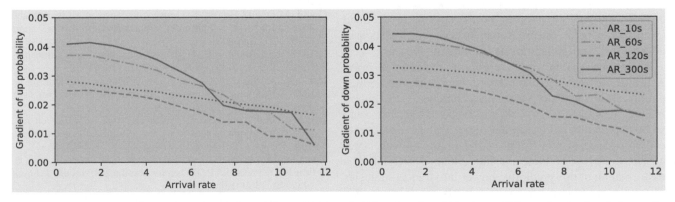

Figure 17. The average gradient values of up (left) and down (right) probability of the best bid price at different levels of arrival rate, from Samsung Electronics futures.

time window, making bid price and ask price more volatile. Besides the overall influence of arrival rates, arrival rates with the time windows of 60 s or under are more influential than arrival rates with longer time windows. The reader is reminded that the time delay is 0.5 s; however, exactly the same patterns are consistently observed for other time delays, too. This tendency tells us that a rapid increase of arrival rates within the last 1 min induces additional volatility to the market.

To further illustrate the effects of arrival rates, we record average gradient values for the up and down probabilities of the best bid with respect to different levels of arrival rates in figure 17. In other words, the figure shows a version of figure 16 conditional on the size of an arrival rate of a specific time window. From the two plots, we notice that the average gradient values are positive at all levels, i.e. added volatilities due to increased order arrivals. However, their effects on up/down probabilities diminish as arrival rates become larger. This indicates that a few extra order arrivals affect price volatility most when the arrival rate is low compared to when order arrivals are already quite high.

5. Conclusion

This paper introduced an efficient neural network architecture and training scheme for order book data. Multi-task training is a simple and easy way to improve the training performance and stability with little extra cost. Preprocessing input features helped the network learn time-sensitive features. This approach with a multi-layer perceptron model performed better than a recurrent neural network model.

Using the proposed approach, the high-frequency lead–lag relationship between spot and futures markets was examined for 110 pairs of assets. Unlike previous works that captured linear interdependence, the lead–lag relationship was calculated directly by comparing the predictive power of the neural networks with different input data. We also observed that such a lead–lag relationship persists across different market activity levels.

Lastly, we identified the market features that drive price movements by looking into the gradient information from trained neural networks. Many known market characteristics including bid/ask imbalance and mean reversion are observed from gradient plots. Other market features which have received little attention in the literature were identified as well. For instance, the order imbalances on the bid (or ask) side have non-negligible impacts on price movements.

The findings in this work are only a small part of many possibilities that we can explore with neural networks which we may call financial deep learning techniques. Other important market characteristics such as order book resilience could also be explored based on similar ideas. We also believe that the performance of prediction can be improved with larger datasets, model ensembles, and fine-tuning. Nevertheless, a transformation of this predictive power into trading strategies in dynamic and adaptive financial markets seems to remain a huge challenge, in which universal and promising outputs are yet to be seen.

Acknowledgments

The authors thank their project counterpart for providing us with valuable datasets. Constructive comments from Prof. Jinwoo Shin are greatly appreciated. Author names are in alphabetical order.

Disclosure statement

No potential conflict of interest was reported by the authors.

Funding

This work was supported by the National Research Foundation of Korea (NRF-2019R1A2C1003144).

ORCID

Geonhwan Ju ⓘ https://orcid.org/0000-0001-9661-5162
Kyoung-Kuk Kim ⓘ https://orcid.org/0000-0002-9661-8707
Dong-Young Lim ⓘ http://orcid.org/0000-0002-4677-965X

References

Abhyankar, A., Linear and nonlinear Granger causality: Evidence from the U.K. stock index futures market. *J. Futures Mark.*, 1999, **18**, 519–540.

Bollerslev, T. and Melvin, M., Bidask spreads and volatility in the foreign exchange market: An empirical analysis. *J. Int. Econ.*, 1994, **36**(3), 355–372.

Cao, C., Hansch, O. and Wang, X., The information content of an open limit-order book. *J. Futures Mark.*, 2009, **29**(1), 16–41.

Cartea, Á., Jaimungal, S. and Penalva, J., *Algorithmic and High-frequency Trading*, 2015 (Cambridge University Press: Cambridge).

Cont, R., Kukanov, A. and Stoikov, S., The price impact of order book events. *J. Financial Econom.*, 2013, **12**(1), 47–88. doi:10.1093/jjfinec/nbt003.

Dixon, M., Sequence classification of the limit order book using recurrent neural networks. *J. Comput. Sci.*, 2017, **24**, 277–286.

Glorot, X. and Bengio, Y., Understanding the difficulty of training deep feedforward neural networks. Proceedings of the Thirteenth International Conference on Artificial Intelligence and Statistics, 2010, pp. 249–256.

Gould, M.D. and Bonart, J., Queue imbalance as a one-tick-ahead price predictor in a limit order book. *Mark. Microstruc. Liquid.*, 2016, **2**(2), 1650006.

Huth, N. and Abergel, F., High frequency lead/lag relationships – empirical facts. *J. Empir. Finance*, 2014, **26**, 41–58.

Ioffe, S. and Szegedy, C., Batch normalization: Accelerating deep network training by reducing internal covariate shift. arXiv preprint arXiv:1502.03167, 2015.

Judge, A. and Reancharoen, T., An empirical examination of the lead–lag relationship between spot and futures markets: Evidence from Thailand. *Pacific-Basic Financ. J.*, 2014, **29**, 335–358.

Kawaller, I.G., Koch, P.D. and Koch, T.W., The temporal price relationship between S&P 500 futures and the S&P index. *J. Financ.*, 1987, **42**, 1309–1329.

Kearns, M. and Nevmyvaka, Y., Machine learning for market microstructure and high frequency trading. In *High Frequency Trading – New Realities for Traders, Markets and Regulators*, edited by D. Easley, M. Lopez de Prado, and M. OHara, 2013 (Risk Books: London).

Kercheval, A.N. and Zhang, Y., Modelling high-frequency limit order book dynamics with support vector machines. *Quant. Finance*, 2015, **15**, 1315–1329.

Li, Y. and Ma, W., Applications of artificial neural networks in financial economics: A survey. *Int. Symp. Comput. Intell. Design*, 2010, **1**, 211–214.

Min, J.H. and Najand, M., A further investigation of the lead–lag relationship between the spot market and stock index futures: Early evidence from Korea. *J. Futures Mark.*, 1999, **19**(2), 217–232.

Sapankevych, N.I. and Sankar, R., Time series prediction using support vector machines: A survey. *IEEE Comput. Intell. Mag.*, 2009, **4**(2), 24–38.

Simonyan, K., Vedaldi, A. and Zisserman, A., Deep inside convolutional networks: Visualising image classification models and saliency maps. ICLR Workshop, 2014.

Sirignano, J., Deep learning for limit order books. *Quant. Finance*, 2018, **19**(4), 549–570.

Sirignano, J. and Cont, R., Universal features of price formation in financial markets: Perspectives from deep learning. Working paper, 2018.

Stoll, H.R. and Whaley, R.E., The dynamics of stock index and stock index futures returns. *J. Financ. Quant. Anal.*, 1990, **25**(4), 441–468.

Wang, D., Tu, J., Chang, X. and Li, S., The lead–lag relationship between the spot and futures markets in China. *Quant. Finance*, 2017, **17**, 1447–1456.

Wyart, M., Bouchaud, J., Kockelkoren, J., Potters, M. and Vettorazzo, M., Relation between bidask spread, impact and volatility in order-driven markets. *Quant. Finance*, 2008, **8**(1), 41–57.

Yang, T. and Zhu, L., A reduced-form model for level-1 limit order books. *Market Microstruct. Liquid.*, 2016, **2**(2), 1650008.

Zhou, B. and Wu, C., Intraday dynamic relationships between CSI 300 index futures and spot markets: A high-frequency analysis. *Neural Comput. Appl.*, 2016, **27**, 1007–1017.

Zumbach, G., How trading activity scales with company size in the FTSE 100. *Quant. Finance*, 2004, **4**(4), 441–456.

A non-linear causality test: a machine learning approach for energy futures forecast

GERMÁN G. CREAMER ⓘ and CHIHOON LEE ⓘ

(*Received 28 June 2018; accepted 6 May 2019; published online 10 July 2019*)

This paper proposes a multivariate distance nonlinear causality test (MDNC) using the partial distance correlation in a time series framework. Partial distance correlation as an extension of the Brownian distance correlation calculates the distance correlation between random vectors X and Y controlling for a random vector Z. Our test can detect nonlinear lagged relationships between time series, and when integrated with machine learning methods it can improve the forecasting power. We apply our method as a feature selection procedure and combine it with the support vector machine and random forests algorithms to study the forecast of the main energy financial time series (oil, coal, and natural gas futures). It shows substantial improvement in forecasting the fuel energy time series in comparison to the classical Granger causality method in time series.

1. Introduction

A significant challenge for current financial time series econometric models is to capture extreme events and nonlinear relationships generated by the complex forces acting on financial markets. For example, during the past 120 years there has been a steady stream of financial and banking crises, stock market bubble bursts, and credit crunches that seem to happen ever more often (Reinhart and Rogoff 2009, Gorton 2012). The effects of these catastrophic events are intensified by the fact that the contemporary time series econometric models often fail to anticipate sudden changes in data, leaving participants exposed to massive losses. The ramifications of these losses have substantial economic and social impact (Hurd and Rohwedder 2010, Butrica *et al.* 2011, Bosworth 2012, Deaton 2012). In response to these limitations, there is a growing interest in exploring nonlinear forecasting methods, especially after the financial credit crisis of 2007–09 which showed the limitation of the existent forecasting models.

We propose in this paper a multivariate distance nonlinear causality (MDNC) test based on the partial distance correlation that expands the scope of the widely used Granger causality test for an autoregressive model to the nonlinear regression model. While the Granger causality has become a standard methodological concept, it has also received criticisms mainly due to the oversimplified nature of the linear (or, parametric) dependence structure in the model. In contrast, the MDNC test is nonparametric and can be used to select the most influential lead-lagged variables, from multivariate time series, in explaining the response variable (or, vector). The proposed MDNC approach can discover nonlinear dependencies between two random vectors while controlling the influence of the third random vector in a nonparametric manner. A sequence of such tests selects a set of significant predictor variables, by entering predictors using the empirical bootstrap based p-values, selected in a stepwise forward manner, until there is no variable left to enter anymore.

We apply the MDNC test to a real dataset of coal, oil and gas futures to forecast the direction of such energy futures returns. More precisely, we use the MDNC test as a feature selection procedure and illustrate that this can improve the forecasting power of a nonlinear machine learning method such as the support vector machine and random forests. We further test for any improvement in the forecast of these energy futures using those selected nonlinear dependencies compared to a prediction based only on linear relationships such as those identified by the Granger causality test

The distance covariance and correlation, developed by Székely *et al.* (2007) and Székely and Rizzo (2009), have received considerable interest as appealing measures of dependence between two random vectors. We refer the reader in particular to Davis *et al.* (2018) for their recent developments in time series contexts. Creamer and Creamer (2016) computed nonlinear autocorrelation of financial variables via the distance correlation, and Creamer *et al.* (2013) also used the distance correlation to forecast return and volatility, while Creamer (2018) included it as part of a market risk forecasting system. Zhou (2012) applied distance correlation to evaluate financial time series introducing the auto distance correlation function. Fokianos and Pitsillou (2017) tested the pairwise dependence of time series with the distance covariance. However, none of these studies have explored the problem of variable selection via testing hypotheses of zero partial distance correlations, detecting nonlinear causality in a multivariate time series framework.

The rest of the paper is organized as follows. Section 2 introduces the linear Granger causality test, proposes MDNC, and also briefly describes support vector machine as a nonlinear forecasting method; Section 3 presents the financial time series data used; Section 4 explains in detail the estimation techniques; Section 5 shows the results of the tests, and Section 6 discusses the results.

2. Methods

2.1 Granger causality

Granger causality (Granger 1969, 1980, 2001) is a prevalent methodology used in economics, financial econometrics, as well as in many other areas of study such as neuroscience, to evaluate the linear causal relationship between two or more variables. According to the basic definition of Granger causality, the forecasting of the variable Y_t with an autoregressive process using Y_{t-l} as its lag-l value ($l = 1, \ldots, L$), should be compared with another autoregressive process using Y_{t-l} and the vector $(X_{t-1}, \ldots, X_{t-L})$ of potential explanatory variables. Thus, X_{t-l} Granger causes Y_t when X_{t-l} takes place before Y_t, and X_{t-l} has unique information to forecast Y_t that is not present in other variables.

Typically, Granger causality is tested using an autoregressive model with and without the vector $(X_{t-1}, \ldots, X_{t-L})$, such as in the following bivariate example:

$$Y_t = \sum_{l=1}^{L} \alpha_l Y_{t-l} + \epsilon_1,$$

$$Y_t = \sum_{l=1}^{L} \alpha_l Y_{t-l} + \sum_{l=1}^{L} \beta_l X_{t-l} + \epsilon_2$$

where the residual ϵ_j is a white noise: $\epsilon_j \sim N(0, \sigma^2), j = 1, 2$. We say X_{t-l} Granger causes Y_t if the null hypothesis $H_0 : \beta_l = 0$ is rejected based on the suitable F-test. The order L of the autoregressive model is selected according to either the Akaike information criterion or the Bayesian information criterion.

2.2. Multivariate distance nonlinear causality test

We propose a multivariate distance nonlinear causality test (MDNC) to detect the nonlinear causality of (controlling) multivariate time series, such as the lagged values of (multivariate) X, on the current value of Y, given the past lagged values of Y. We use a modified version for time series analysis of the partial distance correlation as proposed by Székely and Rizzo (2014) to select the most relevant lagged variables via a stepwise process.

The distance correlation (dCor) characterizes multivariate independence for random vectors X, Y and is equal to zero if and only if X and Y are independent. We summarize a few essential defining properties and computing formulas of the partial distance correlation (pdCor) for easy reference; see Székely and Rizzo (2014) for the formal definitions. The pdCor is a measure of dependence between two random vectors X and Y considering a third (controlling) random vector Z from the joint distribution (X, Y, Z). This correlation is based on an unbiased distance covariance statistic that extends the original Brownian distance correlation and Brownian distance covariance introduced by Székely and Rizzo (2009). Similar to the classical notion of partial correlation, the pdCor is defined via appropriate orthogonal projections and inner product. Letting (x, y, z) a random sample observed from the joint distribution of (X, Y, Z), the sample partial distance covariance (pdCov) is defined by

$$\text{pdCov}(x, y; z) = (P_{z^\perp}(x) \cdot P_{z^\perp}(y)),$$

where

$$P_{z^\perp}(x) = \widetilde{A} - \frac{(\widetilde{A} \cdot \widetilde{C})}{(\widetilde{C} \cdot \widetilde{C})} \widetilde{C}, \quad P_{z^\perp}(y) = \widetilde{B} - \frac{(\widetilde{B} \cdot \widetilde{C})}{(\widetilde{C} \cdot \widetilde{C})} \widetilde{C}$$

denote the orthogonal projection of $\widetilde{A}(x)$ onto $(\widetilde{C}(z))^\perp$ and the orthogonal projection of $\widetilde{B}(y)$ onto $(\widetilde{C}(z))^\perp$, respectively. Here, the (so-called $\mathcal{U}$-centered) matrices $\widetilde{A}, \widetilde{B}, \widetilde{C}$ are elements of suitable Hilbert spaces generated by the Euclidean distance matrices of n sample points $\{x_1, \ldots, x_n\}$, $\{y_1, \ldots, y_n\}$, and $\{z_1, \ldots, z_n\}$, respectively. Then, the sample partial distance correlation (pdCor) is defined as the cosine of the angle θ between the 'vectors' $P_{z^\perp}(x)$ and $P_{z^\perp}(y)$ in the suitable Hilbert space:

$$\text{pdCor}(x, y; z) = \frac{(P_{z^\perp}(x) \cdot P_{z^\perp}(y))}{|P_{z^\perp}(x)||P_{z^\perp}(y)|}$$

for $|P_{z^\perp}(x)||P_{z^\perp}(y)| \neq 0$ and otherwise $\text{pdCor}(x, y; z)$ is defined as zero. For all distributions with finite first moments, the *population* $\text{pdCor}(X, Y; Z)$ can be defined similarly for variables X, Y, Z in arbitrary dimensions (see Section 4 of Székely and Rizzo 2009).

We describe the detailed steps for our proposed multivariate distance nonlinear causality (MDNC) test in figure 1. Given the time series X, Y, Z (they could be multivariate), our goal is to detect any significant (nonlinear) lag effect of series X on the current value of Y, given some past values of Y *and* the previously selected lagged variables of X; henceforth, we use Z to denote the collection of such control variables, i.e. we remove (control for) the effect of Z on Y.

1. (Initialization) Fix $t \geq 2$ and $d, L \geq 1$. Let S be an empty set. (This set would be updated in a later step to include the relevant independent variables, i.e., predictors.) Given the lagged variables $(Y_{t-1}, \ldots, Y_{t-d})$, let $Z = (Y_{t-1}, \ldots, Y_{t-d})$. For the (multivariate) time series $(X^1, \ldots, X^K)$, consider the lag indices $i = 1, \ldots, L$.

2. (Hypothesis testing) Consider all candidate predictor variables (initially, there are KL of them) individually and carry out a sequence of hypothesis tests $H_0 : \mathrm{pdCor}(X_i^j, Y_t; Z) = 0$ vs. $H_0 : \mathrm{pdCor}(X_i^j, Y_t; Z) \neq 0$. Select the significant predictor variables, X_i^j's, that reject the null hypothesis.

3. (Updating) Update the set S so that S includes the significant lagged variables, X_i^j's, selected from the step 2 and also update the controlling series $Z = \{(Y_{t-1}, \ldots, Y_{t-d})\} \cup S$.

4. Repeat the steps 2 and 3 above until the set S can no longer be updated.

The output is the set S of significant lagged variables X_i^j's.

Figure 1. Multivariate distance nonlinear causality test (MDNC).

For the step 2 of hypothesis testing (figure 1), we employ the moving block bootstrap (MBB) introduced by Kunsch (1989) and Liu and Singh (1992) to obtain the empirical p-values of the tests. The MBB extends the bootstrap ideas to time series proposed by Efron (1979). This algorithm samples with replacement blocks of fixed length from a time series by randomly selecting endpoints. The blocks are copied in a sequence creating a bootstrap sample, and this process is repeated B times. The empirical p-value is calculated as below, using B samples of fixed block size with replacements generated by the MBB:

$$\hat{p} = \frac{1 + \sum_{b=1}^{B} I(T_b > T_0)}{1 + B}$$

where T_0 and T_b are calculated as the test statistic $\mathrm{pdCov}(x, y; z) = (P_{z^\perp}(x) \cdot P_{z^\perp}(y))$ from the complete dataset and from the bth bootstrap sample, respectively. The null hypothesis H_0 is rejected whenever $\hat{p} \leq \alpha$ for a fixed significance level α.

Some interpretations regarding a relationship between two time series X and Y, controlling for Z, are as follows.

- If $\mathrm{pdCor}(X_{t-l}, Y_t; Y_{t-1} \ldots Y_{t-d}, Z) \neq 0$ and $l \geq 1$ where Z is a lagged independent variable or the set of lagged independent variables, (i.e. predictors) previously selected, we conclude that X_{t-l} leads the series Y_t.
- If, in addition, $\mathrm{pdCor}(X_t, Y_{t-l}; X_{t-1}, \ldots, X_{t-d}, Z) = 0$ and $l \geq 1$, then there is a unidirectional relationship from X_{t-l} to Y_t.
- If $\mathrm{pdCor}(X_{t-l}, Y_t; Y_{t-1}, \ldots, Y_{t-d}, Z) \neq 0$, $\mathrm{pdCor}(X_t, Y_{t-l}; X_{t-1}, \ldots, X_{t-d}, Z) \neq 0$ and $l \geq 1$, then there is a feedback relationship between X and Y.
- If $\mathrm{pdCor}(X_{t-l}, Y_t; Y_{t-1}, \ldots, Y_{t-d}, Z) = 0$ and $\mathrm{pdCor}(X_t, Y_{t-l}; X_{t-1}, \ldots, X_{t-d}, Z) = 0$ then there is no lead-lag relationship between X and Y.

2.3. Support vector machine

Based on the set of selected lagged variables from the MDNC tests, we are to study its forecasting power using nonlinear, nonparametric machine learning algorithms, such as the support vector machine (SVM) and random forests (RF) briefly introduced in this and the following section.

SVM was proposed by Vapnik (1995) as a distribution-free classification method based on the use of kernel functions to pre-process data in a higher dimensional space than the original. This transformation allows for an optimal hyperplane to separate the data into two categories or values. SVM is a generalized linear model that finds an optimal hyperplane, which maximizes the margin between itself and the nearest training examples while ensuring the accuracy of correct classification. A hyperplane is defined as: $\{X : F(X) \doteq X^T \beta + \beta_0 = 0\}$, where $\|\beta\| = 1$. The strong prediction rule learned by SVM model is $\mathrm{sign}(F(X))$; see Hastie *et al.* (2008). The training examples that are closest to the hyperplane are called support vectors. The support vectors are determined by solving a quadratic programming problem.

For nonlinearly separable data, SVM uses nonlinear kernel functions to transform training data to a higher dimensional feature space in which the data become more separable.

2.4. Random forests

The random forests algorithm is a variant of bagged decision trees proposed by Breiman (2001). This algorithm generates multiple classification or regression trees from bootstrap samples of the training data. For each node of each tree, RF selects the best split among a subset of all the features based on a random vector θ_i sampled independently with the same distribution for any tree that is part of the forest. As a result, each regression tree generates an estimate of the numerical value of the dependent variable or each classification tree predicts a class $h(x, \theta_i)$ according to the majority vote of all the classification trees.

3. Data: energy financial time series

We apply the fuel futures—coal, oil and natural gas—to the proposed MDNC test and connect with the known interrelationship among these time series as recognized by the previous studies. Mohammadi (2011) finds that, in the case of the U.S. market, the oil and natural gas prices are globally and regionally determined, respectively, and the long-term contracts determine the coal prices. Mohammadi (2009), using cointegration analysis, exposes a close relationship between electricity and coal prices and an insignificant relationship between electricity and oil and/or natural gas prices. Both Asche *et al.* (2003) and Bachmeier and Griffin (2006) find very weak linkages among oil, coal and natural gas prices, using cointegration analysis, while crude oil and several refined product prices are integrated, and Hartley *et al.* (2008) notice an indirect relationship between natural gas and oil prices. Furthermore, Aruga and Managi (2011) detect a weak market integration among a large group of energy products: WTI oil, Brent oil, gasoline, heating oil, coal, natural gas, and ethanol futures prices.

Mjelde and Bessler (2009) observe that oil, coal, natural gas and uranium markets are not entirely cointegrated, while Asche *et al.* (2006) indicate that the U.K. energy market between 1995 and 1998 was highly integrated when the demand was for energy rather than for a particular source of energy. Brown and Yucel (2008) show that oil and natural gas prices have been independent since 2000; however, when an error correction model takes into consideration weather and inventories, crude oil prices affect natural gas prices. Similar results are obtained by Ramberg (2010) using cointegration analysis. Amavilah (1995) observes that oil prices influence uranium prices.

Causality analysis is used to evaluate the relationship between spot and future commodity prices. Asche *et al.* (2008), using a nonlinear Granger causality test, shows that neither futures nor the spot crude oil market leads the relationship. Cointegration analysis and Granger causality are the foundation of most of these studies, but none have used a nonlinear correlation measure to evaluate the lead-lag relationship among the energy fuels time series.

We analyze the daily time series of one month forward futures log prices of the fossil fuel series for the period from January 3, 2006, to December 31, 2012 on the West Texas Intermediate oil (WTI), the Central Appalachian bituminous coal (Coal) and natural gas (Gas) from the New York Mercantile Exchange (NYMEX). We have selected a sample that includes the period two years before and after the financial crisis of 2007–2009 to evaluate the causality among future prices during different economic terms.

4. Estimation techniques

4.1. Stationarity, cointegration and causality tests

We first check the weak stationarity condition of the considered time series, using the augmented Dickey-Fuller

Unit Root (ADF) test, which implies that both the mean and variance are time-invariant. This indicates that all log price series are non-stationary (table 1(a)) and, as expected after taking the first difference of the log prices, the log return series are stationary with a 99% confidence level for all periods (table 1(b)). Next, we use the log returns to conduct the proposed causality tests. These series have some critical autoregressive effects according to the autocorrelation function (ACF) and the partial ACF; however, the emphasis of this paper is on the lagged cross-correlation.

We have evaluated the Granger causality and the multivariate distance nonlinear causality test (MDNC) between each pair of the energy futures series up to seven lags. To control for the autocorrelation effect, we include seven lags of the dependent variable for our MDNC calculations, and Granger causality automatically included the lag of the dependent variable that was under study. For MDNC, we calculate the p-value of our tests applying the MBB using 100 samples with replacement and multiple blocks of 10 observations each. The p-value was evaluated with the significance level $\alpha = 0.05$.

We have also tested the cointegration of different pairs using the Johansen test (Johansen 1988a, 1988b) to determine the necessity of a vector autoregressive (VAR) error correction model. Two-time series are cointegrated when each is unit root nonstationary, and a linear combination of both is unit root stationary. In practical terms, it implies that prices may diverge in the short term, but they tend to converge in the long-term. Since none of the log price pairs were cointegrated in the different periods at the 5% significance level according to the Johansen test, we use the VAR model of the log return series to run the Granger causality test with seven lags, instead of using the VAR error correction model.

We evaluate the results of all the tests using the relevant variables detected during our entire period of analysis (2006–2012). For this purpose, we have used the seven lags of the dependent variable, i.e. the predicted variable, for all the tests and included the additional variables selected by each method to predict the *direction* (up or down) of the log return of the fuel series using RF and SVM. However, if there is a difference in the number of variables when we compare the Granger causality and the MDNC test, we reduce the number of lags of the target variable until both MDNC and Granger causality tests have the same number of variables.

4.2. Heston model

In case that there is any doubt about the non-linear relationship between the energy time series, we apply the MDNC and

Table 1. The t ratio's of the ADF unit root tests by the energy product and period for log prices and log returns.

	2006–12	Pre-crisis	Crisis	Recovery	2006–12	Pre-crisis	Crisis	Recovery
	(a) Log Prices				(b) Log returns			
WTI	− 1.70	− 0.91	0.10	− 1.37	− 13.25**	− 6.72**	− 7.25**	− 10.19**
Coal	− 2.13	− 2.43	− 0.91	− 2.91	− 10.93**	− 6.22**	− 8.56**	− 10.34**
Gas	− 2.76	− 3.02	− 0.07	− 2.40	− 11.09**	− 6.85**	− 8.02**	− 9.77**

Note: The null hypothesis is the presence of a unit root or that the series is non-stationary. *: $p \leq 0.05$, **: $p \leq 0.01$.

Granger causality tests to a simulated dataset that includes interaction between two energy time series and non-linear effects as defined by a bi-variate driftless Heston model.

The Heston (1993) model prices European call options using stochastic volatility and arbitrary values of volatility and asset returns. We implement a bivariate version of this model as presented by Abbas-Turki and Lamberton (2014). Let $(W_t^1, W_t^2, \widetilde{W}_t^1, \widetilde{W}_t^2)$ be a standard four-dimensional Brownian motion (i.e. those four Brownian motions are independent and standard one-dimensional Brownian motion). Given the parameters $(\mu_i, \theta_i, \kappa_i, \sigma_i, \rho_i)$, $i = 1, 2$, $\rho \in [-1, 1]$, the bivariate asset price process (S_t^1, S_t^2) is given as a solution of the following stochastic differential equations:

$$dS_t^1 = \mu_1 S_t^1 \, dt + \sqrt{v_t^1} S_t^1 \, dW_t^1,$$

$$dS_t^2 = \mu_2 S_t^2 \, dt + \sqrt{v_t^2} S_t^2 (\rho \, dW_t^1 + \sqrt{1 - \rho^2} \, dW_t^2).$$

Here, the bivariate variance process (v_t^1, v_t^2) follows

$$dv_t^1 = \kappa_1 (\theta_1 - v_t^1) \, dt + \sigma_1 \sqrt{v_t^1} dB_t^1,$$

$$dv_t^2 = \kappa_2 (\theta_2 - v_t^2) \, dt + \sigma_2 \sqrt{v_t^2} dB_t^2,$$

where $B_t^1 = \rho_1 W_t^1 + \sqrt{1 - \rho_1^2} \widetilde{W}_t^1$, $B_t^2 = \rho_2 (\rho W_t^1 + \sqrt{1 - \rho^2} W_t^2) + \sqrt{1 - \rho_2^2} \widetilde{W}_t^2$, θ_i : long-term variance for asset i, ρ_i : volatility-spot correlation for asset i, ρ: spot-spot correlation between two assets, μ_i : drift of asset i, σ_i : volatility of volatility for asset i, κ_i : mean reversion rate for asset i.

In particular, we simulate the series of coal and gas using the data of 2006. Our dataset has 100 observations where the base model has a volatility-spot correlation (ρ_i) of -0.5, a spot-spot correlation (ρ) of 0.5, and a long-term variance (θ) of 26.3 and 1.1 for coal and gas, respectively. We also calibrate our model using a modified version of the quasi-Newton method (Byrd et al. 1995) to obtain the volatility-mean reversion coefficient (κ) of 2.17 and 2.21, and a volatility of volatility (σ) of 1.17 and 0.27 for coal and gas, respectively. Finally, we forecast the prices based on the average of 100 different paths generated by a Montecarlo simulation of the Heston model.

4.3. Non-parametric forecasting and cross-validation

We have selected RF and SVM as our non-parametric forecasting methods because of their capacity to choose features and to model both linear and nonlinear relationships. In particular, RF deals with problems of multicollinearity by randomly selecting a fixed number of variables and generating different trees using bootstrap samples. In the case of linear SVM, the use of an elastic-net penalty, which is a combination of lasso and ridge penalty, can mitigate the impact of correlated features. The limitation with this approach is that a linear SVM may miss the contribution of variables that have a high nonlinear correlation. Therefore, we also run a nonlinear SVM with a radial basis function (RBF) kernel because of its interpretation as a similarity measure, its simplicity and popularity

as a Gaussian kernel, and its capacity to uncover new nonlinear relations. It is possible that some of the energy products show multicollinearity using a linear test, however a nonlinear algorithm may uncover new nonlinear relationships selecting the best variables considering both linear and nonlinear effects.

We use the variables chosen during the full period of our analysis (2006–12) and forecast the next 6 months (124 days) as our test dataset. This dataset starts with an entry corresponding to January 2012 and moves with an increasing window from 2 to 25 days. Based on these forecasts, we run two cross-validation (CV) exercises: (a) 24 samples (windows) CV and calculate the performance indicators using the complete test dataset for each window and compare the means of 24 samples for each test, and (b) 240 samples CV (10 folds × 24 windows) for each moving window and split the forecast in 10 folds of about 12 observations each and employ about 291 observations for training (approximately 14 months). Thus, we use 240 samples to calculate the average of the performance indicators.

We also split the first training sample into new training (11 months) and validation (3 months) datasets to calibrate our models according to their capacity to reduce the validation error. For RF, we explore optimal combinations of the number of trees (# trees) and number of variables (# variables). For the linear SVM, we find optimal values for the regularization parameter λ that controls the importance of penalties for misclassification and α, the elastic-net mixing parameter, which controls the contribution from the lasso ($\alpha = 1$) and ridge ($\alpha = 0$) regularization. For the nonlinear SVM with the RBF kernel, we calculate the γ coefficient as $1/p$ where p is the total number of variables, and test the optimal values for each energy product of C, the cost of constraints violation according to the Lagrange optimization. As a result of the calibration process, we selected the following models for our tests:

(1) RF, with 500 trees as an average of the optimal number of trees for each energy product, and number of variables $= \sqrt{p}$ where p is the total number of variables.

(2) RF, with 600, 100, and 700 trees and 4, 5, and 7 variables for coal, WTI and gas respectively.

(3) RF, with 700, 200, and 800 trees for coal, WTI and gas respectively and number of variables $= \sqrt{p}$.

(4) SVM with the RBF kernel, C (cost) $= 1, 3.5$, and 1 for coal, WTI and gas respectively.

(5) Linear SVM elastic-net, with $\lambda : 0.0066$ and $\alpha : 0.1$, 0.2, and 0.1 for coal, WTI and gas respectively.

We test the mean differences of the test error and lift between the MDNC and the Granger causality test of the folds used in each cross-validation exercise. Lift is a measure of the performance of a classifier model to forecast a variable given the prior probability or the average of the past values of the target variable:

$$\text{Lift} = \frac{p(\hat{Y} = + \mid Y = +)}{p(\hat{Y} = +)}$$

Table 2. Descriptive statistics of log returns.

	2006–12			Pre-crisis		
	Coal	WTI	Gas	Coal	WTI	Gas
Mean (%)	− 0.01	− 0.02	− 0.06	− 0.07	0.00	− 0.08
Standard deviation	1.84	2.39	3.22	1.14	1.92	3.90
Coeff. of variation	− 173.39	− 112.42	− 53.26	− 16.95	488.65	− 46.42
Min	− 28.71	− 13.07	− 14.89	− 5.19	− 8.47	− 10.78
Max	29.35	16.41	26.87	9.53	7.37	24.96
	Crisis			Post-crisis		
Mean (%)	0.01	− 0.07	− 0.16	0.02	0.07	− 0.02
Standard deviation	3.49	3.59	3.06	1.44	2.08	3.39
Coeff. of variation	578.61	− 52.10	− 19.02	58.90	29.91	− 226.03
Min	− 28.71	− 13.07	− 14.89	− 6.95	− 9.26	− 9.78
Max	29.35	16.41	9.84	11.57	10.53	26.87

Table 3. Correlation matrix of log returns.

	2006–12			Pre-crisis			Crisis			Post-crisis		
	Coal	WTI	Gas	Coal	WTI	Gas	Coal	WTI	Gas	Coal	WTI	Gas
Coal	1.00	0.27	0.17	1.00	0.09	0.18	1.00	0.33	0.21	1.00	0.33	0.25
WTI	0.27	1.00	0.21	0.09	1.00	0.29	0.33	1.00	0.30	0.33	1.00	0.19
Gas	0.17	0.21	1.00	0.18	0.29	1.00	0.21	0.30	1.00	0.25	0.19	1.00

Table 4. Multivariate distance nonlinear causality (MDNC) and Granger causality of log returns.

Periods	Lags/Effects	1	2	3	4	5	6	7
2006–12	WTI → Coal	**±	**±	**±	**±	**±	**±	**±
	Gas → Coal	**						**
	Coal → WTI	**	**	**	**	**	**	
	Coal → Gas		**	**		**±	±	⊥
Pre-crisis	WTI → Coal	**			**			
1/2006-5/07	Gas → Coal	**	**					
	Coal → WTI				**			
	Gas → WTI	**	** ⊥					
	Coal → Gas				**		**	
	WTI → Gas	**			**			
Crisis	WTI → Coal	**±	**±	**±	**±	**±	**±	±
6/2007-3/09	Gas → Coal	**					**	**
	Coal → WTI	**	**	**	**	**	**	
	Gas → WTI							**
	Coal → Gas			**		**±	±	**±
	WTI → Gas				**	**		**
Recovery	Gas → WTI		**	**				
3/2009–12/12	Coal → Gas		** ⊥					
	WTI → Gas					**		⊥

Note: For the *p*-values of MDNC: * : $p \leq 0.05$, ** : $p \leq 0.01$, and Granger causality: ⊥: $p \leq 0.05$, ±: $p \leq 0.01$.

where $\hat{Y}$ and Y are the prediction and the class to be predicted, respectively, and $+$ denotes the positive class. The lift curve is a variation of the receiver operating characteristic curve. We use lift as a performance indicator because of its capacity to recognize an improvement in the forecast in comparison to a random alternative, and its extended use in business problems, especially for marketing

4.4. Software

We implement the Granger causality, the Brownian partial distance correlation, the nonlinear support vector machine, the linear support vector machine with regularization, the

Johansen test, the non-stationarity (Augmented Dickey-Fuller) test, random forests and the performance indicators using the MSBVAR, Energy, E1071, sparseSVM, URCA, Tseries, randomForest and ROCR packages for R, respectively.†

5. Results

We split the data into the following periods: January 3, 2006–May 31, 2007 (pre-crisis period), June 1, 2007–March 6, 2009 (financial crisis period), and March 9, 2009–December 31, 2012 (recovery period) according to the low

† Information about R can be found at < http://cran.r-project.org > .

Table 5. Correlation between energy time series (coal, WTI and gas) and lagged values (columns) with different moments (M; rows) of the independent time series for the period 2006–2012.

	M	Coal 1	Coal 2	Coal 3	Coal 4	Coal 5	Coal 6	Coal 7	WTI 1	WTI 2	WTI 3	WTI 4	WTI 5	WTI 6	WTI 7	Gas 1	Gas 2	Gas 3	Gas 4	Gas 5	Gas 6	Gas 7
Coal	1								0.008	0.010	0.042	0.018	0.006	0.021	0.028	-0.001	0.008	-0.029	0.027	-0.027	0.014	0.009
Coal	2								0.029	0.023	-0.001	-0.026	-0.016	0.005	-0.043	0.012	-0.001	-0.037	0.011	0.022	0.002	-0.023
Coal	3								0.010	0.002	0.026	0.063	-0.009	0.006	0.055	0.006	-0.010	-0.034	0.008	-0.011	0.005	-0.001
Coal	4								0.021	-0.006	0.021	0.015	-0.013	-0.001	-0.009	0.012	0.009	-0.034	0.017	0.032	0.010	-0.006
Coal	5								0.007	-0.011	0.024	0.077	-0.010	0.002	0.048	0.011	-0.013	-0.027	0.013	-0.007	0.000	-0.005
Coal	6								0.011	-0.013	0.023	0.046	-0.009	-0.002	0.014	0.012	0.009	-0.030	0.017	0.032	0.005	-0.006
Coal	7								0.003	-0.015	0.024	0.077	-0.008	0.002	0.041	0.012	-0.014	-0.020	0.016	-0.006	-0.001	-0.006
WTI	1	-0.053	-0.045	0.008	0.020	-0.050	0.018	0.003								0.005	-0.009	-0.011	-0.015	0.016	0.005	0.012
WTI	2	-0.028	-0.037	0.005	0.073	0.008	0.005	0.024								0.036	0.023	0.001	-0.049	0.015	-0.031	0.010
WTI	3	-0.105	-0.080	0.034	0.007	-0.076	-0.004	0.051								0.011	-0.008	0.058	-0.021	0.041	0.010	0.022
WTI	4	-0.027	-0.068	0.033	0.081	-0.022	-0.009	0.026								0.016	0.057	0.064	-0.025	0.030	-0.031	0.024
WTI	5	-0.109	-0.072	0.042	0.008	-0.074	-0.011	0.057								0.011	-0.006	0.101	-0.020	0.040	0.002	0.024
WTI	6	-0.029	-0.068	0.043	0.083	-0.053	-0.012	0.026								0.012	0.059	0.096	-0.019	0.033	-0.018	0.026
WTI	7	-0.110	-0.062	0.046	0.010	-0.078	-0.011	0.058								0.010	-0.005	0.121	-0.019	0.040	0.003	0.026
Gas	1	0.013	-0.019	-0.075	0.042	0.021	0.041	0.036	-0.003	-0.034	0.011	0.001	-0.019	-0.074	0.010							
Gas	2	0.000	0.013	0.010	0.012	-0.001	-0.010	-0.007	-0.021	0.014	-0.048	-0.030	0.034	0.005	-0.034							
Gas	3	0.021	0.038	-0.011	-0.024	0.004	-0.016	0.035	0.013	0.022	0.005	0.022	0.040	-0.056	-0.014							
Gas	4	0.009	0.031	0.008	0.014	0.010	-0.039	0.003	-0.023	0.036	-0.040	-0.024	0.047	0.008	-0.042							
Gas	5	0.022	0.062	0.009	-0.026	0.007	-0.041	0.038	0.008	0.038	0.001	0.021	0.048	-0.051	-0.025							
Gas	6	0.010	0.048	0.010	0.013	0.013	-0.046	0.005	-0.015	0.040	-0.038	-0.010	0.048	0.007	-0.040							
Gas	7	0.022	0.069	0.010	-0.026	0.012	-0.046	0.039	0.001	0.040	0.000	0.022	0.048	-0.050	-0.030							

Note: Lagged values in color are selected by MDNC. Colored data bars represent the values of the lags. The higher the value, the longer the bar.

Table 6. Correlation between coal and gas time series simulated by the Heston model with high (0.85) and low (0.15) spot-spot correlation and lagged values (columns) with different moments (M; rows) of the independent time series using data of the year 2006.

Spot-Spot Correlation		M	Coal 1	Coal 2	Coal 3	Coal 4	Coal 5	Coal 6	Coal 7	Gas 1	Gas 2	Gas 3	Gas 4	Gas 5	Gas 6	Gas 7
0.85	Coal	1								-0.055	0.037	0.224	-0.289	0.250	-0.277	-0.079
	Coal	2								-0.002	-0.235	-0.033	0.013	0.083	-0.281	-0.052
	Coal	3								0.009	0.287	0.184	-0.180	0.336	-0.242	-0.088
	Coal	4								0.045	-0.296	0.051	-0.018	0.150	-0.291	-0.079
	Coal	5								0.026	0.374	0.156	-0.131	0.313	-0.209	-0.098
	Coal	6								0.051	-0.336	0.104	-0.044	0.200	-0.261	-0.101
	Coal	7								0.028	0.392	0.147	-0.104	0.291	-0.196	-0.107
	Gas	1	-0.075	0.005	-0.212	0.106	0.119	0.027	0.022							
	Gas	2	0.089	0.070	-0.201	0.065	0.116	0.160	-0.041							
	Gas	3	-0.077	0.016	-0.157	0.167	-0.025	0.089	0.123							
	Gas	4	0.079	0.098	-0.134	0.150	0.150	0.200	-0.127							
	Gas	5	-0.089	0.046	-0.108	0.188	-0.085	0.122	0.155							
	Gas	6	0.081	0.085	-0.080	0.185	0.151	0.194	-0.155							
	Gas	7	-0.091	0.060	-0.071	0.194	-0.111	0.137	0.168							
0.15	Coal	1								-0.095	-0.065	0.109	0.136	0.178	0.004	-0.181
	Coal	2								0.045	-0.272	0.033	-0.013	-0.044	-0.122	0.018
	Coal	3								0.100	-0.013	0.185	0.084	0.046	0.039	-0.147
	Coal	4								0.047	-0.231	0.003	-0.014	-0.109	-0.113	-0.020
	Coal	5								0.184	-0.011	0.200	0.052	-0.039	0.047	-0.140
	Coal	6								0.059	-0.208	-0.011	-0.035	-0.156	-0.090	-0.053
	Coal	7								0.213	-0.024	0.186	0.027	-0.072	0.043	-0.137
	Gas	1	-0.034	0.133	-0.145	0.045	0.071	-0.052	0.097							
	Gas	2	0.065	0.023	-0.095	-0.059	-0.108	0.037	0.090							
	Gas	3	-0.005	0.071	-0.135	0.157	0.022	0.001	0.061							
	Gas	4	0.083	0.023	-0.031	-0.033	-0.194	0.044	0.062							
	Gas	5	0.011	0.054	-0.139	0.192	-0.045	0.032	0.051							
	Gas	6	0.090	0.010	-0.014	-0.021	-0.239	0.051	0.031							
	Gas	7	0.033	0.048	-0.136	0.192	-0.098	0.044	0.040							

Note: Lagged values in color are selected by MDNC. Colored data bars represent the values of the lags. The higher the value, the longer the bar.

Table 7. Multivariate distance nonlinear causality (MDNC) and Granger causality of returns for coal and gas generated by a bivariate Heston Model.

	Coeff.	Lags/Effects	1	2	3	4	5	6	7
Base model:		Gas → Coal	** ⊥	* ⊥	* ⊥	** ⊥	⊥	** ⊥	⊥
		Coal → Gas						** ⊥	⊥
Volatility-spot correlation	− 0.85	Gas → Coal	**		** ⊥	** ⊥	⊥	** ⊥	** ⊥
		Coal → Gas		**		**	**		**
	− 0.15	Gas → Coal		**	**		**		
		Coal → Gas							
Volatility-mean reversion coeff.	3	Gas → Coal	** ⊥	** ⊥	⊥	⊥			
		Coal → Gas					*		**
	1.5	Gas → Coal		** ⊥	** ⊥		**		**
		Coal → Gas	** ⊥					**	
Spot-spot correlation	0.85	Gas → Coal	**						
		Coal → Gas	**		**		**		
	0.15	Gas → Coal		**		**		**	**
		Coal → Gas		**					

Note: The base model has a volatility-spot correlation (ρ_i) of − 0.5, a spot-spot correlation (ρ) of 0.5, and a volatility-mean reversion coefficient (κ) of 2.17 and 2.21 for coal and gas respectively. For the p-values of MDNC: *: $p \leq 0.05$, **: $p \leq 0.01$, and Granger causality: ⊥: $p \leq 0.05$, ±: $p \leq 0.01$.

Table 8. 10-fold cross-Validation with an increasing forecasting moving window from 2 to 25 observations [240 samples CV (10 folds × 24 windows)]: Means of error rate and lift for log return prediction.

		Error rate			Lift		
		Coal	WTI	Gas	Coal	WTI	Gas
1. RF, # trees: 500	MDNC	0.46***	0.45***	0.49***	1.14***	1.06	1.07***
# variables: $\sqrt{p}$	Granger	0.49	0.50	0.53	0.91	1.02	0.96
2. RF, # variables: 4, 5,7	MDNC	0.49***	0.51	0.49	0.91**	0.98	1.02**
# trees/product: 600, 100, 700	Granger	0.51	0.48	0.50	0.86	1.05	0.99
3. RF, # variables: $\sqrt{p}$	MDNC	0.50***	0.51	0.48***	0.88***	0.98	1.05***
# trees/product: 700, 200, 800	Granger	0.52	0.48	0.51	0.76	1.06	0.97
4. SVM with RBF kernel	MDNC	0.49***	0.38***	0.56***	0.92***	1.16***	0.90**
C by product: 1, 3.5, 1	Granger	0.51	0.50	0.57	0.72	1.00	0.88
5. Linear SVM elastic − net	MDNC		0.39***	0.53*		1.14***	0.95***
α/product: 0.1, 0.2, 0.1; λ: 0.006	Granger		0.47	0.54		1.01	0.93

Note: Prediction of test sample of 124 days (6 months) using multivariate distance nonlinear causality (MDNC) and Granger causality. RF stands for random forest, SVM for support vector machine, p is total number of variables, # variables and # trees are number of variables and trees used by RF. Every model includes the parameters selected by the calibration process as described in Section 4. The three values for each parameter included in several models represent the values for coal, WTI and gas respectively. *: $p \leq 0.1$, **: $p \leq 0.05$, ***: $p \leq 0.01$ of t-test mean difference between MDNC and Granger causality.

and high points of the SP 500 index. We notice the most dispersed series measured by the coefficient of variation is coal during the complete period of analysis (2006–2012); see table 2. According to table 3, the correlation between gas and coal log return increases and the correlation between gas and WTI log return decreases. Similarly, the correlation between WTI and coal log returns increases during the crisis period. These cross-correlation changes suggest a high interrelationship among the three fossil fuel series.

During the complete period 2006–2012, WTI and Coal show a two-way feedback relationship according to the MDNC tests, whereas only the WTI → Coal relationship is recognized by the Granger causality test; see table 4 where we use the symbol → to denote a relationship. More precisely, $X \rightarrow Y$ indicates that X Granger causes Y, or Y is dependent on X, when Granger causality or MDNC are used, respectively.

Coal also Granger causes Gas for the lags 5, 6 and 7. Additionally, MDNC acknowledges the following dependencies (all relevant lags are listed in parentheses): Gas $(1, 7) \rightarrow$ Coal, and Coal $(2, 3, 5) \rightarrow$ Gas. Similar relationships are observed during the crisis period (2008–2009). Hence, the crisis years dominate the complete period of analysis. In the pre-crisis period, Granger causality only recognizes the relationship Gas $(2) \rightarrow$ WTI, while the MDNC test can detect the following significant relationships: WTI $(1,4) \rightarrow$ Gas, Coal $(4, 6) \rightarrow$ Gas, Gas $(1, 2) \rightarrow$ Coal, WTI $(1, 4) \rightarrow$ Coal, Coal $(4) \rightarrow$ WTI, and Gas $(1, 2) \rightarrow$ WTI. During the recovery period, the two methods discover fewer relationships than in the other two periods. However, the MDNC finds about twice the number of relevant relationships than the other method based on Granger causality.

In general, the MDNC detects most of the relationships recognized by the other method as well as some new relationships. For instance, the MDNC identifies the effect

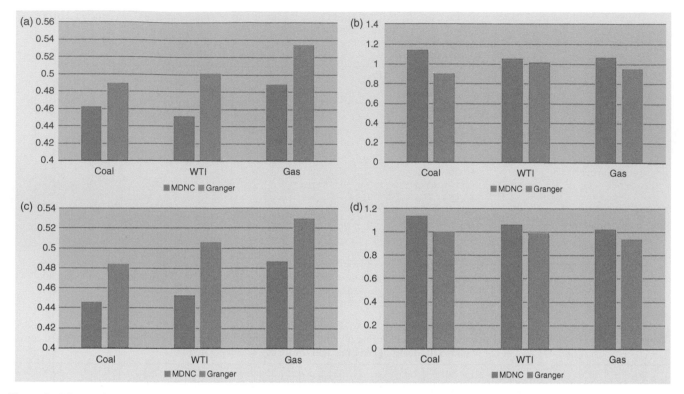

Figure 2. Means of error rate and lift of cross-validation for log return prediction of 124 days (6 months) test dataset, using multivariate distance nonlinear causality (MDNC) and Granger causality for an increasing moving window from 2 to 25 observations. The forecasting algorithm is random forests with 500 trees and $\sqrt{p}$ variables where p is the total number of variables. (a) and (b) are the results of 10-fold cross-validation for each of the 24 moving windows [240 samples CV (10 folds × 24 windows)]. (c) and (d) are the results of cross-validation using each of the entire 24 moving windows (24 samples CV). The p-value of t-test mean difference between MDNC and Granger causality is ≤ 0.01 for all the cases (c) and (d). For (a) and (b), the significance levels are reported in the first model (first two rows) of table 8.

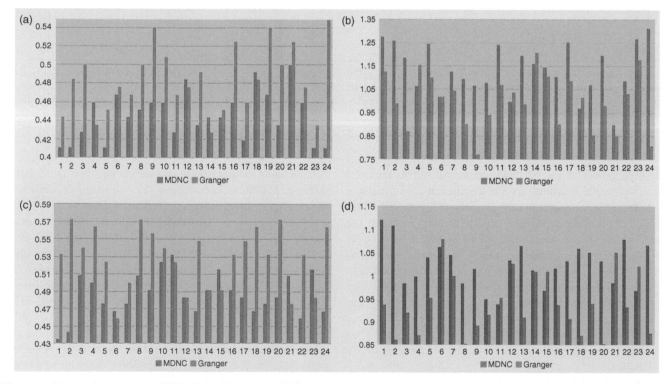

Figure 3. Means of error rate and lift of 24-folds cross-validation (24 moving windows) for log return prediction of coal (a and b) and gas (c and d) of 124 days (6 months) test dataset for every moving window using multivariate distance nonlinear causality (MDNC) and Granger causality. The forecasting algorithm is random forests with 500 trees and $\sqrt{p}$ variables where p is the total number of variables.

of crude oil on natural gas for all the periods and several lags as explored by Brown and Yucel (2008), Hartley *et al.* (2008) and Huntington (2007) while Granger causality only recognizes one relevant during the recovery period.

5.1. Higher moments and Heston model

We studied whether the results that we obtained could be associated with higher moments of the leading variable. Table 5 shows the Pearson correlation between an energy time series and lagged values (columns) with different moments (rows) of the other two time series for the complete period 2006–2012. The values in yellow correspond to the selection made by MDNC while colored data bars represent the values of the lags. The higher the value, the longer the bar. The table shows that the strongest effects are mostly associated with the high moments of different lags while the second moment, typical of the Heston model, is relatively large in only one case.

Our simulations of the bi-variate driftless Heston model of coal and gas with different levels of the volatility-mean reversion coefficient (3, around 2.2, 1.5), the volatility-spot correlation (-0.85, -0.5, -0.15), and the spot-spot correlation (0.85, 0.5, 0.15) are in table 7. We find that high absolute values of these coefficients show non-trivial dependence between the two assets using the Granger causality and MDNC tests. The main difference between the high and low values of these coefficients is the lagged effect. The simulations with high absolute values of these coefficients show at least a relevant effect of the first lagged explanatory variable while most of the simulations with low values show relevant coefficients only at or after the second lag. Table 6 presents a visual example of this effect when the simulations are calculated with a high and low spot-spot correlation coefficient. Even though we can detect dependence between the variables, as the model is a Martingale, we cannot expect to derive any profitable trading strategy from the simulations generated by the Heston model.

This exercise shows a limitation of the application of the MDNC test if the only objective is to generate trading strategies from time series that can be characterized by a driftless Heston model. However, it still shows that MDNC can detect dependencies between variables that were not detected by the Granger causality test. The source of the superiority of lead-lag selections based on MDNC test lies on its capability of detecting an *arbitrary* dependence structure between the two random elements. Note the MDNC test is *nonparametric* and does not assume any linear (or nonlinear) (auto-)regression model structure, such as in the (generalized) Granger causality models.

5.2. Cross-validation using non-parametrics methods

We evaluate the effectiveness of our approach forecasting log return with RF and SVM using the variables selected by Granger causality as the benchmark and assess whether the variables chosen by MDNC show significantly better results using the error rate and lift as the performance indicators. In doing so, for the fair comparison, we use the same number of features selected by the two methods. As the Granger

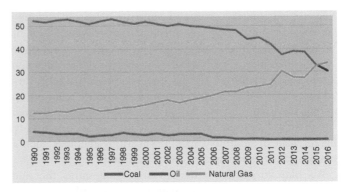

Figure 4. Evolution of net generation of electricity by energy source. Source: US Energy Information Administration.

causality does not reveal any relevant lagged variable to forecast WTI for the entire period 2006–12, we compare MDNC against a baseline model with the first seven lags of WTI.

Using the 240 samples CV (10 folds × 24 windows), the RF with 500 trees (model 1) and SVM with RBF kernel (model 4) introduced in Section 4 show the best and very similar results (table 8), so the rest of our discussion will be limited to the results of these models. The linear SVM elastic-net also shows some positive results for WTI and gas, however it does not show significant results for coal. We assume that as a linear algorithm, it is not able to capture the nonlinear effect of the variables detected by the nonlinear algorithms.

The log returns using the SVM with the RBF kernel forecast the series of coal, WTI and gas significantly better when the MDNC test selects the variables rather than the Granger causality test according to the error rate and lift. RF with 500 trees offers even better results than SVM for most of the cases; see table 8) and figure 2(a), (b). Hence, the introduction of the significant lagged variables detected by the MDNC improves the prediction of these time series. In the case of 24 samples CV, the MDNC is also the best method for feature selection according to both algorithms; see figures 2(c), (d) and 3. These last figures only present the results of RF with 500 trees as SVM with the RBF kernel generates similar results. In conclusion, the MDNC is the dominant method for feature selection across the different windows and cross-validation methods.

6. Discussion

The use of a nonlinear causality test is especially relevant for energy futures considering that their prices might be affected by geopolitical forces such as the decision of an oil cartel to limit oil production or a political crisis in the Middle East. These nonlinear relationships may have an impact on the selection of inputs used to generate electricity in the U.S. In this respect, we can see that the composition of the inputs used to produce electricity has substantially changed in the last few years. Since 1990, the contribution of natural gas has increased while the coal importance has decreased in a similar proportion probably due to the decline in natural gas prices since December 2005 to April 2012 (see figure 4).

In conclusion, the proposed multivariate distance nonlinear causality test shows a substantial improvement on the forecast of the fuel energy time series in comparison to Granger causality. The MDNC recognizes relationships similar to those identified by the linear Granger causality test. Additionally, MDNC uncovers new nonlinear relationships among oil, coal, and natural gas futures. These results indicate that the feature selection capacity of MDNC can improve the forecast of nonlinear machine learning methods such as random forests and support vector machines.

We plan to continue this research, integrating the multivariate distance nonlinear causality test with Markovian stochastic models to strengthen their nonlinear forecasting and feature selection capacity in a time series nonlinear framework.

Acknowledgments

The authors thank Maria Rizzo, Hamed Ghoddusi, Dror Kennett, Alex Moreno, Gary Kazantsev, two anonymous referees, and the participants of the Eastern Economics Association meeting 2014, and the 11th International Conference on Computational and Financial Econometrics 2017, for their comments and suggestions; and to Patrick Jardine for proofreading this paper. The opinions presented are the exclusive responsibility of the author.

Disclosure statement

No potential conflict of interest was reported by the authors.

ORCID

German G. Creamer ⓘ http://orcid.org/0000-0002-3159-5153
Chihoon Lee ⓘ http://orcid.org/0000-0001-5448-2787

References

Abbas-Turki, L. and Lamberton, D., European options sensitivity with respect to the correlation for multidimensional Heston models. *Int. J. Theor. Appl. Financ.*, 2014, **17**(3), 1450015.

Amavilah, V., The capitalist world aggregate supply and demand model for natural uranium. *Energy Econom.*, 1995, **17**(3), 211–220.

Aruga, K. and Managi, S., Linkage among the U.S. energy futures markets. Paper prepared for the 34th IAEE International Conference Institutions, Efficiency and Evolving Energy Technologies, Stockholm, 2011.

Asche, F., Gjolberg, O. and Volker, T., Price relationships in the petroleum market: An analysis of crude oil and refined product prices. *Energy Econom.*, 2003, **25**, 289–301.

Asche, F., Osmundsen, P. and Sandsmark, M., The UK market for natural gas, oil, and electricity: Are the prices decouples? *Energy J.*, 2006, **27**, 27–40.

Asche, F., Gjolberg, O. and Volker, T., The relationship between crude oil spot and futures prices: Cointegration, linear and nonlinear causality. *Energy Econom.*, 2008, **30**, 2673–2685.

Bachmeier, L. and Griffin, J., Testing for market integration: Crude oil, coal, and natural gas. *Energy J.*, 2006, **27**, 55–71.

Bosworth, B., Economic consequences of the great recession: Evidence from the panel study of income dynamics. Working Paper 2012-4, Boston College Center for Retirement Research, Boston, 2012.

Breiman, L., Random forests. *Mach. Learn.*, 2001, **45**(1), 5–32.

Brown, S. and Yucel, M., What drives natural gas prices? *Energy J.*, 2008, **29**, 45–60.

Butrica, B.A., Johnson, R.W. and Smith, K.E., Potential Impacts of the Great Recession on Future Retirement Incomes. Pension Research Council, 2011.

Byrd, R.H., Lu, P., Nocedal, J. and Zhu, C., A limited memory algorithm for bound constrained optimization. *SIAM J. Sci. Comput.*, 1995, **16**(5), 1190–1208.

Creamer, G.G., Network structure and market risk in the European equity market. *IEEE Syst. J.*, 2018, **12**(2), 1090–1098.

Creamer, G.G. and Creamer, B., A non-linear lead lag dependence analysis of energy futures: Oil, coal and natural gas. In *Handbook of High-Frequency Trading and Modeling in Finance*, edited by I. Florescu, M.C. Mariani, H.E. Stanley and F.G. Viens, pp. 61–72, 2016 (Wiley: Hoboken, NJ).

Creamer, G.G., Ren, Y. and Nickerson, J.V., Impact of dynamic corporate news networks on asset return and volatility. IEEE International Conference on Social Computing, Washington, DC, pp. 809–814, 2013.

Davis, R.A., Matsui, M., Mikosch, T. and Wan, P., Applications of distance correlation to time series. *Bernoulli*, 2018, **24**(4A), 3087–3116.

Deaton, A., The financial crisis and the well-being of Americans 2011 OEP Hicks lecture. *Oxf. Econ. Pap.*, 2012, **64**(1), 1–26.

Efron, B., Bootstrap methods: Another look at the jackknife. *Ann. Stat.*, 1979, **7**(1), 1–26.

Fokianos, K. and Pitsillou, M., Consistent testing for pairwise dependence in time series. *Technometrics*, 2017, **59**(2), 262–270.

Gorton, G., *Misunderstanding Financial Crises: Why We Don't See Them Coming*, 2012 (Oxford University Press: Oxford).

Granger, C., Investigating causal relations by econometric models and cross-spectral methods. *Econometrica*, 1969, **37**(3), 424–438.

Granger, C.W.J., Testing for causality: A personal viewpoint. *J. Econom. Dyn. Control*, 1980, **2**, 329–352.

Granger, C.W.J., *Essays in Econometrics: The Collected Papers of Clive W.J. Granger*, 2001 (Cambridge University Press: Cambridge).

Hartley, P., Medlock III, K.B. and Rosthal, J.E., The relationship of natural gas to oil prices. *Energy J.*, 2008, **29**(3), 47–65.

Hastie, T., Tibshirani, R. and Friedman, J., *The Elements of Statistical Learning: Data Mining, Inference and Prediction*, 2nd Edition, 2008 (Springer-Verlag: New York).

Heston, S.L., A closed-form solution for options with stochastic volatility with applications to bond and currency options. *Rev. Financ. Stud.*, 1993, **6**(2), 327–343.

Huntington, H., Industrial natural gas consumption in the united states: An empirical model for evaluating future trends. *Energy Econom.*, 2007, **29**(4), 743–759.

Hurd, M.D. and Rohwedder, S., Effects of the financial crisis and great recession on American households. Tech. rep., National Bureau of Economic Research, 2010.

Johansen, S., Estimation and hypothesis testing of cointegration vectors in Gaussian vector autoregressive models. *Econometrica*, 1988a, **59**(6), 1551–1580.

Johansen, S., Statistical analysis of cointegration vectors. *J. Econom. Dyn. Control*, 1988b, **12**(2–3), 231–254.

Kunsch, H., The jackknife and the bootstrap for general stationary observations. *Ann. Stat.*, 1989, **17**(3), 1217–1241.

Liu, R.Y. and Singh, K., Moving blocks jackknife and bootstrap capture weak dependence. In *Exploring the Limits of Bootstrap*, edited by R. LePage and L. Billard, pp. 225–248, 1992 (Wiley: New York, NY).

Mjelde, J. and Bessler, D., Market integration among electricity markets and their major fuel source markets. *Energy Econom.*, 2009, **31**, 482–491.

Mohammadi, H., Electricity prices and fuel costs: Long-run relations and short-run dynamics. *Energy Econom.*, 2009, **31**, 503–509.

Mohammadi, H., Long-run relations and short-run dynamics among coal, natural gas and oil prices. *Appl. Econ.*, 2011, **43**, 129–137.

Ramberg, D.J., The relationship between crude oil and natural gas spot prices and its stability over time. Master of Science Thesis, Massachusetts Institute of Technology, 2010.

Reinhart, C.M. and Rogoff, K.S., *This Time is Different: Eight Centuries of Financial Folly*, 2009 (Princeton University Press: Princeton, NJ).

Székely, G.J. and Rizzo, M.L., Brownian distance covariance. *Ann. Appl. Stat.*, 2009, **3**(4), 1236–1265.

Székely, G.J. and Rizzo, M.L., Partial distance correlation with methods for dissimilarities. *Ann. Stat.*, 2014, **42**(6), 2382–2412.

Székely, G.J., Rizzo, M.L. and Bakirov, N.K., Measuring and testing dependence by correlation of distances. *Ann. Stat.*, 2007, **35**, 2769–2794.

Vapnik, V., *The Nature of Statistical Learning Theory*, 1995 (Springer-Verlag: New York).

Zhou, Z., Measuring nonlinear dependence in time-series, a distance correlation approach. *J. Time Ser. Anal.*, 2012, **33**, 438–457.

The QLBS Q-Learner goes NuQLear: fitted Q iteration, inverse RL, and option portfolios

IGOR HALPERIN

(*Received 23 July 2018; accepted 6 May 2019; published online 10 July 2019*)

The QLBS model is a discrete-time option hedging and pricing model that is based on Dynamic Programming (DP) and Reinforcement Learning (RL). It combines the famous Q-Learning method for RL with the Black–Scholes (–Merton) (BSM) model's idea of reducing the problem of option pricing and hedging to the problem of optimal rebalancing of a dynamic replicating portfolio for the option, which is made of a stock and cash. Here we expand on several NuQLear (Numerical Q-Learning) topics with the QLBS model. First, we investigate the performance of Fitted Q Iteration for an RL (data-driven) solution to the model, and benchmark it versus a DP (model-based) solution, as well as versus the BSM model. Second, we develop an Inverse Reinforcement Learning (IRL) setting for the model, where we only observe prices and actions (re-hedges) taken by a trader, but not rewards. Third, we outline how the QLBS model can be used for pricing portfolios of options, rather than a single option in isolation, thus providing its own, data-driven and model-independent solution to the (in)famous volatility smile problem of the Black–Scholes model.

1. Introduction

In Halperin (2017), we presented the QLBS model—a discrete-time option hedging and pricing model rooted in Dynamic Programming (DP) and Reinforcement Learning (RL). It combines the famous Q-Learning method for RL (Watkins 1989, Watkins and Dayan 1992) with the Black–Scholes (–Merton) model's idea of reducing the problem of option pricing and hedging to the problem of optimal rebalancing of a dynamic replicating portfolio for an option, which is made of a stock and cash (Black and Scholes 1973, Merton 1974).

In a nutshell, the celebrated Black–Scholes–Merton (BSM) model, also known as the Black–Scholes (BS) model (Black and Scholes 1973, Merton 1974), shows that even though the option price can (and will) change in the future because it depends on a future stock price which is also unknown, a *unique* fair option price can be found by using the principle of one price for identical goods, alongside with the method of pricing by replication. This assumes a continuous re-hedging and a special (lognormal) choice of stock price dynamics. However, such apparent uniqueness of option prices also means that, under these assumptions, options are completely *redundant*, as they can be always perfectly replicated by a simple portfolio made of a stock and cash.

As argued in more detail in Halperin (2017), an apparent redundancy of options in the BSM model is due to the fact that it is formulated in the *continuous time* limit $\Delta t \rightarrow 0$, where hedges are rebalanced continuously—and at zero cost. In such academic limit, an option becomes risk-free, and hence completely redundant, as it is just *equal*, at any time t, to a dynamic portfolio of a stock and cash. In any other case, i.e. when a time step $\Delta t > 0$, risk of a mis-hedge in an option position cannot be completely eliminated, but at best can be *minimized* by a proper choice in an offsetting position in a stock that underlies the option, i.e. by an optimal hedge.

However, re-balancing of option hedges *always* happens with some finite frequency $\Delta t > 0$, e.g. daily, monthly, etc. Therefore, keeping a time-step Δt finite while controlling risk in an option position may be important for realism of modeling. While the classical BSM model gives rise to elegant closed-form expressions for option prices and hedges in the mathematical limit $\Delta t \rightarrow 0$, it makes its theoretical *'risk-neutral'* option prices and hedges quite problematic in practice, even as a 'zero-order' approximation to the real world.

Indeed, as financial markets are precisely in the business of *trading risk*, any meaningful 'zero-order' approximation should account for risk inherently present in financial options and other derivative instruments. One could argue that using an equilibrium 'risk-neutral' framework for option pricing and hedging in a risky option trading business is akin to explaining a biological system starting with equilibrium thermodynamics. While it would be absurd to describe life as a 'correction' to non-life (which is the only possible state with equilibrium thermodynamics), various volatility smile models developed in continuous-time Mathematical Finance do essentially the same thing for financial risk in option pricing.†

Indeed, the BSM model rests on *two* critical assumptions: (1) continuous re-hedging is possible, which produces an equilibrium 'risk-neutral' option price, and (2) the world is log-normal with a fixed volatility which means a flat volatility surface as a function of option strike and maturity. Because *both* these assumptions are violated in practice, the original BSM model contradicts data, see e.g. Wilmott (2000). This puts it in between of a pure mathematical model, and a technical tool to quote market option prices as BS implied volatilities, and risk-manage options using their sensitivities with respect to the stock volatility ('vega'-sensitivity), and other BS sensitivity parameters ('the Greeks'). A mismatch with the market data is 'fixed' by switching to local or stochastic volatility models that 'match the market' much better than the original BSM model.

However, no matter how well stochastic volatility models fit market prices, they entirely miss the *first* question that needs an answer for trading, namely the question of expected *mis-hedging risk* in any given option contract. Their straight-face answer to such a basic question would be 'Right now, you have no mis-hedging risk in this option, sir!'‡

Needless to say, in physics a quantum model that tweaked the Planck constant $\hbar$ to achieve consistency with data would be deemed nonsensical, as the Planck constant is a *constant* that cannot change, thus any 'sensitivity with respect to $\hbar$' would be meaningless (but see Scherrer).

Yet, a likely questionable adjustment to the original BSM model via promoting a *model constant* (volatility) to a *variable* (local or stochastic volatility), to reconcile the model with market data, has become a market standard since 1974. The main reason for this is a common belief that advantages of analytical tractability of the classical BSM model in the continuous-time limit $\Delta t \rightarrow 0$ outweigh its main drawbacks such as inconsistency with data, thus calling for 'fixes' in the original continuous-time model, such as the introduction of non-constant volatilities.

---

† 'Economics ended up with the theory of rational expectations, which maintains that there is a single optimum view of the future, that which corresponds to it, and eventually all the market participants will converge around that view. This postulate is absurd, but it is needed in order to allow economic theory to model itself on Newtonian Physics.' (G. Soros). I thank Vivek Kapoor for this reference.

‡ Note that we focus here on mis-hedging risk and leave aside other sources of risk in options such as bid-ask spreads, transaction costs or volatility risk. The reason is that while the latter can be added as additional risks to make a final model more realistic, an option pricing model that produces a measure of mis-hedging risk seems a *minimal* first adjustment that needs to be done with the classical BS model. This is because the classical BS model claims a strict equivalence between a European option and its replicating portfolio, with a vanishing mis-hedging risk, in the continuous-time limit $\Delta t \rightarrow 0$. In this limit, the option is strictly redundant, as it has exactly *zero* risk of mis-hedging (while simultaneously neglecting other risks as well). We thank the anonymous referee for reminding us about importance of other sources of option risk.

However, this introduces a theoretical (and practical!) nightmare on the modeling side, when mis-hedging risk (as well as other risks), unceremoniously thrown away in the classical BSM model and other continuous-time models of Mathematical Finance but present in the market data, try to make it back to the game, via mismatches between the model and market behavior. This results in what was colorfully described as 'Greek tragedies' for practitioners by Das (2006).

The main issue with these models is that they lump together two different problems with the original BSM model: (i) the absence of mis-hedging risk in the limit $\Delta t \rightarrow 0$, and (ii) differences between real-world stock price dynamics and lognormal dynamics assumed in the BSM model. Unlike the latter, the QLBS model tackles these two problems sequentially.

It starts with a discrete-time version of the BSM model, and re-states the problem of optimal option hedging and pricing as a problem of *risk minimization by hedging* in a sequential Markov Decision Process (MDP). When transition probabilities and a reward function are *known*, such MDP dynamics can be solved by means of DP. This produces a semi-analytical solution for the option price and hedge, which only involves matrix linear algebra for a numerical implementation (Halperin 2017).

On the other hand, we might know only the general *structure* of a MDP model, but *not* its specifications such as transition probability and reward function. In this case, we should solve a Bellman optimality equation for such MDP model relying only on *samples* of data. This is a setting of *Reinforcement Learning*, see e.g. a book by Sutton and Barto (2018).

It turns out that in such *data-driven* and *model-free* setting, the MDP problem for the optimal option price and hedges in the QLBS model can be solved (also semi-analytically) by the celebrated *Q-Learning* method of Watkins (1989), Watkins and Dayan (1992). In recognition of the fact that Q-Learning produces both the optimal price and optimal hedge in such time-discretized (and distribution-free) version of the BS model, we called the model developed in Ref. Halperin (2017) the QLBS model. Because Q-Learning is distribution-free, the RL formulation of the QLBS model is capable of addressing model risk inherent in parametric model-based specifications of price dynamics. Note that as the QLBS model still relies on a parametric specification of the reward function, we do not claim that our approach is completely model-independent. Model risk is mitigated by reliance on a distribution-free Q-Learning approach that does not require specifying a model for the asset price.

While Halperin (2017) focused on Mathematical Q-Learning ('MaQLear') for the QLBS model, here we expand on several topics with a Numerical Q-Learning ('NuQLear') analysis of the model. First, we investigate the performance of Fitted Q Iteration (FQI) for a RL (data-driven) solution to the model, and benchmark it versus a DP (model-based) solution, as well as versus the BSM model. Second, we extend the model to a setting of Inverse Reinforcement Learning (IRL), where we only observe prices and actions (re-hedges) taken by a trader, but not rewards. Third, we outline how the QLBS model can be used for pricing portfolios of options, rather than a single option in isolation. This requires mutual consistency of pricing of different options in a portfolio. We show

how the QLBS model can address this problem, i.e. solve the (in)famous volatility smile problem of the Black–Scholes model.

The paper is organized as follows. In Section 2, we give a summary of the QLBS model, and present both a DP-based and RL-based solutions for the model. An IRL formulation for the model is developed in Section 3. 'NuQLear' experiments are presented in Section 4. Section 5 outlines how option hedging and pricing can be done in a multi-asset (portfolio) setting of the model. Finally, we conclude in Section 6.

2. The QLBS model

The QLBS model starts with a discrete-time version of the BSM model, where we take the view of a seller of a European option (e.g. a put option) with maturity T and a terminal payoff of $H_T(S_T)$ at maturity, that depends on a final stock price S_T at that time. To hedge the option, the seller use the proceeds of the sale to set up a replicating (hedge) portfolio Π_t made of the stock S_t and a risk-free bank deposit B_t. The value of the hedge portfolio at any time $t \leq T$ is

$$\Pi_t = a_t S_t + B_t \qquad (1)$$

where a_t is a position in the stock at time t, taken to hedge risk in the option. As at $t = T$ the option position should be closed, we set $a_T = 0$, which produces a terminal condition at $t = T$:

$$\Pi_T = B_T = H_T(S_T) \qquad (2)$$

Instead of (non-stationary) stock price S_t, we prefer to use time-homogeneous variables X_t as state variables in the model, where X_t and S_t are related as follows:

$$X_t = -\left(\mu - \frac{\sigma^2}{2}\right)t + \log S_t \quad \Leftrightarrow \quad S_t = e^{X_t + \left(\mu - \frac{\sigma^2}{2}\right)t} \qquad (3)$$

2.1. Optimal value function

As was shown in Halperin (2017), the problem of optimal option hedging and pricing in such discrete-time setting can be formulated as a problem of Stochastic Optimal Control (SOC) where a value function to be *maximized* is given by the following expression:

$$V_t^\pi(X_t) = \mathbb{E}_t\left[-\Pi_t - \lambda \sum_{t'=t}^T e^{-r(t'-t)} Var\left[\Pi_{t'} \mid \mathcal{F}_{t'}\right] \Bigg| \mathcal{F}_t\right] \qquad (4)$$

where λ is a Markowitz-like risk aversion parameter (Markowitz 1959), $\mathcal{F}_t$ means an information set of all Monte Carlo (or real) paths of the stock at time t, and the uppercase π stands for a *policy* $\pi(t, X_t)$ that maps the time t and the current

state $X_t = x_t$ into an action $a_t \in \mathcal{A}$:

$$a_t = \pi(t, x_t) \qquad (5)$$

As shown in Halperin (2017), the value function (4) satisfies the following Bellman equation:

$$V_t^\pi(X_t) = \mathbb{E}_t^\pi\left[R(X_t, a_t, X_{t+1}) + \gamma V_{t+1}^\pi(X_{t+1})\right] \qquad (6)$$

where γ stands for a discount factor, and the one-step time-dependent random reward is defined as follows:

$$R_t(X_t, a_t, X_{t+1}) = \gamma a_t \Delta S_t(X_t, X_{t+1}) - \lambda Var\left[\Pi_t \mid \mathcal{F}_t\right]$$
$$= \gamma a_t \Delta S_t(X_t, X_{t+1}) - \lambda \gamma^2 \mathbb{E}_t$$
$$\times \left[\hat{\Pi}_{t+1}^2 - 2a_t \Delta \hat{S}_t \hat{\Pi}_{t+1} + a_t^2 \left(\Delta \hat{S}_t\right)^2\right] \qquad (7)$$

where $\hat{\Pi}_{t+1} \equiv \Pi_{t+1} - \bar{\Pi}_{t+1}$, where $\bar{\Pi}_{t+1}$ is the sample mean of all values of Π_{t+1}, and similarly for $\Delta \hat{S}_t$. For $t = T$, we have $R_T = -\lambda Var[\Pi_T]$ where Π_T is determined by the terminal condition (2).

An *optimal policy* $\pi_t^\star(\cdot \mid X_t)$ is determined as a policy that maximizes the value function $V_t^\pi(X_t)$:

$$\pi_t^\star(X_t) = \arg\max_\pi V_t^\pi(X_t) \qquad (8)$$

The optimal value function $V_t^\star(X_t)$ corresponding to the optimal policy satisfies the Bellman optimality equation

$$V_t^\star(X_t) = \mathbb{E}_t^{\pi^\star}\left[R_t(X_t, a_t = \pi_t^\star(X_t), X_{t+1}) + \gamma V_{t+1}^\star(X_{t+1})\right] \qquad (9)$$

Once it is solved, the (ask) option price is minus the optimal value function: $C_t^{(ask)} = -V_t^\star(X_t)$.

If the system dynamics are known, the Bellman optimality equation can be solved using methods of Dynamic Programming such as Value Iteration. If, on the other hand, dynamics are unknown and the optimal policy should be computed using *samples*, which is a setting of Reinforcement Learning, then a formalism based on an action-value function, to be presented next, provides a better framework for Value Iteration methods.

2.2. Action-value function

The action-value function, or Q-function, is defined by an expectation of the same expression as in the definition of the value function (4), but conditioned on both the current state X_t *and* the initial action $a = a_t$, while following a policy π afterwards:

$$Q_t^\pi(x, a)$$
$$= \mathbb{E}_t[-\Pi_t(X_t) \mid X_t = x, a_t = a]$$
$$- \lambda \mathbb{E}_t^\pi\left[\sum_{t'=t}^T e^{-r(t'-t)} Var\left[\Pi_{t'}(X_{t'}) \mid \mathcal{F}_{t'}\right] \Bigg| X_t = x, a_t = a\right] \qquad (10)$$

The Bellman equation for the Q-function reads (Halperin 2017)

$$Q_t^\pi(x, a) = \mathbb{E}_t\left[R_t(X_t, a_t, X_{t+1})|X_t = x, a_t = a\right]$$
$$+ \gamma \mathbb{E}_t^\pi\left[V_{t+1}^\pi(X_{t+1})\big|X_t = x\right] \quad (11)$$

An optimal action-value function $Q_t^\star(x, a)$ is obtained when (10) is evaluated with an optimal policy $\pi_t^\star$:

$$\pi_t^\star = \arg\max_\pi Q_t^\pi(x, a) \quad (12)$$

The optimal value- and state-value functions are connected by the following equations

$$V_t^\star(x) = \max_a Q_t^\star(x, a)$$
$$Q_t^\star(x, a) = \mathbb{E}_t[R_t(x, a, X_{t+1})] + \gamma \mathbb{E}\left[V_{t+1}^\star(X_{t+1})\big|X_t = x\right] \quad (13)$$

The Bellman Optimality equation for the action-value function is obtained by substituting the first of equations (13) into the second one:

$$Q_t^\star(x, a) = \mathbb{E}_t\Bigg[R_t(X_t, a_t, X_{t+1}) + \gamma \max_{a_{t+1}\in\mathcal{A}}$$
$$\times\ Q_{t+1}^\star(X_{t+1}, a_{t+1})\big|X_t = x, a_t = a\Bigg],$$
$$t = 0, \dots, T - 1 \quad (14)$$

with a terminal condition at $t = T$ given by

$$Q_T^\star(X_T, a_T = 0) = -\Pi_T(X_T) - \lambda\,\mathrm{Var}\left[\Pi_T(X_T)\right] \quad (15)$$

where Π_T is determined by the terminal condition (2). A 'greedy' policy $\pi^\star$ that is used in the QLBS model always seeks an action that maximizes the action-value function in the current state:

$$\pi_t^\star(X_t) = \arg\max_{a_t\in\mathcal{A}} Q_t^\star(X_t, a_t) \quad (16)$$

2.3. DP solution for the optimal Q-function

If transition probabilities to compute the expectation in the right-hand side of the Bellman optimality equation (14) are *known*, then the Bellman equation (14) can be solved, jointly with the optimal policy (16), using backward recursion starting from $t = T - 1$ and the terminal condition (15). This can be used for benchmarking in our test environment where we *do* know these probabilities, and know the rewards function (7).

Substituting the one-step reward (7) into the Bellman optimality equation (14) we obtain

$$Q_t^\star(X_t, a_t) = \gamma \mathbb{E}_t\left[Q_{t+1}^\star(X_{t+1}, a_{t+1}^\star) + a_t\Delta S_t\right]$$
$$- \lambda\gamma^2 \mathbb{E}_t\left[\hat{\Pi}_{t+1}^2 - 2a_t\hat{\Pi}_{t+1}\Delta\hat{S}_t + a_t^2\left(\Delta\hat{S}_t\right)^2\right],$$
$$t = 0, \dots, T - 1 \quad (17)$$

Note that the first term $\mathbb{E}_t[Q_{t+1}^\star(X_{t+1}, a_{t+1}^\star)]$ can depend on the current action only through the conditional probability $p(X_{t+1}|X_t a_t)$. However, the next-state probability can depend on the current action, a_t, only when there is a feedback loop of trading in option underlying stock on the stock price. In the present framework, we follow the standard assumptions of the Black–Scholes model that assumes an option buyer or seller do not produce any market impact.

Neglecting the feedback effect, the expectation $\mathbb{E}_t[Q_{t+1}^\star(X_{t+1}, a_{t+1}^\star)]$ does not depend on a_t. Therefore, with this approximation, the action-value function $Q_t^\star(X_t, a_t)$ is *quadratic* in the action variable a_t.

As $Q_t^\star(X_t, a_t)$ is a quadratic function of a_t, the optimal action (i.e. the hedge) $a_t^\star(S_t)$ that maximizes $Q_t^\star(X_t, a_t)$ is computed analytically:

$$a_t^\star(X_t) = \frac{\mathbb{E}_t\left[\Delta\hat{S}_t\hat{\Pi}_{t+1} + \frac{1}{2\gamma\lambda}\Delta S_t\right]}{\mathbb{E}_t\left[\left(\Delta\hat{S}_t\right)^2\right]} \quad (18)$$

Plugging equation (18) back into equation (17), we obtain an explicit recursive formula for the *optimal* action-value function:

$$Q_t^\star(X_t, a_t^\star) = \gamma \mathbb{E}_t\left[Q_{t+1}^\star(X_{t+1}, a_{t+1}^\star) - \lambda\gamma\hat{\Pi}_{t+1}^2\right.$$
$$\left. + \lambda\gamma\left(a_t^\star(X_t)\right)^2\left(\Delta\hat{S}_t\right)^2\right],\ t = 0, \dots, T - 1 \quad (19)$$

where $a_t^\star(X_t)$ is defined in equation (18).

In practice, the backward recursion expressed by equations (19) and (18) is solved in a Monte Carlo setting, where we assume to have access to N simulated (or real) paths for the state variable X_t Halperin (2017). In addition, we assume that we have chosen a set of basis functions $\{\Phi_n(x)\}$.

We can then expand the optimal action (hedge) $a_t^\star(X_t)$ and optimal Q-function $Q_t^\star(X_t, a_t^\star)$ in basis functions, with time-dependent coefficients:

$$a_t^\star(X_t) = \sum_n^M \phi_{nt}\Phi_n(X_t)\ ,\quad Q_t^\star(X_t, a_t^\star) = \sum_n^M \omega_{nt}\Phi_n(X_t) \quad (20)$$

Coefficients ϕ_{nt} and ω_{nt} are computed recursively backward in time for $t = T - 1, \dots, 0$. The results are given by the following expressions:

$$\phi_t^\star = \mathbf{A}_t^{-1}\mathbf{B}_t \quad (21)$$

where

$$A_{nm}^{(t)} = \sum_{k=1}^N \Phi_n\left(X_t^k\right)\Phi_m\left(X_t^k\right)\left(\Delta\hat{S}_t^k\right)^2$$
$$B_n^{(t)} = \sum_{k=1}^N \Phi_n\left(X_t^k\right)\left[\hat{\Pi}_{t+1}^k\Delta\hat{S}_t^k + \frac{1}{2\gamma\lambda}\Delta S_t^k\right] \quad (22)$$

and

$$\omega_t^\star = \mathbf{C}_t^{-1}\mathbf{D}_t \quad (23)$$

where

$$C_{nm}^{(t)} = \sum_{k=1}^{N} \Phi_n\left(X_t^k\right) \Phi_m\left(X_t^k\right)$$

$$D_n^{(t)} = \sum_{k=1}^{N} \Phi_n\left(X_t^k\right) \left(R_t\left(X_t^k, a_t^{k\star}, X_{t+1}^k\right) \right.$$

$$\left. + \gamma \max_{a_{t+1} \in \mathcal{A}} Q_{t+1}^{\star}\left(X_{t+1}^k, a_{t+1}\right) \right) \qquad (24)$$

Equations (21) and (23), computed jointly and recursively for $t = T - 1, \ldots, 0$, provide a practical implementation of the DP-based solution to the QLBS model using expansions in basis functions. This approach can be used to find optimal price and optimal hedge when the dynamics are *known*. For more details, see Halperin (2017).

2.4. RL solution for QLBS: fitted Q iteration

Reinforcement Learning (RL) solves the same problem as Dynamic Programming (DP), i.e. it finds an optimal policy. But unlike DP, RL does *not* assume that transition probabilities and reward function are known. Instead, it relies on *samples* to find an optimal policy.

Our setting assumes a *batch-mode* learning, when we only have access to some historically collected data. The data available is given by a set of N trajectories for the underlying stock S_t (expressed as a function of X_t using equation (3)), hedge position a_t, instantaneous reward R_t, and the next-time value X_{t+1}:

$$\mathcal{F}_t^{(n)} = \left\{ \left(X_t^{(n)}, a_t^{(n)}, R_t^{(n)}, X_{t+1}^{(n)} \right) \right\}_{t=0}^{T-1}, \quad n = 1, \ldots, N \quad (25)$$

We assume that such dataset is available either as a simulated data, or as a real historical stock price data, combined with real trading data or artificial data that would track the performance of a hypothetical stock-and-cash replicating portfolio for a given option.

We use a popular batch-model Q-Learning method called Fitted Q Iteration (FQI) (Ernst *et al.* 2005, Murphy 2005). A starting point in this method is a choice of a parametric family of models for quantities of interest, namely optimal action and optimal action-value function. We use linear architectures where functions sought are *linear* in adjustable parameters that are next optimized to find the optimal action and action-value function.

We use the same set of basis functions $\{\Phi_n(x)\}$ as we used above in Section 2.3. As the optimal Q-function $Q_t^{\star}(X_t, a_t)$ is a quadratic function of a_t, we can represent it as an expansion in basis functions, with time-dependent coefficients parametrized by a matrix $\mathbf{W}_t$:

$$Q_t^{\star}(X_t, a_t) = \left(1, a_t, \frac{1}{2}a_t^2\right) \begin{pmatrix} W_{11}(t) & W_{12}(t) & \cdots & W_{1M}(t) \\ W_{21}(t) & W_{22}(t) & \cdots & W_{2M}(t) \\ W_{31}(t) & W_{32}(t) & \cdots & W_{3M}(t) \end{pmatrix}$$

$$\times \begin{pmatrix} \Phi_1(X_t) \\ \vdots \\ \Phi_M(X_t) \end{pmatrix}$$

$$\equiv \mathbf{A}_t^T \mathbf{W}_t \Phi(X_t) \equiv \mathbf{A}_t^T \mathbf{U}_W(t, X_t) \qquad (26)$$

Equation (26) is further re-arranged to convert it into a product of a parameter vector and a vector that depends on both the state and the action:

$$Q_t^{\star}(X_t, a_t) = \mathbf{A}_t^T \mathbf{W}_t \Phi(X) = \sum_{i=1}^{3} \sum_{j=1}^{M} \left(\mathbf{W}_t \odot \left(\mathbf{A}_t \otimes \Phi^T(X) \right) \right)_{ij}$$

$$= \vec{\mathbf{W}}_t \cdot \text{vec}\left(\mathbf{A}_t \otimes \Phi^T(X) \right) \equiv \vec{\mathbf{W}}_t \vec{\Psi}(X_t, a_t) \quad (27)$$

Here $\odot$ stands for an element-wise (Hadamard) product of two matrices. The vector of time-dependent parameters $\vec{\mathbf{W}}_t$ is obtained by concatenating columns of matrix $\mathbf{W}_t$, and similarly, $\vec{\Psi}(X_t, a_t) = vec(\mathbf{A}_t \otimes \Phi^T(X))$ stands for a vector obtained by concatenating columns of the outer product of vectors $\mathbf{A}_t$ and $\Phi(X)$.

Coefficients $\vec{\mathbf{W}}_t$ can then be computed recursively backward in time for $t = T - 1, \ldots, 0$ (Halperin 2017):

$$\vec{\mathbf{W}}_t^{\star} = \mathbf{S}_t^{-1} \mathbf{M}_t \qquad (28)$$

where

$$S_{nm}^{(t)} = \sum_{k=1}^{N} \Psi_n\left(X_t^k, a_t^k\right) \Psi_m\left(X_t^k, a_t^k\right)$$

$$M_n^{(t)} = \sum_{k=1}^{N} \Psi_n\left(X_t^k, a_t^k\right) \left(R_t\left(X_t^k, a_t^k, X_{t+1}^k\right) \right.$$

$$\left. + \gamma \max_{a_{t+1} \in \mathcal{A}} Q_{t+1}^{\star}\left(X_{t+1}^k, a_{t+1}\right) \right) \qquad (29)$$

To perform the maximization step in the second equation in (29) analytically, note that because coefficients $\mathbf{W}_{t+1}$ and hence vectors $\mathbf{U}_W(t+1, X_{t+1}) \equiv \mathbf{W}_{t+1}\Phi(X_{t+1})$ (see equation (26)) are known from the previous step, we have

$$Q_{t+1}^{\star}\left(X_{t+1}, a_{t+1}^{\star}\right) = \mathbf{U}_W^{(0)}(t+1, X_{t+1}) + a_{t+1}^{\star} \mathbf{U}_W^{(1)}(t+1, X_{t+1})$$

$$+ \frac{\left(a_{t+1}^{\star}\right)^2}{2} \mathbf{U}_W^{(2)}(t+1, X_{t+1}) \qquad (30)$$

It is important to stress here that while this is a quadratic expression in $a_{t+1}^{\star}$, it would be *wrong* to use a point of its maximum as a function of $a_{t+1}^{\star}$ as such optimal value in equation (30). This would amount to using the same dataset to estimate both the optimal action and the optimal Q-function, leading to an overestimation of $Q_{t+1}^{\star}(X_{t+1}, a_{t+1}^{\star})$ in equation (29), due to Jensen's inequality and convexity of the $\max(\cdot)$ function. The correct way to use equation (30) is to plug there a value of $a_{t+1}^{\star}$ computed using the analytical solution equation (18) (implemented in the sample-based approach in equation (21)), applied at the previous time step. Due to the availability of the analytical optimal action (18), a potential overestimation problem, a classical problem of

Q-Learning that is sometimes addressed using such methods as Double Q-Learning van Hasselt (2010), is avoided in the QLBS model, leading to numerically stable results.

Equation (28) gives the solution for the QLBS model in a *model-free* and *off-policy* setting, via its reliance on Fitted Q Iteration which *is* a model-free and off-policy algorithm (Ernst *et al.* 2005, Murphy 2005).

3. Inverse reinforcement learning in QLBS

Inverse reinforcement learning (IRL) provides a very interesting and useful extension of the (direct) RL paradigm. In the context of batch-mode learning used in this paper, a setting of IRL is nearly identical to the setting of RL (see equation (25)), except that there is no information about rewards:

$$\mathcal{F}_t^{(n)} = \left\{ \left(X_t^{(n)}, a_t^{(n)}, X_{t+1}^{(n)} \right) \right\}_{t=0}^{T-1}, \quad n = 1, \ldots, N \qquad (31)$$

The objective of IRL is typically two-fold: (i) find rewards $R_t^{(n)}$ that would be most consistent with observed states and action, and (ii) (the same as in RL) find the optimal policy and action-value function. One can distinguish between *on-policy* IRL and *off-policy* IRL. In the former case, we know that observed actions were *optimal* actions. In the latter case, observed actions may *not* necessarily follow an optimal policy, and can be sub-optimal or noisy.

In general, IRL is a harder problem than RL. Indeed, not only we have to find optimal policy from data, which is the same task as in RL, but we also have to do it without observing rewards. Furthermore, the other task of IRL is to find a (or the?) reward function corresponding to an observed sequence of states and actions. It appears that information about rewards is frequently missing in many potential real-world applications of RL/IRL. In particular, this is typically the case when RL methods are applied to study human behavior, see e.g. Liu *et al.* (2013). IRL is also widely used in robotics as a useful alternative to direct RL methods via training robots by demonstrations, see e.g. Kober *et al.* (2013).

It appears that IRL offers a very attractive, at least conceptually, approach for many financial applications that consider rational agents involved in a sequential decision process, where no information about rewards received by an agent is available to a researcher. Some examples of such (semi-) rational agents would be loan or mortgage borrowers, deposit or saving account holders, credit card holders, consumers of utilities such as cloud computing, mobile data, electricity, etc.

In the context of trading applications, such IRL setting may arise when a trader wants to learn a strategy of a counterparty. She observes counterparty's actions in their bilateral trades, but not counterparty's rewards. Clearly, if she reverse-engineered most likely counterparty's rewards from observed actions to find counterparty's objective (strategy), she could use it to design her own strategy. This is a typical IRL problem.

While typically IRL is a harder problem than RL, and *both* are computationally *hard*, in the QLBS model both are about equally *easy*, due to a quadratic form of both the reward function (7) and action-value function (17). Moreover, the general IRL setting, where only states and actions, but not rewards, are observed in a dataset, is exactly in between of our two previous settings: a DP setting where we only observe states, and a RL setting where we observe states, actions, and rewards.

The main difference is that in the DP setting we know model dynamics, including in particular the risk aversion parameter λ, while in the setting of RL or IRL λ is unknown. Therefore, we will first assume that λ is *known*, and outline how IRL should proceed with the QLBS model, and then we will discuss ways to estimate λ from data.

In the IRL setting, once we have observed states X_t and actions a_t, rewards R_t corresponding to these actions can be obtained, if λ is known, in the same way they were computed in equation (7). The only difference is that while in the DP solution of Section 2.3 we computed rewards (7) for *optimal* actions (18), in the IRL setting we would use *observed* actions a_t to plug into equation (7) to compute the corresponding rewards. After that, the algorithm proceeds in the same way as the FQI solution of Section 2.4, using these computed rewards instead of observed rewards in equation (29). Clearly, this produces *identical* RL and IRL solutions of the QLBS model, as long as λ implied in observed rewards R_t in the RL case is the same λ used in equation (7) by the IRL solution.

This means that the first problem of IRL, i.e. finding a reward function, amounts for the QLBS model to finding just *one* parameter λ using equation (7). This can be done using an approach that we present next.

3.1. Maximum entropy IRL

A simple method to estimate the one-step reward function (7) by estimating its parameter λ is based on a highly tractable version of a popular Maximum Entropy (MaxEnt) IRL method (Ziebart *et al.* 2008) that was developed in Halperin (2017) in a different context.

We start with writing expected rewards corresponding to equation (7) as follows

$$\bar{R}_t(X_t, a_t) \equiv \mathbb{E}_t \left[R_t(X_t, a_t, X_{t+1}) \right]$$
$$= c_0(\lambda) + a_t c_1(\lambda) - \frac{1}{2} a_t^2 c_2(\lambda) \qquad (32)$$

where, omitting for brevity the dependence on X_t, we defined

$$c_0(\lambda) = -\lambda \gamma^2 \mathbb{E}_t \left[\hat{\Pi}_{t+1}^2 \right],$$
$$c_1(\lambda) = \gamma \mathbb{E}_t \left[\Delta S_t + 2\lambda \gamma \Delta \hat{S}_t \hat{\Pi}_{t+1} \right],$$
$$c_2(\lambda) = 2\lambda \gamma^2 \mathbb{E}_t \left[\left(\Delta \hat{S}_t \right)^2 \right] \qquad (33)$$

The MaxEnt method of Halperin (2017) assumes that one-step probabilities of observing different actions a_t in data are described by an exponential model

$$p_\lambda (a_t | X_t) = \frac{1}{Z_\lambda} e^{\bar{R}_t(X_t, a_t)}$$
$$= \sqrt{\frac{c_2(\lambda)}{2\pi}} \exp \left[-\frac{c_2(\lambda)}{2} \left(a_t - \frac{c_1(\lambda)}{c_2(\lambda)} \right)^2 \right] \qquad (34)$$

where Z_λ is a normalization factor.

Thus, by combining an exponential distribution of the Max-Ent method with the quadratic expected reward (32), we ended up with a Gaussian action distribution (34) for IRL in QLBS. Clearly this is very good news given the amount of tractability of Gaussian distributions. Using equation (34), the log-likelihood of observing data $\{X_t^{(k)}, a_t^{(k)}\}_{k=1}^N$ is (omitting a constant factor $-\frac{1}{2}\log(2\pi)$ in the second expression)

$$
\begin{aligned}
LL(\lambda) &= \log \prod_{k=1}^N p_\lambda \left(a_t^{(k)} \middle| X_t^{(k)} \right) \\
&= \sum_{k=1}^N \left(\frac{1}{2} \log c_2^{(k)}(\lambda) - \frac{c_2^{(k)}(\lambda)}{2} \left(a_t^{(k)} - \frac{c_1^{(k)}(\lambda)}{c_2^{(k)}(\lambda)} \right)^2 \right)
\end{aligned}
\tag{35}
$$

where $c_i^{(k)}(\lambda)$ with $i = 1, 2$ stands for expressions (33) evaluated on the k-th path. As this is a concave function of λ, its unique maximum can be easily found numerically using standard optimization packages.

Note that optimization in equation (35) refers to one particular value of t, therefore this calculation can be repeated independently for different times t, producing a curve $\lambda_{impl}(t)$ that could be viewed as a term structure of implied risk aversion parameter.

It can also be noticed that while equation (34) describes a *probabilistic* Gaussian policy (action probability), in Section 2.4 we used the *deterministic* 'greedy' policy (16). Therefore, if we used a value of λ estimated with equation (35) in the IRL algorithm described above, this may not produce the same result as the RL approach of Section 2.4. Policy assumptions can be made more consistent between the RL and IRL approaches if instead of Q-Learning (in the form of Fitted Q Iteration) that we used in Section 2.4, we switched to G-Learning (Fox *et al.* 2015) that replaces the 'greedy max' term in equation (29) with a 'soft-greedy max' term for a G-function:

$$
\max_{a_{t+1} \in \mathcal{A}} Q_{t+1}^\star (X_{t+1}, a_{t+1}) \to
$$

$$
-\frac{1}{\beta} \log \left(\int p(a|X_{t+1}) e^{-\beta G_{t+1}(X_{t+1}, a)} da \right)
\tag{36}
$$

where β is an 'inverse temperature' parameter of G-Learning (Fox *et al.* 2015). We leave G-Learning in the QLBS model for a future research.

4. NuQLear experiments

We illustrate the numerical performance of the model in different settings (DP, RL, IRL) using simulated stock price histories S_t with the initial stock price $S_0 = 100$, stock drift $\mu = 0.05$, and volatility $\sigma = 0.15$. Option maturity is $T = 1$ year, and a risk-free rate is $r = 0.03$. We consider an ATM ('at-the-money') European put option with strike $K = 100$. Re-hedges are done bi-weekly (i.e. $\Delta t = 1/24$). We use $N = 50,000$ Monte Carlo scenarios for a path of the stock, and report results obtained with two MC runs (each having N

paths), where the error reported is equal to one standard deviation calculated from these runs. In our experiments, we use pure risk-based hedges, i.e. omit the second term in the numerator in equation (18), in order to make comparison with the BSM model.

We use 12 basis functions chosen to be cubic B-splines on a range of values of X_t between the smallest and largest values observed in a dataset.

4.1. DP solution

In our experiments below, we pick the Markowitz risk aversion parameter $\lambda = 0.001$. This provides a visible difference of QLBS prices from BS prices, while being not too far away from BS prices. The dependence of the ATM option price on λ is shown in figure 1.

Simulated path and solutions for optimal hedges, portfolio values, and Q-function values corresponding to the DP solution of Section 2.3 are illustrated in figure 2. In the numerical implementation of matrix inversion in equations (21) and (23), we used a regularization by adding a unit matrix with a regularization parameter of 10^{-3}.

The resulting QLBS ATM put option price is 4.90 ± 0.12 (based on two MC runs), while the BS price is 4.53.

4.2. On-policy RL/IRL solutions

We first report results obtained with *on-policy* learning with $\lambda = 0.001$. In this case, optimal actions and rewards computed as a part of a DP solution are used as inputs to the Fitted Q Iteration algorithm Section 2.4 and the IRL method of Section 3, in addition to the paths of the underlying stock. Results of two MC runs with Fitted Q Iteration algorithm of Section 2.4 are shown (respectively, in the left and right columns, with a random selection of a few trajectories) in figure 3. Similarly to the DP solution, we add a unit matrix with a regularization parameter of 10^{-3} to invert matrix $\mathbf{C}_t$

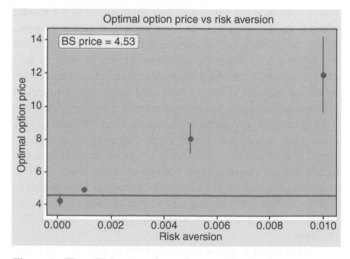

Figure 1. The ATM put option price vs risk aversion parameter. The time step is $\Delta t = 1/24$. The horizontal red line corresponds to the continuous-time BS model price. Error bars correspond to one standard deviation of two MC runs.

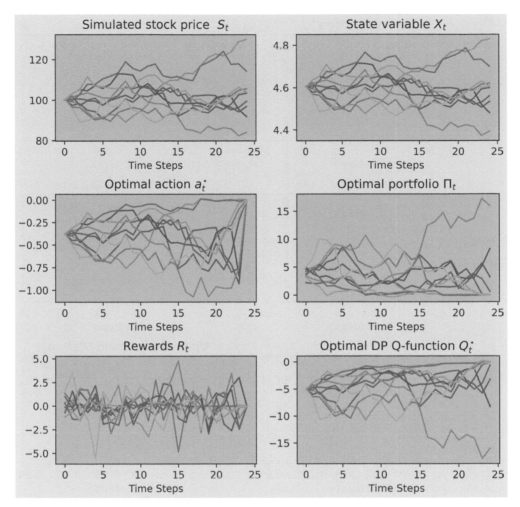

Figure 2. DP solution for the ATM put option on a sub-set of MC paths.

in equation (28). Note that because here we deal with *on-policy* learning, the resulting optimal Q-function $Q_t^\star(X_t, a_t)$ and its optimal value $Q_t^\star(X_t, a_t^\star)$ are virtually identical in the graph.

The resulting QLBS RL put price is 4.90 ± 0.12 which is identical to the DP value. As expected, the IRL method of Section 3 produces the same result.

4.3. Off-policy RL solution

In the next set of experiments, we deal with *off-policy* learning. The risk aversion parameter is $\lambda = 0.001$. To make off-policy data, we multiply, at each time step, optimal hedges computed by the DP solution of the model by a random uniform number in the interval $[1 - \eta, 1 + \eta]$ where $0 < \eta < 1$ is a parameter controlling the noise level in the data. We will consider the values of $\eta = [0.15, 0.25, 0.35, 0.5]$ to test the noise tolerance of our algorithms. Rewards corresponding to these sub-optimal actions are obtained using equation (7). In figure 4, we show results obtained for off-policy learning with 10 different scenarios of sub-optimal actions obtained by random perturbations of a fixed simulated dataset. Note that the impact of sub-optimality of actions in recorded data is rather mild, at least for a moderate level of noise. This is as expected as long as Fitted Q Iteration is an *off-policy* algorithm. This implies that when dataset is large enough, the QLBS model

can learn even from data with purely random actions. In particular, if the world is lognormal, it can learn the BSM model itself (Halperin 2017).

Results of two MC runs for off-policy learning with the noise parameter $\eta = 0.5$ with Fitted Q Iteration algorithm are shown in figure 5.

5. Option portfolios

While above and in Halperin (2017), we looked at the problem of hedging and pricing of a single European option by an option seller that *does not* have any pre-existing option portfolio, here we outline a simple generalization to the case when the option seller *does* have such pre-existing option portfolio, or alternatively if she wants to sell a few options simultaneously.

In this case, she needs to worry about *consistency* of pricing and hedging of *all* options in her new portfolio. In other words, she has to solve the dreaded *volatility smile problem* for her particular portfolio. Here we outline how she can do it using the QLBS model, with an objective to argue that flexibility and a data-driven nature of the model should facilitate adaptation to arbitrary consistent volatility surfaces. Detailed numerical examples of option portfolios are left here for future work.

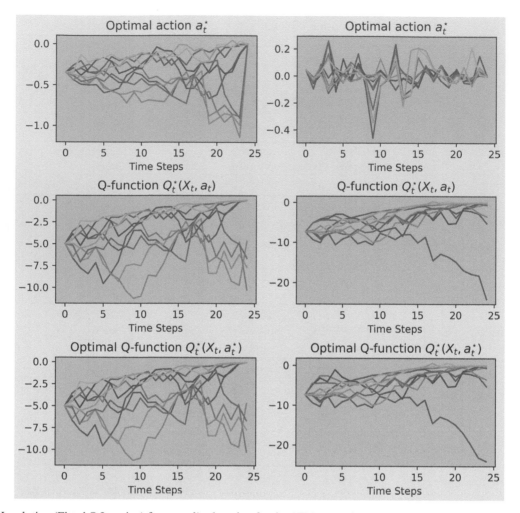

Figure 3. RL solution (Fitted Q Iteration) for *on-policy* learning for the ATM put option on a sub-set of MC paths for two MC runs.

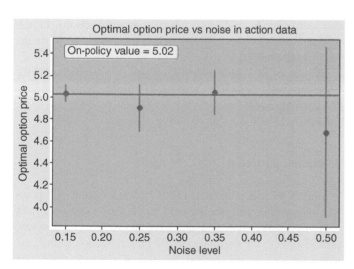

Figure 4. Means and standard deviations of option prices obtained with *off-policy* FQI learning with data obtained by randomization of DP optimal actions by multiplying each optimal action by a uniform random variable in the interval $[1 - \eta, 1 + \eta]$ for $\eta = [0.15, 0.25, 0.35, 0.5]$. Error bars are obtained with 10 scenarios for each value of η. The horizontal red line show the value obtained with *on-policy* learning corresponding to $\eta = 0$.

Assume the option seller has a pre-existing portfolio of K options with market prices $C_1, \ldots, C_K$. All these options reference an underlying state vector (market) $\mathbf{X}_t$ which can

be high-dimensional such that each particular option C_i with $i = 1, \ldots, K$ references only one or a few components of market state $\mathbf{X}_t$.

Alternatively, we can add vanilla option prices as components of the market state $\mathbf{X}_t$. In this case, our dynamic replicating portfolio would include vanilla options, along with underlying stocks. Such hedging portfolio would provide a dynamic generalization of static option hedging for exotics introduced by Carr *et al.* (1998).

We assume that we have a historical dataset $\mathcal{F}$ that includes N observations of trajectories of tuples of vector-valued market factors, actions (hedges), and rewards (compare with equation (25)):

$$\mathcal{F}_t^{(n)} = \left\{ \left(\mathbf{X}_t^{(n)}, \mathbf{a}_t^{(n)}, \mathbf{R}_t^{(n)}, \mathbf{X}_{t+1}^{(n)} \right) \right\}_{t=0}^{T-1}, \quad n = 1, \ldots, N \quad (37)$$

Now assume the option seller wants to add to this pre-existing portfolio another (exotic) option C_e (or alternatively, she wants to sell a portfolio of options $C_1, \ldots, C_K, C_e$). Depending on whether the exotic option C_e was traded before in the market or not, there are two possible scenarios. We will look at them one by one.

In the first case, the exotic option C_e was previously traded in the market (by the seller herself, or by someone else). As long as its deltas and related P&L impacts marked by a trading desk are available, we can simply extend vectors of actions

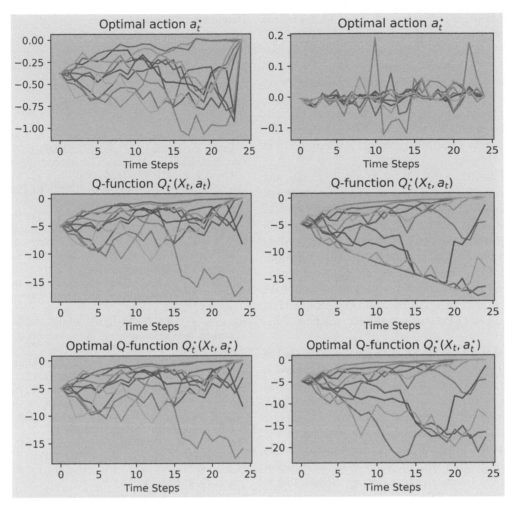

Figure 5. RL solution (Fitted Q Iteration) for *off-policy* learning with noise parameter $\eta = 0.5$ for the ATM put option on a sub-set of MC paths for two MC runs.

$\mathbf{a}_t^{(n)}$ and rewards $\mathbf{R}_t^{(n)}$ in equation (37), and then proceed with the FQI algorithm of Section 2.4 (or with the IRL algorithm of Section 3, if rewards are not available). The outputs of the algorithm will be optimal price P_t of the whole option portfolio, plus optimal hedges for all options in the portfolio. Note that as long as FQI is an *off-policy* algorithm, it is quite forgiving to human or model errors: deltas in the data should not even be perfectly mutually consistent (see single-option examples in the previous section). But of course, the more consistency in the data, the less data is needed to learn an optimal portfolio price P_t.

Once the optimal time-zero value P_0 of the total portfolio $C_1, \ldots, C_K, C_e$ is computed, a market-consistent price for the exotic option is simply given by a subtraction:

$$C_e = P_0 - \sum_{i=1}^{K} C_i \qquad (38)$$

Note that by construction, the price C_e is consistent with *all* option prices $C_1, \ldots, C_K$ and *all* their hedges, to the extent they are consistent between themselves (again, this is because Q-Learning is an off-policy algorithm).

Now consider a different case, when the exotic option C_e was *not* previously traded in the market, and therefore there are no available historical hedges for this option. This can be handled by the QLBS model in essentially the same way as in the previous case. Again, because Q-Learning is an *off-policy* algorithm, it means that a delta and a reward of a *proxy* option C'_e (that *was* traded before) to C_e could be used in the scheme just described in lieu of their actual values for option C_e. Consistently with a common sense, this will just slow down the learning, so that more data would be needed to compute the optimal price and hedge for the exotic C_e. On the other hand, the closer the traded proxy C'_e to the actual exotic C_e the option seller wants to hedge and price, the more it helps the algorithm on the data demand side. Finally, when rewards for the C'_e are not available, we can use the IRL methods of Section 3.

6. Summary

In this paper, we have provided further extensions of the QLBS model developed in Halperin (2017) for RL-based, data-driven and model-independent option pricing, including some topics for 'NuQLear' (Numerical Q-Learning) experimentations with the model. In particular, we have checked the convergence of the DP and RL solutions of the model to the BSM results in the limit $\lambda \to 0$.

We looked into both *on-policy* and *off-policy* RL for option pricing, and showed that Fitted Q Iteration (FQI) provides a reasonable level of noise tolerance with respect to possible sub-optimality of observed actions in our model, which is in agreement with general properties of Q-Learning being an *off-policy* algorithm. This makes the QLBS model capable of learning to hedge and price even when traders' actions (re-hedges) are sub-optimal or not mutually consistent for different time steps, or, in a portfolio context, between different options.

We formulated an IRL approach for the QLBS model, and showed that when the Markowitz risk aversion parameter λ is *known*, the IRL and RL algorithms produce identical results, by construction. On the other hand, when λ is *unknown*, it can be separately estimated using Maximum Entropy (Max-Ent) IRL (Ziebart *et al.* 2008) applied to one-step transitions as in Halperin (2017). While this does *not* guarantee identical results between the RL and IRL solutions of the QLBS model, this can be assured again by using G-Learning (Fox *et al.* 2015) instead of Q-Learning in the RL solution of the model.

Finally, we outlined how the QLBS model can be used in the context of option portfolios, while leaving detailed numerical examples for future work. By relying on Q-Learning and Fitted Q Iteration, which are *model-free* methods, the QLBS model provides its own, data-driven and model-independent solution to the (in)famous volatility smile problem of the Black–Scholes model. While fitting the volatility smile and pricing options consistently with the smile is the *main objective* of Mathematical Finance option pricing models, this is just a *by-product* for the QLBS model. This is because the latter is distribution-free, and is therefore capable of adjusting to *any* smile (a set of market quotes for vanilla options). As was emphasized in the Introduction and in Halperin (2017), the *main* difference between continuous-time 'risk-neutral' option pricing models of Mathematical Finance (including the BSM model and its various local and stochastic volatility extensions, jump-diffusion models, etc.) and the QLBS model is that while the former try to 'match the market', they remain clueless about the expected mis-hedging risk in option positions, while the QLBS model makes the *risk-return* analysis of option replicating portfolios the *main focus* of option hedging and pricing, similarly to how such analysis is applied for stocks in the classical Markowitz portfolio theory (Markowitz 1959).

Disclosure statement

No potential conflict of interest was reported by the author.

References

Black, F. and Scholes, M., The pricing of options and corporate liabilities. *J. Political Econ.*, 1973, **81**(3), 637–654.

Carr, P., Ellis, K. and Gupta, V., Static hedging of exotic options. *J. Finance*, 1998, **53**(3), 1165–1190.

Das, S., *Traders, Guns, and Money*, 2006 (FT Prentice Hall: Harlow, UK).

Ernst, D., Geurts, P. and Wehenkel, L., Tree-based Batch model reinforcement learning. *J. Mach. Learn. Res.*, 2005, **6**, 405–556.

Fox, R., Pakman, A. and Tishby, N., Taming the noise in reinforcement learning via soft updates. Available online at: https://arxiv.org/pdf/1512.08562.pdf, 2015.

Halperin, I., Inverse reinforcement learning for marketing. Available online at: https://papers.ssrn.com/sol3/papers.cfm?abstract_id=3087057, 2017.

Halperin, I., QLBS: Q-Learner in the Black-Scholes (-Merton) worlds. Available online at: https://papers.ssrn.com/sol3/papers.cfm?abstract_id=3087076, 2017.

Kober, J., Bagnell, J.A. and Peters, J., Reinforcement learning in robotics: A survey. *Int. J. Robot. Res.*, 2013, **32**(11), 1238–1278.

Liu, S., Araujo, M., Brunskill, E., Rosetti, R., Barros, J. and Krishnan, R., Undestanding sequential decisions via inverse reinforcement learning. IEEE 14th International Conference on Mobile Data Management, Milan, Italy, 2013.

Markowitz, H., *Portfolio Selection: Efficient Diversification of Investment*, 1959 (John Wiley: New York).

Merton, R., Theory of rational option pricing. *Bell J. Econ. Manag. Sci.*, 1974, **4**(1), 141–183.

Murphy, S.A., A generalization error for Q-Learning. *J. Mach. Learn. Res.*, 2005, **6**, 1073–1097.

Scherrer, R.J., Time variation of a fundamental dimensionless constant. Available online at: http://lanl.arxiv.org/pdf/0903.5321.

Sutton, R.S. and Barto, A.G., *Reinforcement Learning: An Introduction*, 2nd ed., 2018 (MIT Press: Cambridge, MA).

van Hasselt, H., Double Q-Learning, advances in neural information processing systems. Available online at: http://papers.nips.cc/paper/3964-double-q-learning.pdf, 2010.

Watkins, C.J., Learning from delayed rewards. Ph.D. Thesis, Kings College, Cambridge, May, 1989.

Watkins, C.J. and Dayan, P., Q-Learning. *Mach. Learn.*, 1992, **8**(3–4), 179–192.

Wilmott, P., *Paul Wilmott on Quantitative Finance*, 2000 (John Wiley & Sons Ltd: Chichester).

Ziebart, B.D., Maas, A., Bagnell, J.A. and Dey, A.K., Maximum entropy inverse reinforcement learning. *AAAI*, 2008, **8**, 1433–1438.

Detection of false investment strategies using unsupervised learning methods

MARCOS LÓPEZ DE PRADO and MICHAEL J. LEWIS

(Received 25 May 2018; accepted 6 May 2019; published online 10 July 2019)

In this paper we address the problem of selection bias under multiple testing in the context of investment strategies. We introduce an unsupervised learning algorithm that determines the number of effectively uncorrelated trials carried out in the context of a discovery. This estimate is critical for computing the familywise false positive probability, and for filtering out false investment strategies.

1. Introduction

Finance lacks laboratories where experiments can be conducted while controlling for environmental conditions. For example, we cannot test the cause of the Flash Crash by reproducing the events of that date, while subtracting the trades of individual participants in order to derive a cause-effect mechanism. This elementary exercise, so common in Physics laboratories such as Berkeley Lab or CERN, is unavailable to financial researchers (López de Prado 2016b, 2017, 2018a).

In absence of this essential scientific tool, financial researchers often resort to conducting backtests, which are simulations of how an investment portfolio would have performed under a particular historical scenario. The performance of such a portfolio is often measured in terms of the Sharpe ratio (SR), which has become *de facto* the most popular investment performance metric. The distributional properties of the SR are well-known, allowing researchers to use this statistic to test the profitability of a strategy for a given confidence level (Lo 2002, Bailey and López de Prado 2012).

A false positive occurs when a statistical test rejects a true null hypothesis. The probability of obtaining a false positive is set by the significance level (usually 5%). This false positive probability does not remain constant, and it necessarily increases as more than one test is conducted on the same data. The implication is that, applying the same rejection threshold for the null hypothesis under multiple testing will grossly underestimate the probability of obtaining a false positive. The practice of carrying out multiple tests without adjusting the rejection threshold is so widespread and misleading that the American Statistical Association considers it unethical (American Statistical Association 1997). In particular, if we test multiple strategies on the same data, we should demand an increasing SR for the same false positive probability (Bailey *et al.* 2014, Bailey and López de Prado 2014, Bailey *et al.* 2017).

Backtest overfitting occurs when a researcher makes a false discovery (finds a false positive) as a result of selecting the best outcome out of a multiplicity of backtests conducted on the same dataset. As soon as a researcher executes more than one backtest on a given dataset, backtest overfitting is taking place with a non-null probability. The goal of this paper is to provide a practical methodology that will allow researchers to compute and report the probability that an investment strategy is a false positive, while controlling for selection bias under multiple testing (SBuMT).

The rest of the paper is organized as follows: Section 2 reviews the literature. Section 3 lists the contributions made by this paper. Section 4 describes the distributional properties of the SR. Section 5 computes the probability that a strategy is a false positive in a single-test setting. Section 6 states the false strategy theorem. Section 7 explains how to compute the probability that a strategy is a false positive in a multiple-test setting. Section 8 provides practical solutions to the estimation of the probability of a false positive. Section 9 demonstrates empirically the accuracy of these practical solutions. Section 10 summarizes our findings.

2. Review of the literature

In a series of papers, William Sharpe introduced the notion of measuring the performance of portfolio managers in terms of their risk-adjusted returns (Sharpe 1966, 1975, 1994). This makes intuitive sense, since the portfolio that maximizes returns subject to a level of risk is a member of the Markowitz's efficient frontier. This performance measure quickly grew in popularity and became by far the premier statistic used to compare the performance across portfolio managers (Bailey and López de Prado 2012).

Lo (2002) studied the distributional properties of the SR. He concluded that, under the assumption of independent and identically distributed (IID) Normal returns, the SR estimator follows a Normal distribution with mean SR and a standard deviation that depends on the very value of SR and the number of observations. Mertens (2002) found that the Normality assumption on returns could be dropped, and still the estimated SR would follow a Normal distribution. Christie (2005) derived a limiting distribution that only assumes stationary and ergodic returns, thus allowing for time-varying conditional volatilities, serial correlation and even non-IID returns. Surprisingly, Opdyke (2007) proved that the expressions in Mertens (2002) and Christie (2005) are in fact identical. Bailey and López de Prado (2012) derived the probability that the true SR exceeds a given benchmark level, under non-Normal returns.

Until 2014, all estimates of the SR assumed that returns were the result of a single trial. In a world where researchers routinely conduct millions of backtests, clearly that is an unrealistic assumption. To address this problem, Bailey and López de Prado (2014) introduced the *deflated Sharpe ratio* (DSR), which computes the probability that the true SR is positive while controlling for SBuMT.

In this paper we focus on Type I errors (false positives) rather than Type II errors (false negatives), because the former are actual economic losses, whereas the latter are opportunity losses. A hedge fund manager has a vested interest in minimizing Type II errors, while he receives a free call option on Type I errors. In other words, investors participate in the upside and downside, while managers participate only in the upside. Therefore, investors may adopt a 'safety first' principle and concentrate on Type I errors, knowing that financial incentives take care of the Type II errors. For a treatment of both errors, see Harvey and Liu (2018b) and López de Prado and Lewis (2018).

In general terms, the statistics literature on multiple testing works with two different definitions of Type I error: First, the Familywise Error Rate (FWER) is defined as the probability that *at least one* false positive takes place. FWER-based tests are designed to control for a single false positive (Holm 1979). Second, the False Discovery Rate (FDR) is defined as the expected value of the ratio of false positives to predicted positives. FDR-based tests are designed to generate Type I errors

at a constant rate, proportional to the number of predicted positives (Benjamini and Hochberg 1995, Benjamini and Liu 1999, Benjamini and Yekutieli 2001). In most scientific and industrial applications, FWER is considered overly punitive, and authors prefer to use FDR. For example, it would be impractical to design a car model where we control for the probability that a single unit will be defective. However, in the context of finance, we advise against the use of FDR. The reason is, an investor does not typically allocate funds to all strategies with predicted positives within a family of trials, where a proportion of them are likely to be false. Instead, investors are only introduced to the single best strategy out of a family of millions of alternatives. Following the car analogue, in finance there is actually a single car unit produced per model, which everyone will use. If the only produced unit is defective, everyone will crash. For example, investors are not exposed to the dozens of alternative model specifications tried by Fama and French. They have only been told about the one specification that Fama and French found to be best, and they have no ability to invest in their alternative models that passed individual statistical significance tests. Hence we argue that, in the context of financial applications, the more realistic Type I error definition is to control for a single error, not for an error rate. Accordingly, the procedure explained in this paper applies a FWER definition of Type I error.

3. Our contributions

Bailey and López de Prado (2012, 2014) and Bailey et al. (2014) introduced the *False Strategy theorem* (see Section 6.1), and demonstrated how a SR estimate can be used to reject false discoveries under non-Normal returns while controlling for SBuMT. Critically, this theorem required the estimation of two meta-research variables, in the sense that they are variables related to the research process itself, rather than the outcome of the research. These two meta-research variables in question are: (1) The estimation of the number of effectively uncorrelated tests ($E[K]$); and (2) the variance of the SR across the K effectively uncorrelated tests ($E[V[\{SR_k\}]]$). With the help of both variables, we can discount the likelihood of 'lucky findings', that is, random patterns that appear naturally in the data but are meaningless. In this paper we provide practical solutions to the estimation of these two critical meta-research variables.

Important papers on this subject, published by Campbell Harvey and his coauthors, include Harvey and Liu (2015), Harvey et al. (2016) and Harvey and Liu (2018a). Their work shares similarities with ours, particularly as it relates to our concern that the practical totality of academic papers published in financial economics do not control for SBuMT, and the implication that most discoveries in empirical finance are likely to be false. Despite these similarities, our goals and mathematical approaches are different, as explained in Harvey and Liu (2015, Section 3.4).

Particularly relevant is Harvey and Liu (2015), which applies the Šidák correction (Šidák 1967) to estimate the probability of observing a maximal SR that exceeds a given threshold. Their key assumptions are that returns are Normally distributed, and that trials are either independent or there is a constant average correlation between trials. Our method is different in three ways:

1. **We do not assume that returns follow a Normal distribution**. Empirical studies show that hedge fund returns exhibit substantial negative skewness and positive excess kurtosis. Wrongly assuming that returns are Normal underestimates the false positive probability (see Section 5). Our derived probability of a false discovery incorporates information regarding the trials' sample length, and the skewness and kurtosis of the observed returns.

2. **Our method is based on Extreme Value Theory, rather than Šidák's correction**. We derive the probability of a false positive adjusted for SBuMT through the direct application of the False Strategy theorem (see Section 6 herein). Notably, the False Strategy theorem uses the variance of the trials' SRs to accurately estimate the threshold that the maximal SR must exceed to be statistically significant (see Section 6.2). Incorporating this variance information is critical when returns are not drawn from an IID Normal distribution (see Section 4).

3. **We do not assume a constant average correlation across trials**. A family of backtests often contains heterogeneous strategies. Trials that belong to the same strategy tend to be highly correlated among themselves, while trials that belong to different strategies tend to exhibit a lower correlation. This clustering of trials around heterogeneous strategies leads to a hierarchical structure, which can be highly irregular and complex. Assuming a constant correlation across all trials fails to recognize that hierarchical structure, biasing the estimates of the number of independent trials (E[K]) and the false positive probability.

Generally speaking, our approach is data-intensive and closer to the machine learning literature, whereas Harvey *et al.*'s is closer to the econometrics literature. We advise readers to become familiar with both, as they can be seen as complementary. In particular, our unsupervised learning method for estimating the number of effectively uncorrelated tests (E[K]) should be useful to both approaches.

4. The normality of the Sharpe ratio

Consider an investment strategy with excess returns (or risk premia) $\{r_t\}$, $t = 1, \ldots, T$, which follow an IID Normal distribution,

$$r_t \sim \mathcal{N}[\mu, \sigma^2]$$

where $\mathcal{N}[\mu, \sigma^2]$ represents a Normal distribution with mean μ and variance σ^2. The SR (non-annualized) of such strategy is defined as

$$\text{SR} = \frac{\mu}{\sigma}$$

Because parameters μ and σ are not known, SR is estimated as

$$\widehat{\text{SR}} = \frac{E[\{r_t\}]}{\sqrt{V[\{r_t\}]}}$$

Under the assumption that returns follow an IID Normal distribution, Lo (2002) derived the asymptotic distribution of $\widehat{\text{SR}}$ as

$$(\widehat{\text{SR}} - \text{SR}) \xrightarrow{a} \mathcal{N}\left[0, \frac{1 + \frac{1}{2}\text{SR}^2}{T}\right]$$

Equivalently, under the assumption that returns follow an IID Normal distribution, Harvey and Liu (2015) transform $\widehat{\text{SR}}$ into a t-ratio, which follows a t-distribution with $T - 1$ degrees of freedom. In this paper we refrain from following that approach, as empirical evidence shows that hedge fund strategies exhibit substantial negative skewness and positive excess kurtosis (among others, see Brooks and Kat 2002, Ingersoll *et al.* 2007). Wrongly assuming that returns follow an IID Normal distribution can lead to a gross underestimation of the false positive probability.

Under the assumption that returns follow an IID non-Normal distribution, Mertens (2002) derived the asymptotic distribution of $\widehat{\text{SR}}$ as

$$(\widehat{\text{SR}} - \text{SR}) \xrightarrow{a} \mathcal{N}\left[0, \frac{1 + \frac{1}{2}\text{SR}^2 - \gamma_3\text{SR} + \frac{\gamma_4 - 3}{4}\text{SR}^2}{T}\right]$$

where γ_3 is the skewness of $\{r_t\}$, and γ_4 is the kurtosis of $\{r_t\}$ ($\gamma_3 = 0$ and $\gamma_4 = 3$ when returns follow a Normal distribution). Shortly after, Christie (2005) and Opdyke (2007) discovered that, in fact, Mertens' equation is also valid under the more general assumption that returns are stationary and ergodic (not necessarily IID). The key implication is that $\widehat{\text{SR}}$ still follows a Normal distribution even if returns are non-Normal, however with a variance that partly depends on the skewness and kurtosis of the returns. In the next section we utilize this result to express the SR statistic in the probabilistic space. Such metric can be used directly to determine the probability that a discovery made after a single trial is a false positive.

5. The probabilistic Sharpe ratio

The probabilistic Sharpe ratio (PSR) provides an adjusted estimate of the SR, by removing the inflationary effect caused by short series with skewed and/or fat-tailed returns. Given a user-defined benchmark level SR*, PSR estimates the probability that an observed $\widehat{\text{SR}}$ exceeds SR*. Following Bailey and López de Prado (2012), PSR can be estimated as

$$\widehat{\text{PSR}}[\text{SR}^*] = Z\left[\frac{(\widehat{\text{SR}} - \text{SR}^*)\sqrt{T - 1}}{\sqrt{1 - \hat{\gamma}_3\widehat{\text{SR}} + \frac{\hat{\gamma}_4 - 1}{4}\widehat{\text{SR}}^2}}\right]$$

where $Z[.]$ is the CDF of the standard Normal distribution, T is the number of observed returns, $\hat{\gamma}_3$ is the skewness of the returns, and $\hat{\gamma}_4$ is the kurtosis of the returns. Note that $\widehat{\text{SR}}$ is the non-annualized estimate of SR, computed on the same frequency as the T observations. For a given SR*, $\widehat{\text{PSR}}$

increases with greater $\widehat{SR}$ (in the original sampling frequency, i.e. non-annualized), or longer track records (T), or positively skewed returns ($\hat{\gamma}_3$), but it decreases with fatter tails ($\hat{\gamma}_4$).

6. The false strategy theorem

For the reader's convenience, in this section we will discuss the theorem needed to further adjust $\widehat{PSR}$ for the inflationary effect caused by SBuMT. A proof of this statement can be found in Bailey *et al.* (2014).

Given a sample of IID-Gaussian Sharpe ratios, $\{\widehat{SR}_k\}$, $k = 1, \ldots, K$, with $\widehat{SR}_k \sim \mathcal{N}[0, V[\{\widehat{SR}_k\}]]$, then

$$E\left[\max_k \{\widehat{SR}_k\}\right] (V[\{\widehat{SR}_k\}])^{-1/2}$$

$$\approx (1 - \gamma)Z^{-1}\left[1 - \frac{1}{K}\right] + \gamma Z^{-1}\left[1 - \frac{1}{Ke}\right]$$

where $Z^{-1}[.]$ is the inverse of the standard Gaussian CDF, e is Euler's number, and γ is the Euler-Mascheroni constant. The implication is that, unless $\max_k\{\widehat{SR}_k\} \gg E\left[\max_k\{\widehat{SR}_k\}\right]$, the discovered strategy is likely to be a *false positive*. In Section 7 we will evaluate this likelihood.

7. The deflated Sharpe ratio

In accordance with the previous result, we define the deflated Sharpe ratio (DSR) as the probability that the true SR exceeds a user-defined benchmark level SR*, where that level is adjusted to reflect the multiplicity of trials. Following Bailey and López de Prado (2014), DSR can be estimated as $\widehat{PSR}[SR^*]$, where the benchmark SR (SR*), is no longer user-defined. Instead, SR* is estimated as

$$SR^* = \sqrt{V[\{\widehat{SR}_k\}]}$$
$$\times \left((1-\gamma)Z^{-1}\left[1 - \frac{1}{K}\right] + \gamma Z^{-1}\left[1 - \frac{1}{Ke}\right]\right)$$

where $V[\{\widehat{SR}_k\}]$ is the variance across the trials' estimated SR, K is the number of independent trials, $Z[.]$ is the CDF of the standard Normal distribution, γ is the Euler-Mascheroni constant, and $k = 1, \ldots, K$.

The rationale behind DSR is the following: Given a set of SR estimates, $\{\widehat{SR}_k\}$, its expected maximum is greater than zero, even if the true SR is zero. Under the null hypothesis that the actual SR is zero, $H_0 : SR = 0$, we know that the expected maximum SR can be estimated as the SR*. Indeed, *SR** increases quickly as more independent trials are attempted (K), or the trials involve a greater variance ($V[\{\widehat{SR}_k\}]$). In order to reject the null hypothesis that the strategy is uninformed ($H_0 : SR = 0$), the observed SR ($\widehat{SR}$) must be statistically significantly greater than the expected SR after controlling for SBuMT (SR*). Thus, DSR gives us the confidence level, that is, the probability complementary to the false positive rate. For example, in order to reject the null hypothesis, $H_0 : SR = 0$, with a 5% significance level, the observed DSR must exceed 0.95.

8. Practical considerations

In practice, the estimation of the false positive probability requires the evaluation of six variables:

1. $\widehat{SR}$
2. T
3. $\hat{\gamma}_3$
4. $\hat{\gamma}_4$
5. $E[K]$
6. $E[V[\{\widehat{SR}_k\}]]$

Of these six variables, (1)–(4) are either directly observable or can be estimated from the selected strategy. However, (5)–(6) are meta-research variables, in the sense that they are intrinsic to the research process itself, and they cannot be estimated from the selected strategy.

There are two major reasons why (5)–(6) are usually unknown. First, it is common for researchers to hide, not track, not report or underreport (5)–(6). The motivations may vary, and they could range all the way between negligence and outright fraud. Regardless of the motivations, the implication is that ignorance of (5)–(6) makes it impossible to assess whether a discovery is false. Second, even those careful and knowledgeable researchers who track every single trial that takes place face the problem that trials are not usually *independent*. The number of independent trials K is less or equal to the number of trials N. In the following sections, we will show how (5)–(6) can be estimated in practice.

8.1. Estimation of the number of clustered trials, E[K]

While finding independent trials may not be feasible, given that likely all strategies will be dependent to varying degrees, we consider clustering the strategies and using those clusters as a proxy. To that end, our goal is to develop an algorithm that, given N series, will partition them into an optimal number of K subgroups, or clusters. Ideally, each cluster will have high intra-cluster correlations and low inter-cluster correlations. We denote this algorithm ONC, since it searches for the *optimal number of clusters* within a correlation matrix.

Given that our goal is to cluster correlated strategies, we first assume that we have a correlation matrix ρ for our strategies, where ρ_{ij} is the correlation of the returns between strategies i and j. Next, we need a metric for clustering the strategies, specifically one where higher correlations map to smaller (closer) distances. For this, we consider the proper distance matrix D, where

$$D_{i,j} = \sqrt{\frac{1}{2}(1 - \rho_{ij})}$$

for $i, j = 1, \ldots, N$. This definition of distance is a proper metric in the sense that it satisfies the four classical axioms: Non-negativity, identity, symmetric and sub-additivity. Furthermore, we wish to consider a more global distance rather than local distance for improved clustering. Therefore, our clustering will be performed on the final Euclidean distance matrix $\tilde{D}$ where

$$\tilde{D}_{i,j} = \sqrt{\sum_k (D_{ik} - D_{jk})^2}$$

In doing so, ONC works on a distance of distances ($\tilde{D}$), rather than on a simple distance matrix (D). The reason is, while $D_{i,j}$ is a direct function of ρ_{ij} (a single correlation), $\tilde{D}_{i,j}$ incorporates information about the entire system, thereby reducing noise and adding robustness to the procedure (López de Prado 2016a).

With the above formed distance matrix $\tilde{D}$, we next consider the clustering methodology. One possibility would be to use the K-means algorithm on our distance matrix $\tilde{D}$. While K-means is simple and frequently effective, it does have two notable limitations: First, the algorithm requires a user-set number of clusters K, which is not necessarily optimal a priori. Second, the initialization is random, and hence the effectiveness of the algorithm is similarly random.

In order to address these two concerns, we need to modify the K-means algorithm. The first modification is to introduce an objective function, so that we can find the 'optimal K'. For this, we utilize the silhouette score introduced by Rousseeuw (1987). As a reminder, for a given node i and a given clustering, the silhouette score S_i is defined as

$$S_i = \frac{b_i - a_i}{\max\{a_i, b_i\}}$$

where a_i is the average distance between i and all other nodes in the same cluster, and b_i is the smallest average distance between i and all the nodes in any other cluster. Effectively, this is a measure comparing intra-cluster distance and inter-cluster distance. A $S_i = 1$ means that node i is clustered well, while $S_i = -1$ means that i was clustered poorly. Our measure of quality q for a given clustering is thus set to

$$q = \frac{E[\{S_i\}]}{\sqrt{V[\{S_i\}]}}$$

The second modification deals with K-mean's initialization problem. At the base level, our clustering algorithm performs the following operation: First, we are given a $N \times N$ correlation matrix ρ, from which we evaluate the distance matrices D and $\tilde{D}$. Second, we perform a double for ... loop. In the first loop, we try different $k = 2, \ldots, N - 1$ on which to cluster via K-means for one given initialization, and evaluate the quality q for each clustering. The second loop repeats the first loop multiple times, thereby obtaining different initializations. Third, over these two loops, we select the clustering with the highest q. See Snippet 1 in the Appendix for an implementation of this operation in python.

The third modification to K-means deals with clusters of inconsistent quality. The base clustering may capture the more distinct clusters, while missing the less apparent ones. To address this issue, we evaluate the quality q_k of each cluster $k = 1, \ldots, K$ given the clustering and silhouette scores obtained from the base clustering algorithm. We then take the average quality $\bar{q}$, and find the set of clusters with quality below average, $\{q_k | q_k < \bar{q}, k = 1, \ldots, K\}$. Let us denote as K_1 the number of clusters in the set, $K_1 < K$. If the number of clusters to rerun is $K_1 \leq 2$, then we return the clustering given by the base algorithm. However, if $K_1 > 2$, we rerun the clustering of the items in those K_1 clusters, while the rest are considered acceptably clustered.

We rerun the K_1 clusters in a recursive manner, rerunning the clustering on ρ, restricted to the nodes in the K_1 clusters. Doing so will return a, possibly new, optimal clustering for those nodes. To check its efficacy, we compare the average quality of the clusters to redo given the previous clustering to the average quality of the clusters given the new clustering. If the average quality improves for these clusters, we return the accepted clustering from the base clustering concatenated with the new clustering for the nodes redone. Otherwise, we return the clustering formed by the base algorithm. See Snippet 2 in the Appendix for an implementation of this operation in python. Exhibits 1 and 2 outline the structure of the ONC algorithm.

8.2. Estimation of the variance of clustered trials, $E[V[\{\widehat{SR}_k\}]]$

Upon completion of the clustering above, ONC has successfully partitioned our N strategies into K groups, each of which is construed of highly correlated strategies. In this section, our goal is to utilize the clustering to reduce the N strategies to $K \ll N$ cluster-level strategies. Upon creation of these 'cluster strategies', we derive our estimate $E[V[\{\widehat{SR}_k\}]]$ for each $k = 1, \ldots, K$.

For a given cluster k, the goal is to form an aggregate cluster returns time series $S_{k,t}$. This necessitates choosing a weighting scheme for the aggregation. We choose the minimum variance allocation, described in López de Prado (2016a), to mitigate the adverse effects of any strategies with larger variance. Let C_k denote the set of strategies in cluster k, $r_{i,t}$ the returns series for strategy i, Σ_k the covariance matrix restricted to strategies in C_k, and $w_{k,i}$, or w_k in vector notation, the weight for strategy $i \in C_k$. Then, we set

$$w_k = \frac{\overset{-1}{\underset{k}{\Sigma}} 1}{1' \overset{-1}{\underset{k}{\Sigma}} 1}$$

$$S_{k,t} = \sum_{i \in C_k} w_{k,i} r_{i,t}$$

where 1 is the characteristic vector of 1s. A robust method of computing w_k can be found in the Appendix. With the cluster returns time series $S_{k,t}$ now computed, we estimate each SR ($\widehat{SR}_k$). However, these $\widehat{SR}_k$ are not yet comparable, as their frequency of trading may vary. To make them comparable, we must first annualize each. Accordingly, we calculate the frequency of trading as

$$\text{Years}_k = \frac{\text{Last Date}_k - \text{First Date}_k}{365.25 \text{ days}}$$

$$\text{Frequency}_k = \frac{T_k}{\text{Years}_k}$$

where T_k is the length of the $S_{k,t}$, and First Date$_k$ and Last Date$_k$ are the first and last dates of trading for $S_{k,t}$, respectively. With this, we estimate the annualized Sharpe Ratio

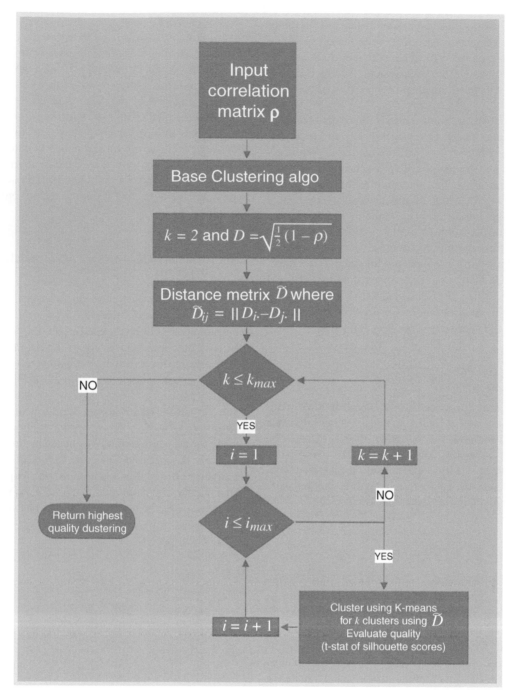

Exhibit 1. Structure of ONC's base clustering stage. This exhibit outlines the workflow within ONC's base algorithm, highlighting the three ways in which it departs from the K-means algorithm: 1) The clustering is done on a distance of distances ($\tilde{D}$), rather than on the distance matrix (D); 2) it optimizes the Silhouette score; 3) it tries alternative initialization points to avoid local optima.

(aSR) as

$$\widehat{\text{aSR}}_k = \frac{E[\{S_{k,t}\}]\text{Frequency}_k}{\sqrt{V[\{S_{k,t}\}]\text{Frequency}_k}} = \widehat{\text{SR}}_k \sqrt{\text{Frequency}_k}$$

With these now comparable $\widehat{\text{aSR}}_k$, we can estimate the variance of clustered trials as

$$E[V[\{\widehat{\text{SR}}_k\}]] = \frac{V[\{\widehat{\text{aSR}}_k\}]}{\text{Frequency}_{k*}}$$

where Frequency_{k*} is the frequency of the selected strategy. We need to express the estimated variance of clustered trials in terms of the frequency of the selected strategy, in order to match the frequency of the $\widehat{\text{SR}}$ estimate used by the DSR equation (recall Sections 5 and 7). Otherwise, SR^* would not be estimated on the same frequency as $\widehat{\text{SR}}$.

9. Experimental validation of $E[K]$

We now design a Monte Carlo experiment to verify the accuracy of the ONC algorithm introduced in Section 8.1. Our goal

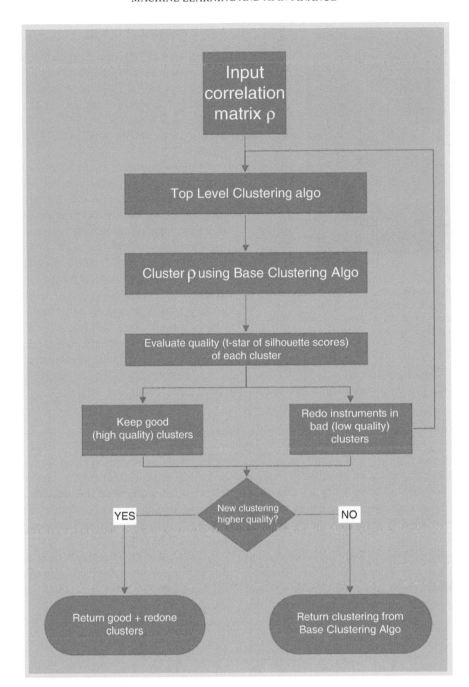

Exhibit 2. *Structure of ONC's higher-level stage.* This exhibit outlines ONC's higher-level clustering, which seeks to reduce discrepancies across clusters quality.

is to create a $N \times N$ correlation matrix ρ from random data with a predefined number of blocks K, where ρ_{ij} is high inside a block and low outside the block. We can then verify that the ONC algorithm recovers the blocks we injected.

9.1. Generation of random block correlation matrices

First, given the tuple (N, M, K), we create a random block covariance matrix of size $N \times N$, made up of K blocks, each of size $\geq M$. To do so, we randomly partition the N indices into K disjoint groups. Note that each block must be of size $M \geq 2$, as blocks of size 1 are difficult to identify as a cluster.

Let us describe the procedure for randomly partitioning N items into K groups, each of size at least M. First, note that this is equivalent to randomly partitioning $N' = N -$

$K(M - 1)$ items into K groups each of size at least 1, so we reduce our analysis to that. Next, consider randomly choosing $K - 1$ distinct items, denoted as a set B, from the set $A = (1, \ldots, N' - 1)$, then add N' to B, so that B is of size K. Thus, B contains $i_1, \ldots, i_K$, where $1 \leq i_1 < i_2 < \ldots < i_K = N'$. Given B, consider the K partition sets $C_1 = 0, \ldots, i_1 - 1$, $C_2 = i_1, \ldots, i_2 - 1, \ldots$, and $C_K = i_{K-1}, \ldots, i_K - 1$. Given the i_j are distinct, each partition contains at least 1 element as desired, and furthermore completely partitions the set $(0, \ldots, N' - 1)$. In doing so, each set C_j contains $i_j - i_{j-1}$ elements for $j = 1, \ldots, K$, letting $i_0 = 0$. We can generalize again by adding $M - 1$ elements to each block.

Let each block $k = 1, \ldots, K$ have size x_k by x_k, where $x_k \geq M$, thus implying $x_1 + \ldots + x_K = N \geq MK$. First, for each block k, we create a time series S of length T that is

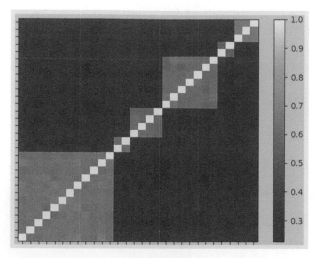

Exhibit 3. *Example of a random block correlation matrix.* This exhibit plots a random block correlation matrix, generated using the method explained in section 9.1. Light colors indicate a high correlation, and dark colors indicate a low correlation. In this example, the number of blocks $K = 6$, each of varying size, with a total of $N = 30$ instruments.

9.2. Extraction of $E[K]$

Using the above described procedure to create random $N \times N$ correlation matrices with K blocks of size at least M, we test the efficacy of the ONC algorithm. For our simulations, we chose $N = 20, 40, 80, 160$. We set $M = 2$, and thus necessarily $\frac{K}{N} \leq \frac{1}{2}$. For each N, we test $K = 3, 6, \ldots$, up to $\frac{N}{2}$. Finally, we test 1000 random generations for each of these parameter sets.

Exhibit 4 displays various boxplots for these simulations. In particular, for $\frac{K}{N}$ in a given bucket, we display the boxplot of the ratio of K predicted by the clustering (denoted $E[K]$) to the actual K tested. Ideally, this ratio should be near 1. We observe that this clustering is very effective, frequently obtaining the correct number of clusters, with some outliers.

As a reminder, in a boxplot, the central box has the bottom set to the 25% percentile of the data (Q1), while the top is set to the 75% percentile (Q3). The interquartile range (IQR) is set to Q3-Q1. The median is displayed as a line inside the box. The 'whiskers' extend to the largest datum less than $Q3 + 1.5IQR$, and the smallest datum greater than $Q1-1.5IQR$. All points outside that range are considered outliers.

made from IID standard Gaussians, then make copies of that to each column of a matrix X of size (T, x_k). Second, we add to each X_{ij} a random Gaussian with standard deviation $\sigma > 0$. By design, the columns of X will be highly correlated for small σ, and less correlated for large σ. Third, we evaluate the covariance matrix Σ_X for the columns of X, and add Σ_X as a block to Σ. Fourth, we add to Σ another covariance matrix with one block but larger σ. Finally, we derive the correlation matrix ρ related to Σ.

By design, ρ will have K blocks with high correlations inside each block, and low correlations otherwise. Exhibit 3 is an example of a correlation matrix constructed this way. See Snippet 3 in the Appendix for an implementation of this operation in python.

10. Conclusions

In this paper we apply the False Strategy theorem, first proved in Bailey *et al.* (2014), to the prevention of false positives in finance. This requires the estimation of two meta-research variables that allow us to discount for the likelihood of 'lucky findings'. We estimate these two meta-research variables with the help of the ONC algorithm.

In particular, ONC extracts from a series of backtests the number of effectively uncorrelated trials. This number is useful in two applications: a) Estimating the expected value of the maximum Sharpe ratio, via the False Strategy Theorem (see Bailey and López de Prado (2014) for an example); and

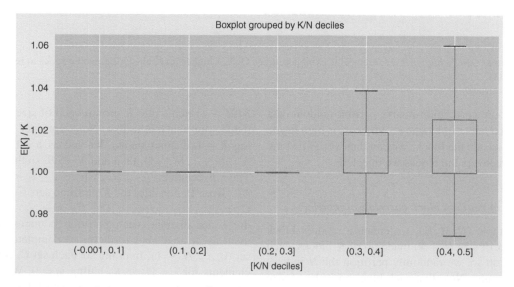

Exhibit 4. *Boxplots of estimated K / actual K for bucketed $\frac{K}{N}$.* This exhibit plots the ratio between the extracted number of clusters (E[K]) and the actual number of clusters (K), for various deciles of K/N, where $N \times N$ is the size of the correlation matrix. These results were obtained from numerous random simulations across a variety of matrix sizes and cluster counts, namely $N = 20, 40, 80, 160$ and $K = 3, 6, \ldots$, up to $\frac{N}{2}$. The ONC algorithm provides an accurate estimation of K across all ratios of clusters per variable.

b) deriving the FWER, via the Šidák correction (see Harvey and Liu (2015) for an example). Monte Carlo experiments demonstrate the precision of this method.

We think that ONC has multiple uses in finance. Many investing problems involve the extraction of an unknown number of clusters. For example, ONC could be used to identify the optimal number of economic sectors from a risk perspective. Risk parity investors could then allocate assets in a more diversified way, where the peer groups are not set in advance. More generally, ONC could be useful in situations where researchers are interested in finding the most uncorrelated groups without a change of basis (like in principal components analysis, PCA). This could be particularly helpful in addressing multicollinearity problems, where the standard PCA solution forces researchers to work with variables removed of economic intuition.

Acknowledgements

We wish to thank Prof. Germán G. Creamer and two anonymous referees for their help and useful comments.

Disclosure statement

No potential conflict of interest was reported by the authors.

References

American Statistical Association, Ethical guidelines for statistical practice. *Committee on Professional Ethics*, 2016. Available online at: http://www.amstat.org/asa/files/pdfs/EthicalGuidelines.pdf

Bailey, D., Borwein, J., López de Prado, M. and Zhu, J., Pseudo-mathematics and financial charlatanism: The effects of backtest overfitting on out-of-sample performance. *Notices Am. Math. Soc.*, 2014, **61**(5), 458–471. Available online at: http://ssrn.com/abstract = 2308659

Bailey, D., Borwein, J., López de Prado, M. and Zhu, J., The probability of backtest overfitting. *J. Comput. Financ.*, 2017, **20**(4), 39–70. Available online at: http://ssrn.com/abstract = 2326253

Bailey, D. and López de Prado, M., The Sharpe ratio efficient frontier. *J. Risk*, 2012, **15**(2), 3–44.

Bailey, D. and López de Prado, M., The deflated Sharpe ratio: Correcting for selection bias, backtest overfitting and non-normality. *J. Portfolio Manage.*, 2014, **40**(5), 94–107.

Benjamini, Y. and Hochberg, Y., Controlling the false discovery rate: A practical and powerful approach to multiple testing. *J. Roy. Stat. Soc. Ser. B*, 1995, **57**, 289–300.

Benjamini, Y. and Liu, W., A step-down multiple hypotheses testing procedure that controls the false discovery rate under independence. *J. Stat. Plan. Inference.*, 1999, **82**, 163–170.

Benjamini, Y. and Yekutieli, D., The control of the false discovery rate in multiple testing under dependency. *Ann. Stat.*, 2001, **29**, 1165–1188.

Brooks, C. and Kat, H., The statistical properties of hedge fund index returns and their implications for investors. *J. Altern. Invest.*, 2002, **5**(2), Fall, 26–44.

Christie, S., Is the Sharpe ratio useful in asset allocation? MAFC Research Paper No. 31, Applied Finance Centre, Macquarie University, 2005.

Harvey, C. and Liu, Y., Backtesting. *J. Portfolio Manage.*, 2015, **42**(1), 13–28.

Harvey, C., Liu, Y. and Zhu, C., … And the cross-section of expected returns. *Rev. Financ. Stud.*, 2016, **29**(1), 5–68. Available online at: https://ssrn.com/abstract = 2249314

Harvey, C. and Liu, Y., Lucky factors. Working paper, 2018a. Available online at: https://ssrn.com/abstract = 2528780

Harvey, C. and Liu, Y., False (and Missed) discoveries in financial economics. Working paper, 2018b. Available online at: https://ssrn.com/abstract = 3073799

Holm, S., A simple sequentially rejective multiple test procedure. *Scand. J. Stat.*, 1979, **6**, 65–70.

Ingersoll, J., Spiegel, M., Goetzmann, W. and Welch, I., Portfolio performance manipulation and manipulation-proof performance measures. *Rev. Financ. Stud.*, 2007, **20**(5), 1504–1546.

Lo, A., The statistics of Sharpe ratios. *Financ. Anal. J.*, 2002, **58**(4), July, 36–52.

López de Prado, M., Building diversified portfolios that outperform out-of-sample. *J. Portfolio Manage.*, 2016a, **42**(4), 59–69.

López de Prado, M., Mathematics and economics: A reality check. *J. Portfolio Manage.*, 2016b, **43**(1), 5–8.

López de Prado, M., Finance as an industrial science. *J. Portfolio Manage.*, 2017, **43**(4), 5–9.

López de Prado, M., *Advances in Financial Machine Learning*, 1st edition, 2018a (Wiley). https://www.amazon.com/dp/1119482089

López de Prado, M. and Lewis, M., What is the Optimal Significance Level for Investment Strategies? Working paper, 2018. Available online at: https://ssrn.com/abstract = 3193697

Mertens, E., Variance of the IID Estimator in Lo (2002). Working paper, University of Basel, 2002.

Opdyke, J., Comparing Sharpe ratios: So where are the *p*-values? *J. Asset Manage.*, 2007, **8**(5), 308–336.

Rousseeuw, P., Silhouettes: A graphical aid to the interpretation and validation of cluster analysis. *Comput. Appl. Math.*, 1987, **20**, 53–65.

Sharpe, W., Mutual fund performance. *J. Bus.*, 1966, **39**(1), 119–138.

Sharpe, W., Adjusting for risk in portfolio performance measurement. *J. Portfolio Manage.*, 1975, **1**(2), Winter, 29–34.

Sharpe, W., The Sharpe ratio. *J. Portfolio Manage.*, 1994, **21**(1), Fall, 49–58.

Šidák, Z., Rectangular confidence regions for the means of multivariate normal distributions. *J. Am. Stat. Assoc.*, 1967, **62**(318), 626–633.

Appendices

A.1. The base clustering algorithm

The purpose of this step is to perform a first-pass estimate of $E[K]$. First, we transform the correlation matrix into a distance matrix. On this distance matrix, we apply the K-means algorithm on alternative target number of clusters. For each target number of clusters, we perform a stochastic optimization, repeating the clustering operation `n_init` times. Among all the clustering alternatives, we choose the solution that achieves the highest quality score, defined as the t-value of the silhouette scores.

```
import numpy as np,pandas as pd
#- - - - - - - - - - - - - - - - - - - - - - - - - - - - - - - - - - -
def clusterKMeansBase(corr0,maxNumClusters = 10,n_init =
    10):
    from sklearn.cluster import KMeans
    from sklearn.metrics import silhouette_samples
    dist,silh = ((1-corr0.fillna(0))/2.)**.5,pd.Series() # distance
    matrix
    for init in range(n_init):
        for i in xrange(2,maxNumClusters + 1): # find optimal num
        clusters
            kmeans_ = KMeans(n_clusters = i,n_jobs = 1,n_init
```

```
             = 1)
           kmeans_ = kmeans_.fit(dist)
           silh_ = silhouette_samples(dist,kmeans_.labels_)
           stat = (silh_.mean()/silh_.std(),silh.mean()/silh.std())
           if np.isnan(stat[1]) or stat[0] > stat[1]:
               silh,kmeans = silh_,kmeans_
       n_clusters = len(np.unique(kmeans.labels_))
       newIdx = np.argsort(kmeans.labels_)
       corr1 = corr0.iloc[newIdx] # reorder rows
       corr1 = corr1.iloc[:,newIdx] # reorder columns
       clstrs = {i:corr0.columns[np.where(kmeans.labels_ = = i)
           [0] ].tolist() for
               i in np.unique(kmeans.labels_) } # cluster members
       silh = pd.Series(silh,index = dist.index)
       return corr1,clstrs,silh
```

Snippet 1 – Base Clustering

A.2. The top-level clustering algorithm

The purpose of this step is to perform a second-pass estimate of $E[K]$. We evaluate the quality score for each cluster within the first-pass solution. Those clusters with quality greater or equal than average remain unchanged. We re-run the base clustering on clusters with below-average quality. The outputs of these re-runs are preserved only if their cluster quality improves.

```
#- - - - - - - - - - - - - - - - - - - - - - - - - - - - - - - - - -
def makeNewOutputs(corr0,clstrs,clstrs2):
    from sklearn.metrics import silhouette_samples
    clstrsNew,newIdx = {},[]
    for i in clstrs.keys():
        clstrsNew[len(clstrsNew.keys())] = list(clstrs[i])
    for i in clstrs2.keys():
        clstrsNew[len(clstrsNew.keys())] = list(clstrs2[i])
    map(newIdx.extend, clstrsNew.values())
    corrNew = corr0.loc[newIdx,newIdx]
    dist = ((1-corr0.fillna(0))/2.)**.5
    kmeans_labels = np.zeros(len(dist.columns))
    for i in clstrsNew.keys():
        idxs = [dist.index.get_loc(k) for k in clstrsNew[i]]
        kmeans_labels[idxs] = i
    silhNew = pd.Series(silhouette_samples(dist,kmeans_labels),
        index = dist.index)
    return corrNew,clstrsNew,silhNew
#- - - - - - - - - - - - - - - - - - - - - - - - - - - - - - - - - -
def clusterKMeansTop(corr0,maxNumClusters = 10,n_init =
    10):
    corr1,clstrs,silh = clusterKMeansBase(corr0,maxNum
        Clusters = corr0.shape[1]-1,n_init = n_init)
    clusterTstats = {i:np.mean(silh[clstrs[i]])/np.std(silh[clstrs[i]])
        for i in clstrs.keys()}
    tStatMean = np.mean(clusterTstats.values())
    redoClusters = [i for i in clusterTstats.keys() if clusterT-
        stats[i] < tStatMean]
    if len(redoClusters) < = 2:
        return corr1,clstrs,silh
    else:
        keysRedo = [];map(keysRedo.extend,[clstrs[i] for i in redo-
            Clusters])
        corrTmp = corr0.loc[keysRedo,keysRedo]
        meanRedoTstat = np.mean([clusterTstats[i] for i in redo-
            Clusters])
        corr2,clstrs2,silh2 = clusterKMeansTop(corrTmp,
            maxNumClusters = corrTmp.shape[1]-1,n_init = n_init)
        # Make new outputs, if necessary
        corrNew,clstrsNew,silhNew = makeNewOutputs(corr0,
            {i:clstrs[i] for i in clstrs.keys() if i not in redoClusters},
            clstrs2)
        newTstatMean = np.mean([np.mean
```

```
           (silhNew[clstrsNew[i]])/np.std(silhNew[clstrsNew[i]])
            for i in clstrsNew.keys()])
        if newTstatMean < = tStatMean:
            return corr1,clstrs,silh
    else:
            return corrNew,clstrsNew,silhNew
```

Snippet 2 – Top Level of Clustering

A.3. Random correlation block-matrices

In this section we present an algorithm for the generation of random correlation block-matrices, with a pre-determined number of clusters. After generating these matrices, we can shuffle their rows (and columns), and apply the ONC algorithm. We can repeat this process thousands of times to evaluate ONC's performance, while controlling for the matrix size and the number of clusters.

```
import numpy as np,pandas as pd
from scipy.linalg import block_diag
from sklearn.utils import check_random_state
#- - - - - - - - - - - - - - - - - - - - - - - - - - - - - - - - - -
def cov2corr(cov):
    # Derive the correlation matrix from a covariance matrix
    std = np.sqrt(np.diag(cov))
    corr = cov/np.outer(std,std)
    corr[corr < -1],corr[corr > 1] = -1,1 # numerical error
    return corr
#- - - - - - - - - - - - - - - - - - - - - - - - - - - - - - - - - -
def getCovSub(nObs,nCols,sigma,random_state = None):
    # Sub correl matrix
    rng = check_random_state(random_state)
    if nCols = = 1:return np.ones((1,1))
    ar0 = rng.normal(size = (nObs,1))
    ar0 = np.repeat(ar0,nCols,axis = 1)
    ar0 + = rng.normal(scale = sigma,size = ar0.shape)
    ar0 = np.cov(ar0,rowvar = False)
    return ar0
#- - - - - - - - - - - - - - - - - - - - - - - - - - - - - - - - - -
def getRndBlockCov(nCols,nBlocks,minBlockSize = 1,
    sigma = 1.,random_state = None):
    # Generate a random correlation matrix with a given number
        of blocks
    rng = check_random_state(random_state)
    parts = rng.choice(range(1,nCols-(minBlockSize-1)*
        nBlocks),nBlocks-1,replace = False)
    parts.sort()
    parts = np.append(parts,nCols-(minBlockSize-1)*nBlocks)
    parts = np.append(parts[0],np.diff(parts)) - 1 + minBlockSize
    cov = None
    for nCols_ in parts:
        cov_ = getCovSub(int(max(nCols_*(nCols_ + 1)/
            2.,100)),nCols_,sigma,random_state = rng)
        if cov is None:cov = cov_.copy()
        else:cov = block_diag(cov,cov_)
    return cov
#- - - - - - - - - - - - - - - - - - - - - - - - - - - - - - - - - -
def randomBlockCorr(nCols,nBlocks,random_state = None,
    minBlockSize = 1):
    # Form block covar
    rng = check_random_state(random_state)
    cov0 = getRndBlockCov(nCols,nBlocks,minBlockSize
        = minBlockSize,
                sigma = .5,random_state = rng) #
                perfect block corr
    cov1 = getRndBlockCov(nCols,1,minBlockSize =
        minBlockSize,
                sigma = 1.,random_state = rng)
                # add noise
    cov0 + = cov1
```

```
corr0 = cov2corr(cov0)
corr0 = pd.DataFrame(corr0)
return corr0
```

Snippet 3 – Random block correlation matrix creation

A.4. Minimum variance allocation

In section 8.2, we wish to evaluate the minimum variance allocation for the strategies within a cluster k of size N_k. Note that the intra-cluster correlations will be high by design, and thus Σ_k may be ill-conditioned and difficult to invert. In practice, one could choose to approximate the weights by setting $w_{k,i}$ proportional to $\frac{1}{\sigma_i^2}$ as is typically done in inverse variance allocations. If more accuracy is desired, consider the following approximation. Let ρ be the average off-diagonal correlation in the correlation matrix for the cluster. Then, the covariance matrix is approximately

$$\sum_k \approx \sum_{\text{approx}} = \begin{pmatrix} \sigma_1^2 & \cdots & \rho\sigma_1\sigma_{N_k} \\ \vdots & \ddots & \vdots \\ \rho\sigma_1\sigma_{N_k} & \cdots & \sigma_{N_k}^2 \end{pmatrix}$$

$$= \rho\sigma\sigma^T + (1-\rho)\begin{pmatrix} \sigma_1^2 & \cdots & 0 \\ \vdots & \ddots & \vdots \\ 0 & \cdots & \sigma_{N_k}^2 \end{pmatrix}$$

where

$$\sigma = \begin{pmatrix} \sigma_1 \\ \vdots \\ \sigma_{N_k} \end{pmatrix}$$

This is a rank one update. If our goal is to take the inverse of Σ_{approx}, we can utilize the Sherman-Morrison (SM) formula. Using the notation

$$\frac{1}{\sigma} = \begin{pmatrix} \frac{1}{\sigma_1} \\ \vdots \\ \frac{1}{\sigma_{N_k}} \end{pmatrix}$$

then the SM formula gives us

$$\sum_{\text{approx}}^{-1} = \frac{1}{1-\rho}\begin{pmatrix} \frac{1}{\sigma_1^2} & \cdots & 0 \\ \vdots & \ddots & \vdots \\ 0 & \cdots & \frac{1}{\sigma_{N_k}^2} \end{pmatrix}$$

$$- \frac{\rho}{(1-\rho)(1+(N_k-1)\rho)}\left(\frac{1}{\sigma}\right)\left(\frac{1}{\sigma}\right)^T$$

When computing the weights allocation, we are trying to evaluate $\Sigma_{\text{approx}}^{-1}1$. In this case, we find that

$$w_{k,i} \sim \frac{1}{\sigma_i^2} - \frac{\rho\sum\limits_{j\in C_k}\frac{1}{\sigma_j}}{(1+(N_k-1)\rho)\sigma_i}$$

As is readily observable, if $\rho = 0$, this reduces to the standard inverse variance allocation. Snippet 4 implements this procedure in python.

```python
import numpy as np,pandas as pd
#- - - - - - - - - - - - - - - - - - - - - - - - - - - - - - - - - -
def getIVP(cov,use_extended_terms = False):
    # Compute the minimum-variance portfolio
    ivp = 1./np.diag(cov)
    if use_extended_terms:
        n = float(cov.shape[0])
        corr = cov2corr(cov)
        # Obtain average off-diagonal correlation
        rho = (np.sum(np.sum(corr))-n)/(n**2-n)
        invSigma = np.sqrt(ivp)
        ivp- = rho*invSigma*np.sum(invSigma)/(1.+(n-1)*rho)
    ivp/ = ivp.sum()
    return ivp
```

Snippet 4 – Obtain minimum variance portfolio

Index

Page numbers in italics and bold denote figures and tables, respectively.